THE MORAL BASIS OF A FREE SOCIETY

BY

H. VERLAN ANDERSEN

COMPILED AND PRESENTED
BY
HANS V. ANDERSEN, JR.

For more books and products of similar interest, see order form in back or write to:

Hans V. Andersen, Jr.
1724 South 165 West
Orem, UT 84058
(801) 224-3368

ISBN: 1-57636-027-X
Library of Congress Catalog Card Number: 96-70759
Suggested Retail: $12.95

Text layout and cover design by:
SunRise Publishing, Orem, Utah

TABLE OF CONTENTS

Introduction v

I   The Reign Of Law 1
II   The Universal Desire For Freedom 9
III   The Natural Laws Governing Freedom 19
IV   Justice According To The Golden Rule 37
V   The United States Constitution 53
VI   Criminal Laws..67
VII   Tort Laws 83
VIII   Contract Laws 95
IX   The Nature Of Wealth 109
X   The Nature Of Property Rights 121
XI   Limitations On Government Power...........................135
XII   Procedures Which Must Be Followed By Government
       In The Exercise Of Its Powers 149
XIII   Administrative Laws And The Law Of Stewardships 163

Appendix I (Unity) 181
Appendix II (Handling Opposition) 189
Appendix III (Justified and Unjustified Warfare) 203
Appendix IV (Who Opposes Socialism) 207
Index 213

Now Ammon being wise, yet harmless, he said unto Lamoni: Wilt thou hearken unto my words, if I tell thee by what power I do these things? And this is the thing that I desire of thee.

And the king answered him, and said: Yea, I will believe all thy words. And thus he was caught with guile.

And Ammon began to speak unto him with boldness, and said unto him: Believest thou that there is a God?

(Alma 18:22-24)

INTRODUCTION

UNNAMED, UNGRADED QUESTIONNAIRE

As a professor in the accounting department, Daddy taught Business Law at BYU for many years. His students were primarily upper division business and accounting majors at BYU, which meant that in most instances they were returned missionaries. My reason for making this observation is that the following explanation by him of the test he gave his students should be of concern for all freedom-loving Americans.

—Hans V. Andersen, Jr.

As a college law teacher, I have made it a practice over the years to give a questionnaire to my students on the first day of class in which they were asked to respond to a number of questions regarding their acceptance or rejection of the proposals contained in the Ten Points of the Communist Manifesto. Of course I did not inform them that they were registering opinions about Communism and the questionnaire revealed that very few had ever read the Communist Manifesto. Their responses were therefore presumably not colored by any anti-communist bias. The results of the poll might be surprising to some. They revealed that on the average, my students were approximately two-thirds communist in their political beliefs. That is, on an average, they accepted about two-thirds of the Communist program for socializing a capitalist nation.

Doubtless, much of the explanation for this apparent discrepancy lies in the fact that people are generally ignorant about Communist practices and methods. They do not realize that the political beliefs they are espousing will lead to the same loss of liberty in America as in Russia. (H. Verlan Andersen, Speech on Socialism, 10/8/79)

(Note: Below is a copy of the questionnaire, referred to above. The percentages to the right show the percent of the students who responded with a "Yes," or "No." The "No Response" would be the difference, if any.)

Please place a check mark in the yes or no column or fill in the blanks to indicate your response to the following questions. Do not place your name on your paper.

A.
1. Have you read the Constitution within the last four years?
Yes/Agree [ ] No/Disagree [ ] No response [ ]   39% 60%
2. Have you ever read the Communist Manifesto?
Yes/Agree [ ] No/Disagree [ ] No response [ ]   12% 86%

B.
Do you favor—
1. Graduated tax rates on income?
Yes/Agree [ ] No/Disagree [ ] No response [ ]   55% 43%
2. An unrestricted power in government to tax inheritances?
Yes/Agree [ ] No/Disagree [ ]   4% 96%
3. A return to the gold and silver standard of the Constitution?
Yes/Agree [ ] No/Disagree [ ] No response [ ]   39% 60%
4. Federal regulation of transportation and communication businesses?
Yes/Agree [ ] No/Disagree [ ]   54% 46%
5. A system of free public education?
Yes/Agree [ ] No/Disagree [ ] No response [ ]   72% 23%

C.
1. For the purpose of providing for the less fortunate, do you feel government should have the power to completely equalize all incomes?
Yes/Agree [ ] No/Disagree [ ]   2% 98%
2. If not, do you believe the poor have some claim on government for their subsistence needs?
Yes/Agree [ ] No/Disagree [ ] No response [ ]   55% 43%

D.
1. Should government have the power to prohibit child labor?
Yes/Agree [ ] No/Disagree [ ] No response [ ]   67% 30%
2. Should government have the power to set minimum wages?
Yes/Agree [ ] No/Disagree [ ] No response [ ]   65% 30%
3. Should government have the power to license every economic activity?
Yes/Agree [ ] No/Disagree [ ] No response [ ]   18% 80%
4. Should government be completely without such licensing power?
Yes/Agree [ ] No/Disagree [ ] No response [ ]   13% 82%
5. If you believe in some, but not complete licensing power, indicate three trades, professions, businesses, etc. which should be licensed:
    a) _____
    b) _____
    c) _____
List three which should not be licensed:
    a) _____
    b) _____
    c) _____

E.
1. Government should have the power to regulate the operation of all economic activities.
Yes/Agree [ ] No/Disagree [ ] No response [ ]   9% 89%
2. Government should not have the power to regulate any legitimate economic activity.
Yes/Agree [ ] No/Disagree [ ] No response [ ]   24% 73%
3. If you believe in some, but not complete government regulation, do you feel you could draw a precise line between those activities which should and should not be regulated?
Yes/Agree [ ] No/Disagree [ ] No response [ ]   17% 79%
4. Government should have the power to set minimum standards for all goods and services.
Yes/Agree [ ] No/Disagree [ ] No response [ ]   43% 41%
5. If you favor a partial, but not complete set of government standards, name three products or services for which standards should be set by government:
   a) _____
   b) _____
   c) _____
Name three products or services for which standards should not be set:
   a) _____
   b) _____
   c) _____

F.
1. Should government have the power to bring waste lands into production and engage in soil conservation programs?
Yes/Agree [ ] No/Disagree [ ] No response [ ]   77% 19%
2. Should government have the power to control natural resources such as rivers, lakes, forests and mineral deposits?
Yes/Agree [ ] No/Disagree [ ] No response [ ]   78% 19%
3. Should governments sell to private individuals all the land they now own except that which is necessary for defense and protection of rights?
Yes/Agree [ ] No/Disagree [ ] No response [ ]   21% 76%

G.
1. I believe that there is a distinct line between those circumstances under which the government should compel people against their will and those where it should not.
Yes/Agree [ ] No/Disagree [ ] No response [ ]   48% 47%
2. I believe that the scriptures provide accurate guidance regarding the distinction between good and bad laws.
Yes/Agree [ ] No/Disagree [ ] No response [ ]   81% 14%

WHY MEN ESTABLISH GOVERNMENTS

One fundamental political truth which will be considered is that men establish governments for the purpose of compelling the citizens to obey a code of private morality. This code is contained in a set of laws which govern human conduct. Such laws may be classified into these two types: (1) Those which condemn and punish certain conduct as evil and harmful; (2) Those which compel the performance of other conduct considered good and beneficial.

When men make laws, and thus determine which conduct is so evil it should be punished and which is so good it should be compelled, they do so by referring to their own religious, ethical or moral beliefs. Indeed there is no other point of reference for distinguishing good from evil. And so no matter who makes the laws, be they kings, dictators, legislatures or the people themselves, they express their most intensely held moral convictions in the laws they favor.

ALL GOVERNMENT ACTION IS EITHER GOOD OR EVIL

A second political fact which may be equally as important as the first is this: Every act which government performs is either morally right or morally wrong. This conclusion is unavoidable because government can act only by using force on humans and force cannot be used on humans without moral consequences.

THE MORAL PROBLEM PLAINLY DISCERNIBLE

If one reflects upon the nature of government and how it functions, the moral problem is clearly seen. It exists to enforce laws which forbid or command certain conduct. But the only type of conduct which a reasonable person would want to forbid is that which he considers evil or wrong, and the only conduct he would want to compel is that which is good.

But the moral problem is most clearly seen when we consider

how laws are enforced. This is done by depriving the disobedient of either his life, his liberty or his property. Every law which can properly be termed such carries one or more of these three penalties. But the problem as to when it is right and when wrong to put a person to death or take from him his liberty or property is of the utmost moral significance. Both humanity and justice dictate that we punish only those who do evil. Anyone who would inflict death, imprisonment or fine for any other reason must regard himself as a murderer, an enslaver, or a thief.

Thus when government enforces a law, its actions are either morally right or morally wrong. Never are they without moral significance. They are good or evil depending upon whether the conduct prohibited or commanded is good or evil. This makes the study of government extremely challenging. There is no latitude for error. The existence of government is justified only because there exists a code of private morality which should be enforced. But if it misconstrues what that code is, to that same extent it violates it.

THE MORAL PROBLEM EXTENDS BEYOND THE IMPOSITION OF PENALTIES

The propriety of inflicting punishment is not the only moral issue which arises when a law is adopted. In addition to this, the effect of the law on the freedom of all who obey it out of fear of punishment must be considered. The primary purpose for passing a law is to induce those to obey it who would not do so unless threatened with death, imprisonment or fine. Thus the object is to deny the people their freedom to do what the law forbids. If the law proscribes only evil, then no one loses a freedom to which he is entitled because no one has the right to do wrong. But if it forbids conduct which is good or innocent, then it takes from the people a freedom which is rightfully theirs and this cannot be considered other than evil.

THE MORAL ISSUE PRESENT IN EVERY BRANCH OF THE LAW

The moral problem in government action is most clearly seen in the field of criminal law where punishments are inflicted. But it is also the central problem of both tort and contract law because when a case arises in these areas, the court is almost always faced with the problem of deciding whether to take property from one party and transfer it to another. This also is a moral issue. It is either right or wrong, just or unjust, good or evil to forcibly take property from A and transfer it to B.

It has been stated that: "Justice is the end of government. It is the end of civil society. It ever has been and ever will be pursued until it be obtained, or until liberty be lost in the pursuit." (Fed. Papers # 51) But the very concept of justice rests upon the assumption that there is a solution to a case which is morally right and that any deviation therefrom is morally wrong. Thus, even in the field of tort and contract law, when government uses force on a litigant, it either dispenses justice or commits an injustice. In other words, it does either good or evil.

THE NECESSITY OF A UNIVERSAL MORAL CODE

A government which pretends to be just to all must see to it that the code of morality expressed by its laws is properly enforceable against everyone. With the exception of infants and mental incompetents, everyone is expected to conform to the laws or suffer punishment. But unless each member of society believes the conduct which the law prohibits to be evil, and that which it commands to be good, some will be punished for doing that which they sincerely consider to be right while others will be compelled to do that which they regard as wrong. This violates our sense of justice and the only solution is to find a moral code which is known and accepted by all people. But does such a code exist?

The position taken herein is that there is a code of moral behavior which may with justice be enforced against all people regardless of the age or country in which they live. This code is based upon the universal need and desire for freedom. While people differ widely in their objectives, everyone wants to be free to achieve his own, whatever they may be. Everyone wants those elements of freedom—life, liberty of action, property and knowledge—without which no objective can be reached.

Not only does each desire to possess these elements, but each is keenly aware of what injures them and considers such actions harmful and evil when committed. Even during infancy and youth we condemn that which injures our bodies, restricts our movements, deprives us of our property and corrupts our knowledge. With respect to those possessions which are necessary to the exercise of freedom, we all have essentially the same moral code: that which denies or injures them is evil and wrong; that which provides, protects and preserves them is good.

When the laws of a nation conform to this universal moral code, they will be respected and upheld because they suit the paramount need and desire of all people. But when they deviate from it, contention and strife are bound to arise because this is the only standard of moral behavior which is known and accepted by all men. In essence this universal moral code is nothing more nor less than the Christian's GOLDEN RULE which, according to Holy Writ, "is the law and the prophets." (Matt. 7:12)

THE TENDENCY TO VIOLATE PRIVATE MORAL PRINCIPLES THROUGH PUBLIC ACTION

Even though it be true that all men share the same moral code with respect to human freedom, history demonstrates that they have a strong disposition to do through government that which would violate that code if done outside its framework. They seem to divorce their ethical from their political principles and become oblivious to the moral consequences of the laws they favor.

How otherwise do we account for the following? If there is a forcible transfer of A's property to B committed outside the framework of government, this is universally regarded as criminal. If done in the name of government, many favor it as an act of charity. How does that which was once evil suddenly become good? Is it because its real nature is hidden by being clothed in the robes of legality?

Is A any less a victim in the latter case than the former? Is the demoralizing effect on B's character any less when government does the taking?

Or, suppose that a number of farmers or some other economic group desiring to maintain at a high level the price of their crops, goods or services, band together and use force to restrain competition. How can people condemn this as criminal racketeering when done by the group itself, but regard it as a proper exercise of a licensing power when done by their servants in government? Is an act any less evil when done by an agent than when done by the principal? Is the injury to the public any less when government forces prices up than when racketeers do?

Let us assume further that someone has been convicted of violating such a licensing law but there is no proof that he either intended evil or caused anyone harm. He had only tried to make a living in the licensed occupation by producing something which the public needed and was willing to purchase from him. How can any moral person approve of punishing him? And, yet by a curious twist of logic many do. If it is inherently unjust to punish an innocent person, can a man-made law change this fundamental truth? Is a punishment any less harmful and wrong when inflicted by government than when inflicted by a racketeer?

And how can one who thoroughly detests having his own business and private affairs regulated, and who has neither the means nor the least inclination to interfere privately in the affairs of his neighbors—how can he favor laws which send an army of bureaucrats to do this very thing? Is it any less expensive when done through government? Are government employees more competent to operate businesses than the owners themselves?

What is his reason for favoring regulatory laws anyway? Is he fearful that his neighbors, if left to run their own affairs might commit crimes? If so, there are criminal laws to punish them. Is he concerned that if not regulated they might cause someone harm? If so, there are tort and contract laws which permit restitution for every compensable injury. And where did he obtain the authority to regulate his neighbors anyway? And if he does not possess it, how can he delegate it to government? If he undertook it himself, he would likely consider himself either a mental incompetent, an insufferably arrogant busybody or a criminal. How can he fail to view himself in this same light when he acts through government?

This embarrassing disparity between private and public morality has extremely important consequences to every citizen. But it has peculiar significance to businessmen and all who are concerned with the operation of the free enterprise system. Let us observe why.

THE DANGERS OF CONFLICT AND CONSTANT CHANGE IN POLITICAL AFFAIRS

When men abandon the principles of private morality in public affairs, they have no standard to adhere to and disagreements arise. It is probable that there is no subject about which there is more dispute today than that of politics. Not only do the laws of the various nations differ radically one from another, but people of the same nation are found to hold widely varying political opinions. Disagreement is so extensive that it is difficult to find even two people who favor exactly the same set of laws.

Much of this contention centers around the role of government in economic affairs. Should it engage in welfare state activities and if so to what extent? What limit, if any, should be placed on the amount taken from the "haves?" To what class of people should aid be extended and to what standard of living should they be raised? Is it proper for government to withhold incomes for such purposes as social security, medicare, old age pensions and unemployment insurance and if so how much? Should wages, hours of labor and working conditions be regulated and, if so, in what particulars? How much education are children (or adults) entitled to at state expense? Which professions, trades and businesses should be licensed and how stiff should licensing requirements be? How thoroughly should the use of property be controlled through zoning laws? To what degree should government dictate the type of products which may be produced and sold, the safety standards which must be observed and the pollution limits which are permissible?

Questions of this type could be continued for pages with no one able to give a logically defensible answer or to explain why the answer he does give should not be something else. Not only are people in hopeless disagreement over such matters but the opinions of any one person are ofttimes subject to constant change. This confusion and uncertainty extends into the ranks of the lawmakers with chaos the result. At each legislative session, they spew forth a veritable torrent of new measures which add to, amend or repeal the equally ill-considered acts of their predecessors. This instability not only threatens to destroy our free enterprise system but also the foundations upon which it rests. Perhaps there is no better description of the dangers flowing from a voluminous and constantly changing set of laws than the one contained in #62 of the Federalist Papers authored by James Madison and Alexander Hamilton from which the following is quoted:

> The internal effects of a mutable policy are still more calamitous. It poisons the blessing of liberty itself. It will be of little avail to the people, that the laws are made by men of their own choice, if the laws be so voluminous that they cannot be read, or so incoherent that they cannot be understood; if they be repealed or revised before they are promulgated, or undergo such incessant changes that no man, who knows what the law is to-day, can guess what it will be to-morrow. Law is defined to be a rule of action; but how can that be a rule, which is little known, and less fixed?
>
> In another point of view, great injury results from an unstable government. The want of confidence in the public councils damps every useful undertaking, the success and profit of which may depend on a continuance of existing arrangements. What prudent merchant will hazard his fortunes in any new branch of commerce when he knows not but that his plans may be rendered unlawful before they can be executed? What farmer or manufacturer will lay himself out for the encouragement given to any particular cultivation or establishment, when he can have no assurance that his preparatory labors and advances will not render him a victim to an inconstant government? In a word, no great improvement or laudable enterprise can go forward which requires the auspices of a steady system of national policy.
>
> But the most deplorable effect of all is that diminution of attachment and reverence which steals into the hearts of the people, towards a political system which betrays so many marks of infirmity, and disappoints so many of their flattering hopes. No government, any more than an individual, will long be respected without being truly respectable; nor be truly respectable, without possessing a certain portion of order and stability.

There is no group which should be more anxiously concerned with finding a solution to the problems enumerated above than the owners and operators of economic enterprises. As Madison and Hamilton have pointed out, the evil effects of multitudinous and unstable laws falls most heavily upon them. Not only are they disabled from making and executing long-range plans, but the freedom to make contracts and manage their own concerns is denied.

If the laws dictate the employment contract by specifying wages, hours and working conditions; if they establish product, safety and pollution standards; if by means of consumer protection acts they govern relations between seller and buyer; if they regulate profits through graduated tax rates and price controls; if they license all businesses and determine who may enter which; if the securities laws control financing; if they do all of this and much, much more, what remains for the businessman to manage? And if the trend continues as in the past, what future is there for those who plan a business career?

As the role of government in economic affairs increases, that of the owner and operator decreases. Their area of decision making will be reduced with every new rule and regulation until they become no more than tools of the bureaucracy, doing their will and carrying out their decrees. At that point, there will be no further need for studying the principles of private business and contract law. Business colleges will then be concerned almost exclusively with teaching the current rules and regulations of government. This possibility should induce every student and practitioner of business to take a strong and continuing interest in political matters.

WHERE DOES ONE FIND THE ANSWER TO THE MORAL PROBLEM OF GOVERNMENT?

To give us that guidance, without which one cannot hope to find the correct answer to political questions which are essentially moral, we shall go to the source of moral law. We shall consult the prophets and the scriptures and those whom they approve. No apology is offered for doing this. Anyone who defends a particular legal philosophy must use some code of ethics as its foundation because that is what a set of laws consists of. Those laws are a concise description of that conduct which they decree to be punishable evil and can have no other source than the code of ethics of those who sponsor them.

If it be objected that the bias of any one particular religion or moral code should not be incorporated into the laws which people of many faiths are compelled to obey, we answer that there is no help for this. No one who favors a particular set of laws can escape that accusation. There can be only one set of laws at a time and, thus, only one moral code, and every member of society must conform to it regardless of his religion or lack thereof. But our particular defense to that charge is that the doctrines of the Latter-day Saint Church are in complete harmony with the moral code expounded in the United States Constitution which every American citizen is obligated to uphold until that document be amended by a three-fourths majority of the states as therein provided. Justification for using the moral code of the Constitution rests in the fact that it is founded on the universal need and desire for freedom and constitutes the only code which may, with justice, be enforced against all men.

But the author has another reason to resort to the teachings of his faith and the Founding Fathers for guidance. He has been instructed by his superiors to do so. Those who teach subjects involving political principles at the Brigham Young University are under direction from the controlling body of this institution to harmonize their teachings with "the principles of government as vouchsafed to us by our Constitutional Fathers." In a letter written in 1967 by the late President David O. McKay to the BYU Administration and Faculty, explicit instructions were given regarding what should and should not be taught here regarding laws and government. This letter was considered of sufficient importance that the entire Board of Trustees approved it;

> . . .as the policy of the Board of Trustees for the guidance of the Board, the University Administration, and present and prospective members of the Faculty.

It may not be inappropriate to present herewith extracts from the letter that its true meaning may be expressed:

> (2) In these days when not only religious standards but some of the Ten Commandments themselves are under attack, I hope that you and the faculty will go the extra mile in seeing that the religious doctrines of our Church are taught in their fullness so that students will have proper religious convictions for all decisions which they have to make. The trends of the time in the opposite direction are so strong that it will require extraordinary vigilance on the part of all of us to resist them. . . . I would urge all members of the faculty, whether they have a Church position or not, to teach principles of the Gospel and standards in every class

whenever the opportunity arises, whether that class be a class in theology or otherwise.

(3) I cannot help but think that there is a direct relationship between the present evil trends which I have above indicated, and the very marked tendency of the people of our country to pass on to the state the responsibility for their moral and economic welfare. This trend to a welfare state in which people look to and worship government more than their God, is certain to sap the individual ambitions and moral fiber of our youth unless they are warned and rewarned of the consequences. History, of course, is replete with the downfall of nations who, instead of assuming their own responsibility for their religious and economic welfare, mistakenly attempted to shift their individual responsibility to the government.

I am aware that a university has the responsibility of acquainting its students with the theories and doctrines which are prevalent in various disciplines, but I hope that no one on the faculty of Brigham Young University will advocate positions which cannot be harmonized with the views of every prophet of the church, from the Prophet Joseph Smith on down, concerning our belief that we should be strong and self-reliant individuals, not dependent upon the largess or benefactions of government. None of the doctrines of our Church give any sanction to the concept of a socialistic state.

It is a part of our "Mormon" theology that the Constitution of the United States was divinely inspired; that our Republic came into existence through wise men raised up for that very purpose. We believe it is the duty of the members of the Church to see that this Republic is not subverted either by any sudden or constant erosion of those principles which gave this Nation its birth.

In these days when there is a special trend among certain groups, including members of faculties of universities, to challenge the principles upon which our country has been founded and the philosophy of our Founding Fathers, I hope that Brigham Young University will stand as a bulwark in support of the principles of government as vouchsafed to us by our Constitutional Fathers.

In accordance with the Board's policy as above set forth, there has been included herein scriptural references and quotes from General Authorities, the Founding Fathers and others, which it is hoped will aid the student in understanding the American Constitutional system of government and the principles of private morality upon which it was built.

There is a law, irrevocably decreed in heaven before the foundations of this world, upon which all blessings are predicated—

And when we obtain any blessing from God, it is by obedience to that law upon which it is predicated.

(D&C 130:20-21)

Therefore, choose you by the voice of this people, judges, that ye may be judged according to the laws which have been given you by our fathers, which are correct, and which were given them by the hand of the Lord.

(Mosiah 29:25)

CHAPTER I
THE REIGN OF LAW

1.1 MAN'S SUBJECTION TO LAW

> All kingdoms have a law given;
> And there are many kingdoms; for there is no space in the which there is no kingdom; and there is no kingdom in which there is no space, either a greater or a lesser kingdom.
> And unto every kingdom is given a law; and unto every law there are certain bounds also and conditions.
> All beings who abide not in those conditions are not justified.
> *(D&C 88:36-39)*

Universally man is subject to the reign of law. In reality he lives in subjection to two sets of laws—those man-made and those existing naturally. This book is devoted primarily to a study of man-made law. However, since natural law reigns supreme in every field, including that of political science, it is appropriate that we commence with a recognition of those natural laws which govern in this field. Indeed, without a knowledge of such laws, the intelligent use of man-made laws would be impossible. Justification for this conclusion lies in the fact that men cannot use their intelligence to solve problems in any field of inquiry, unless those natural laws which govern in that field are understood. Let us pursue this thought by defining natural law and then observing that the use of intelligence is dependent upon its existence.

1.2 DEFINITION OF NATURAL LAW

The term "natural law" is used herein to mean a statement of an unvarying relationship between cause and effect. It is a description of change which, according to all that is known, will invariably follow a given cause. Thus natural laws constitute that entire body of laws which exist independently of man. Their operation is unrelated to the will of democratic majorities, the enactments of legislatures or the decrees of monarchs. They are above and beyond man. He is

1

powerless to alter or affect them in any way. His ignorance of them, his refusal to accept them or his mistaken beliefs regarding how they function have not the slightest effect upon their operation. The only way he can obtain the results which are predicated upon obedience is to learn and obey them.

Civilized man realizes that he lives in a universe governed by immutable, inexorable natural laws. He has learned that to accomplish any given result he must discover and precisely obey the laws upon which that result depends. If he complies partially or imperfectly, he may expect no more than a partial or an imperfect result. Nor is natural law any respecter of persons. It affects everyone the same. No matter in what age or country one lives, to obtain a result he must comply with a law.

The reign of law in the physical world is not questioned by intelligent people. Scientists as well as others have proved over and over again the unvarying nature of the rules which govern changes relating to energy and matter such as the laws of gravity, electricity and thermodynamics. All reliable evidence proves the existence of immutable laws in the physical world and nothing man has observed has disproved their existence. Therefore, they are taken for granted. The large sums of money spent on research is evidence of man's faith in the reign of law. By conducting such research he tries to discover new laws which he assumes to exist and which he knows he must obey to accomplish his purposes. Never yet has he been disappointed in his assumption that natural law governs in the physical world.

1.3 THE USE OF INTELLIGENCE DEPENDENT UPON NATURAL LAW

> And if ye shall say there is no law, ye shall also say there is no sin. If ye shall say there is no sin, ye shall also say there is no righteousness. And if there be no righteousness there be no happiness. And if there be no righteousness nor happiness there be no punishment nor misery. And if these things are not there is no God. And if there is no God we are not, neither the earth; for there could have been no creation of things, neither to act nor to be acted upon; wherefore, all things must have vanished away.
> *(2 Nephi 2:13)*

Intelligence has been defined as: "The ability to apprehend the interrelationships of presented facts in such a way as to guide action toward a desired goal." Using this definition we might define intelligent conduct as "compliance with law to obtain a desired goal." But one cannot work toward a goal unless he can foresee the consequences of his action; and one cannot foresee the consequences of his actions unless natural laws exist which decree that the same results will follow the same causes. From this we must conclude that intelligent conduct is possible only in the presence of natural law. Only where one can predict the consequences of what he does can he "guide action toward a desired goal." Where law prevails and is understood, one is able to predetermine the results which will flow from any given course of conduct and thus choose that course which will accomplish his purposes.

The necessity for natural law is also evident by recognizing that without it there could be no human freedom. When one exercises freedom he chooses between alternatives. This means that he elects to accept the consequences which flow from pursuing one course of action while rejecting those which would result from another. But unless natural laws exist which predetermine the consequences he is choosing between, he could not anticipate them; therefore, a choice would be impossible.

It is difficult, if not impossible to visualize an environment in which law does not exist. But if such were possible, chaos would reign. Nothing could be depended upon to happen the same way twice. Past events and conditions would bear no relation to future occurrences. Man could not survive in such an environment. Being unable to foresee the results of his actions he could not feed and clothe himself. Memory, judgment, knowledge, foresight, reason and other qualities of the mind would be of no avail. In the absence of law, intelligent conduct would be impossible and intelligence unusable.

1.4 NATURAL LAW IN THE FIELD OF GOVERNMENT

There is a law, irrevocably decreed in heaven before the foundations of this world, upon which all blessings are predicated—

And when we obtain any blessing from God, it is by obedience to that law upon which it is predicated.

> It is impossible for a man to be saved in ignorance.
> *(D&C 130:20, 21; 131:6)*

Does the conclusion that intelligence cannot be exercised in the absence of natural law apply in the field of government? That is, in adopting man-made laws to achieve a given purpose is it essential to discover and obey certain laws before the attainment of that purpose is possible? While the supremacy of law in the physical realm is generally accepted, there may be those who question its existence in the area of human relations. But as has been demonstrated above, if natural law does not prevail here, the conscious achievement of goals in this field is impossible. Unless we proceed under the assumption that natural laws exist which enable us to set goals for our law-making and work toward them, it is idle to study the subject.

Obedience to law is the sum of intelligent existence. Anyone who assumes that there is no need to learn and obey the natural laws of some particular field such as government has, in effect, concluded that it is impossible to work toward goals in that field. Man is continually striving to bring about change; but every change occurs in strict accordance with law. Therefore to produce any desired change, whether in the physical world or in our political and social affairs, those laws which govern its occurrence must be discovered and obeyed. This constitutes the purpose of intelligent life.

1.5 SUPREMACY OF NATURAL LAW OVER MAN-MADE LAW LONG RECOGNIZED

> Therefore I will be your king the remainder of my days; nevertheless, let us appoint judges, to judge this people according to our law; and we will newly arrange the affairs of this people, for we will appoint wise men to be judges, that will judge this people according to the commandments of God.
> Therefore, choose you by the voice of this people, judges, that ye may be judged according to the laws which have been given you by our fathers, which are correct, and which were given them by the hand of the Lord. *(Mosiah 29:11, 25)*

The proposition that natural law controls in all areas, including that of government has long been recognized by the sages, prophets and great thinkers of the past. The people of the Old Testament regarded God as the Source of their civil laws. The Ten Commandments which came to them through their prophet, Moses (Ex. 20), constituted the essence of their legal code and was enforced among the people just as civil laws are enforced by governments today. Even the penalties which were imposed for violation were accepted by them as having been divinely revealed (Deut. 5:1-33). To the Israelites, the laws of God and the laws of nature were one and the same—immutable, inexorable and eternal.

The notion that there is a law of nature which emanates from God and governs political activities had its advocates among the Romans. Cicero, a statesman and orator of some stature, proclaimed his acceptance of this belief in the following passage:

> Of all these things respecting which learned men dispute there is none more important than clearly to understand that we are born for justice, and that right is founded not in opinion but in nature. There is indeed a true law (lex), right reason, agreeing with nature and diffused among all, unchanging, everlasting, which calls to duty by commanding, deters from wrong by forbidding. . . It is not allowable to alter this law nor to deviate from it. Nor can it be abrogated. Nor can we be released from this law either by the senate or by the people. Nor is any person required to explain or interpret it. Nor is it one law at Rome and another at Athens, one law today and another thereafter; but the same law, everlasting and unchangeable, will bind all nations and all times; and there will be one common Lord and Ruler of all, even God, the framer and proposer of this law. (De Legibus ll, 4, 10)

Accompanying and following the Reformation, the doctrine of a supreme and controlling law of nature found acceptance and reiteration by recognized authorities in the fields of social and political science. The English philosopher, John Locke, sometimes called "the intellectual ruler of the eighteenth century," had this to say in his *Second Essay Concerning Civil Government* which made its appearance around 1689:

> Thus the law of Nature stands as an eternal rule to all men, legislators as well others. The rules that they make for other men's actions, must. . . be conformable to the law of Nature—i.e., to the will of God, of which that is a declaration, and the fundamental law of Nature being the preservation of mankind, no human sanction can be good or valid against it. (Second Essay Concerning Civil Government, Para. 135)

Sir William Blackstone, a famous English jurist, and one of the best legal minds in any country, wrote this in his *Commentaries on the Laws of England* published in 1765:

> Man, considered as a creature, must necessarily be subject to the laws of his Creator. . . This will of his Maker is called the law of nature. . . This law of nature, being co-eval with mankind, and dictated by God himself, is of course superior in obligation to any other. It is binding over all the globe, in all countries, and at all times; no human laws are of any validity, if contrary to this; and such of them as are valid derive all their force and all their authority, mediately and immediately, from this original. . . Upon these two foundations, the law of nature and the law of revelation, depend all human laws; that is to say no human laws should be suffered to contradict these. . . nay, if any human law should allow or enjoin us to commit it, we are bound to transgress that human law, or else we offend both the natural and the divine. (Vol. I, pp. 41-43)

It is generally conceded that both Locke and Blackstone wielded an immense influence on the thinking of the men who established the United States Constitutional system of government. Certainly these "Founding Fathers" believed in the supremacy of natural law. The Declaration of Independence is itself an affirmation of the view that natural law is superior to the authority of civil rulers. In this document the doctrine of the "Law of Nature" is transmuted into the doctrine of the "unalienable rights of man" the essence of which is contained in the following excerpt:

> We hold these truths to be self-evident, that all men are created equal; that they are endowed by their Creator with certain unalienable rights; that among these are life, liberty, and the pursuit of happiness. That, to secure these rights, governments are instituted among men, deriving their just powers from the consent of the governed; that, whenever any form of government becomes destructive of these ends, it is the right of the people to alter or to abolish it . . . (Declaration of Independence)

The thought here expressed, that men possess from their Creator certain unalienable rights which government should protect but never deny, is a statement of the Natural Law concept in slightly different form. Here, as in the other quotes, it is asserted that there are natural limitations on the power of civil rulers. Deviation from these natural laws (or the protection of natural rights) is not allowable. But if such does occur it is the right of the people to abolish their government and replace it with one which exercises only those powers rightfully possessed.

In the foregoing quotes the authors have not only asserted the supremacy of natural law in the field of government, but have taken the position that such natural laws are religious or moral in nature. This may seem strange to some. Let us, by defining man-made laws and observing how they are enforced, demonstrate that not only is it proper to require man-made laws to conform to natural moral law, but that it is contrary to all logic when they fail to do so.

1.6 MAN-MADE LAW

A man-made law is a rule of human conduct prescribed by the state and enforced by an adequate penalty for disobedience. It is an enactment by government which forbids the individual to do as he pleases in the matter regulated and threatens him with physical punishment if he disobeys. The penalty provided in the law directs the officers of government to punish the offender in one or more of three ways:

(1) Inflict injury on his body including death;
(2) Deprive him of his liberty by imprisonment or some other restraint;
(3) Deprive him of his property.

A law may be mandatory in that it commands the individual to take some affirmative action such as pay taxes or serve in the armed forces; or it may be prohibitive in that it forbids murder, robbery, arson or some other act. There are two essential parts to every man-made law: (1) The regulation of human conduct; (if it does not do this there is nothing to obey) (2) A penalty for disobedience; (if no penalty is imposed one is as free to do as he pleases after the law is passed as before). As was stated by Hamilton in the *Federalist Papers:*

> Government implies the power of making laws. It is essential to the idea of law, that it be attended with a sanction; or, in other words, a penalty or punishment for disobedience. If there be no penalty annexed for disobedience, the resolutions or commands which pretend to be laws will, in fact, amount to nothing more than advice or recommendation. (Fed. Papers #15)

1.7 CIVIL LAWS ARE MORAL LAWS

> And that they had altered and trampled under their feet the laws of Mosiah, or that which the Lord commanded him to give unto the people; and they saw that their laws had become corrupted, and that they had become a wicked people, insomuch that they were wicked even like unto the Lamanites.
>
> For as their laws and their governments were established by the voice of the people, and they who chose evil were more numerous than they who chose good, therefore they were ripening for destruction, for the laws had become corrupted. *(Helaman 4:22; 5:2)*

The foregoing analysis indicates that man-made laws are essentially moral laws because their enforcement involves the taking of human life, liberty or property rights. Governments act legally only in accordance with law. But every law regulates human conduct by commanding or forbidding certain actions and directing the executive arm to execute, jail or fine those who disobey. Indeed the only reason for adopting a law is to compel those to obey it who would not do so unless threatened with violence. Thus, every law affects at least one of those three possessions which men value above all others. If the law is obeyed out of fear, then freedom is affected by the threat of violence. If the law is violated, then either freedom, life, or property is taken as punishment.

But there is no question which has greater moral implications than that of determining when it is proper to deprive a human being of his life, his liberty, or the means by which he sustains life and exercises liberty. Therefore, civil laws are moral laws by very definition. Those natural laws then which control in the field of political science constitute a moral code. The man-made laws which should conform thereto are also a code of moral behavior.

CHAPTER II

THE UNIVERSAL DESIRE
FOR FREEDOM

2.1 THE NEED TO ESTABLISH A COMMON PURPOSE FOR GOVERNMENT

We have seen that the first and most fundamental lesson man can learn is that of obedience to natural law. Until he does this it is impossible for him to knowingly accomplish any purpose whatsoever. This basic truth is the starting point for the acquisition of knowledge in every discipline and applies with as much force to the study of government as to other fields. In view of this fact, we are commencing our study of this subject by seeking to identify those natural laws which must be obeyed to achieve the purposes we seek through the agency of government.

However, before proceeding to this task, it will be necessary to agree upon the purpose or purposes to be accomplished. Unless all men are willing to give priority to a single objective, or unless the various goals set for government are harmonious, it will be impossible to find a set of natural laws, obedience to which will accommodate everyone. An antagonism in purposes would require a sacrifice of one goal to accomplish another—a violation of the natural laws which lead to one result in order to obey those which lead to results inconsistent therewith.

But is there one goal for government which all men agree is transcendent and takes precedence over all others? Or, in lieu thereof, is there a single set of goals which are fully compatible upon which similar agreement may be reached? If not, we face an insuperable obstacle in our attempt to discover a set of natural moral laws which will serve as an unerring guide in the conduct of political affairs. If the services which governments perform do not provide something which all men need and desire—if they do not protect the rights of all men equally—then the dream of "liberty and justice for all" is unattainable.

Men are so diverse in their interests and aims that it may appear impossible to pass a set of civil laws demanding uniformity of conduct which will serve the needs and desires of all people equally. While some are religious, others deny the existence of God; while some are devoted to much learning, others are content to remain uneducated; while some love art, music and the theatre, others prefer science, engineering or sports; while some desire palatial homes, rich food and expensive clothing, others are content with the simpler things of life. Furthermore any one person is subject to constant change so that his objectives and values at one point in life may be replaced by a very different set later on. Do these infinitely diverse and ever-changing purposes and interests make it impossible for the members of society to reach agreement upon a single and controlling purpose for government?

2.2 THE TRANSCENDENT PURPOSE OF GOVERNMENT—INDIVIDUAL FREEDOM

> That every man may act in doctrine and principle pertaining to futurity, according to the moral agency which I have given unto him, that every man may be accountable for his own sins in the day of judgment. *(D&C 101:78)*

> And now I desire that this inequality should be no more in this land, especially among this my people; but I desire that this land be a land of liberty, and every man may enjoy his rights and privileges alike, so long as the Lord sees fit that we may live and inherit the land, yea, even as long as any of our posterity remains upon the face of the land. *(Mos. 29:32)*

> I refer to the fundamental principle of the gospel, free agency. References in the scriptures show that this principle is (1) essential to man's salvation; and (2) may become a measuring rod by which the actions of men, or organizations, of nations may be judged. (President David O. McKay, *Gospel Ideals*, pp. 299-300)

Fortunately there is a common need and desire which all men share and which takes precedence over all other considerations: this is the need and desire to be free. Every person, no matter in what age or country he lives desires his own liberty of action. While men may differ widely in their individual goals, every person wants the freedom to carry out his own purposes whatever they may be. Thus, everyone with a goal will have an accompanying desire to be free to achieve it.

Not only does every person desire freedom for himself but this desire takes precedence over every other consideration. To become and remain free is paramount because when a person is in bondage, he must first free himself before he can pursue any other purpose. This truism applies to partial as well as total restraints. If servitude in any degree makes impossible the attainment of an objective, the removal of the restraint must occur before the goal can be reached.

Assuming that a state of freedom is transcendent above all other needs, it should constitute the supreme and controlling objective of government. No other purpose can be allowed to take precedence over it, and if any other goal is found to be in conflict therewith or to diminish in any degree the freedom of the individual, it must be abandoned as being opposed to the paramount need and desire of all men. So considered, we may establish freedom not only as the supreme but the exclusive purpose of government. If freedom exists, any achievement within the power of man is made possible while without it every other goal is beyond reach.

2.3 THE ELEMENTS OF FREEDOM

We believe that no government can exist in peace, except such laws are framed and held inviolate as will secure to each individual the free exercise of conscience, the right and control of property, and the protection of life. *(D&C 134:2)*

Therefore, it is not right that any man should be in bondage one to another.
And for this purpose have I established the Constitution of this land, by the hands of wise men whom I have up unto this very purpose, and redeemed the land by the shedding of blood. *(D&C 101:79, 80)*

Nevertheless, they durst not lie, if it were known, for fear of the law, for liars were punished; therefore they pretended to preach according to their belief; and now the law could have no power on any man for his belief.
And they durst not steal, for fear of the law, for such were

punished; neither durst they rob, nor murder, for he that murdered was punished unto death. *(Alma 1:17, 18)*

But Ammon said unto him: It is against the law of our brethren, which was established by my father, that there should be any slaves among them; therefore let us go down and rely upon the mercies of our brethren. *(Alma 27:9)*

But if he murdered he was punished unto death; and if he robbed he was also punished; and if he stole he was also punished; and if he committed adultery he was also punished; yea, for all this wickedness they were punished.
For there was a law that men should be judged according to their crimes. Nevertheless, there was no law against a man's belief; therefore, a man was punished only for the crimes which he had done; therefore all men were on equal grounds. *(Alma 30:10, 11)*

Since every person desires freedom, every person desires those possessions without which the exercise of freedom is impossible. They are:

(1) Life and some degree of physical and mental health and strength;
(2) The absence of restraint and coercion by others;
(3) Knowledge of those laws which must be obeyed to achieve one's goals;
(4) The right and control of property.

Let us observe that each of these four possessions is indispensable to the exercise of freedom and that each person wants his own protected against injury and loss in order that he may accomplish his own purposes whatever they may be.

2.4 LIFE

To strive toward any goal one must have some degree of physical and mental health and strength. Therefore, the desire for life is at least as strong as the desire to accomplish goals. Every rational person wants bodily health not only because of the freedom from pain and suffering which it brings but also because the greater the vigor of mind and body the more able one is to accomplish his purposes or exercise his freedom.

Of course, there are those abnormal individuals who intentionally abuse and injure their bodies and some even take measures to bring their existence to an end. But even such people want to determine for themselves when and by what means they shall experience suffering or terminate their lives. They would strenuously object if others undertook to make these decisions for them.

Also, since every person desires to be born with a disease-free body and wants the care, support and protection during infancy and childhood which only the family organization can properly provide, every rational person knows that illicit sex relations are evil and harmful. They are primarily responsible for destroying the family unit and transmitting disease and misery to unborn generations.

And so throughout history moral man has recognized that such crimes as murder, mayhem, assault, battery and adultery are evil and should be punished. They are so regarded because they destroy and injure life—an element of freedom which every person desires and wants protected.

2.5 RESTRAINT AND COERCION

Another desire which all share is freedom from control and regimentation. When a person is restrained or coerced he is compelled to fulfill the purposes of those using the compulsion rather than his own and consequently is unable to exercise his own freedom. Admittedly there are those who prefer to have others direct their lives in some areas, thus saving them the trouble of thinking and making decisions. But even such people want to choose their masters and determine which of their activities are subject to supervision. Thus, while all may not desire the same amount of freedom with its accompanying responsibilities, no one will willingly forego the amount he does want and to this extent the desire to be free from coercion and restraint is universal. Everyone objects to being enslaved and wants protection against those who would place him in bondage or prevent him from accomplishing his purposes.

2.6 KNOWLEDGE

The third element of freedom listed is knowledge—sufficient

knowledge of facts and natural laws to accomplish one's purposes. It will be remembered that natural law reigns supreme in every area in which intelligence can be used and that no goal can be reached without complying with that law upon which the desired result depends. But one cannot knowingly obey a law of which he is ignorant; therefore, a knowledge of law is indispensable to the exercise of freedom and the desire for it is in proportion to the desire for freedom.

That this desire varies from person to person is admitted, but everyone objects to being deceived and having the knowledge he does possess corrupted by falsehood. If one bases his actions on false principles and erroneous information, his efforts are futile, his failure certain and the exercise of freedom is frustrated. Therefore, every person wants to be protected against deception.

2.7 THE RIGHT AND CONTROL OF PROPERTY

The fourth element of freedom, the right and control of property, requires a more extensive discussion than the other three because the need for it is not as easily recognized. However, an accurate understanding of this right and its relationship to the other three elements will demonstrate that without it freedom is impossible.

Property consists of raw materials and energy which have been organized into consumable products such as food, clothing and shelter. Unless one is free to acquire and utilize these forms of wealth, his existence ceases, and it is of the greatest importance to recognize that if he must depend upon others for sustenance he is not free. He is subject to the direction and control of those who support him and will do nearly anything they command merely to stay alive. And it matters not whether it be an individual or an organization such as government which feeds him, his subservience is as certain as his desire for life. When this fact is recognized it is plainly seen that private ownership and control of property is as essential to the exercise of freedom as life itself.

Not only must one own and control his own sustenance to live and labor without domination by others, but he must have the right and control of property to accomplish his every purpose. Property is the means to all ends because no goal of any consequence can be achieved unless one is free to use property to aid him in reaching it.

With property we build our homes and support families; we acquire a farm, an office, a factory, machinery and tools and enter the occupation of our choice; we construct churches and exercise freedom of religion; obtain a printing press, a lecture hall, a radio or television station and exercise freedom of press and speech. We gain an education by using property to pay for instruction and to support ourselves while we learn. Not one of these freedoms can be exercised without the right and control of property. Let us also recognize that it is with property that we purchase the skill, experience and labor of others by which we accomplish objectives which are utterly beyond our individual strength and ability.

A man's property is his life. It is what he spends his productive life to obtain and he uses it to sustain life. It is also his liberty because he uses it to achieve his every goal. It is the limiting factor in his dreams and ambitions. Property is the fruit of labor and naturally belongs to that person whose labor created it. When you take from a person his property, you take from him his life—that part of his life he spent acquiring it. You also deprive him of his liberty— that portion of his liberty he would exercise if permitted to retain it. It is beyond dispute that without the right of private property the other elements of freedom—life, liberty and knowledge—could not exist or would be useless. There are those who try to distinguish between "property rights" and what they term "human rights." But such a distinction does not exist because a property right is a human right and there is no other human right of any value without it.

While men may differ widely in the amount of property they desire to own and control, everyone wants enough to sustain life and enable him to achieve his purposes. Therefore everyone wants his property protected from theft and destruction. This desire is as strong as the desire for life and liberty and is common to every rational person.

2.8 THE INTERRELATIONSHIP AND MUTUAL DEPENDENCE OF THE FREEDOM ELEMENTS

For the earth is full and there is enough and to spare; yea, I prepared all things, and have given unto the children of men to be agents unto themselves. *(D&C 104:17)*

> The fostering of full economic freedom lies at the base of our liberties. Only in perpetuating economic freedom can our social, political and religious liberties be preserved. (President David O. McKay, *Church News*, 3/12/52)

In the foregoing discussion it has been observed that the freedom elements are closely interrelated and mutually dependent one upon another. This fact seems sufficiently important to merit special attention. If it be true that not one of these four possessions is usable unless the other three are present, the necessity of protecting them all becomes most apparent. Viewed in this light, each possession is equally important. No three of them is of value unless the fourth is present. They are mutually dependent.

There is no difficulty in recognizing that the other three elements are valueless without life; and it is also plain that without liberty or knowledge the other elements would be unusable. But the right and control of property is equally necessary for without it life cannot be sustained, liberty exercised, nor knowledge utilized. Let it also be recognized that a partial denial of the right and control of property diminishes the value of the others accordingly. Since a loss of property reduces one's ability to carry out his purposes, the utility of life, liberty and knowledge is reduced in like manner.

2.9 THE NEED AND DESIRE FOR FREEDOM COMMON TO ALL

The foregoing analysis confirms the conclusion that the need and desire for freedom is common to all and is paramount above every other consideration. Every person, regardless of how he may differ otherwise, wants his life, liberty of movement, knowledge and property protected from injury and destruction. This being true, if we make the protection of freedom the overriding purpose of government, we serve the transcendent need and desire of every man, woman and child. As long as government is engaged exclusively in the protection of freedom, no one is compelled to purchase with his tax money a service that he does not want and use. There is a unity and harmony of purpose among all members of society with respect to this government function. Everyone receives that which he values above all else.

2.10 THE UNIVERSAL STANDARD OF MORALITY

> And now, verily I say unto you concerning the laws of the land, it is my will that my people should observe to do all things whatsoever I command them.
> And that law of the land which is constitutional, supporting that principle of freedom in maintaining rights and privileges, belongs to all mankind, and is justifiable before me.
> Therefore, I, the Lord, justify you, and your brethren of my church, in befriending that law which is the constitutional law of the land;
> And as pertaining to law of man, whatsoever is more or less than this, cometh of evil.
> I, the Lord God, make you free, therefore ye are free indeed; and the law also maketh you free. *(D&C 98:4-8)*

> According to the laws and constitution of the people, which I have suffered to be established, and should be maintained for the rights and protection of all flesh, according to just and holy principles; *(D&C 101:77)*

Since each person desires to possess the four elements of freedom, each is acutely aware of those acts and intents which injure or destroy them. He considers as harmful and wrong any act which harms his body, circumscribes his liberty, corrupts his knowledge and deprives him of his property. He regards as evil an intent to commit these acts. No one needs to be taught these feelings and attitudes. We are born with them. They are evident even during infancy and childhood and never change throughout life. The desire for freedom and for those possessions which make its exercise possible is the most fundamental and common characteristic of intelligent life. It is the very nature of man to want to be free.

This common awareness of what is harmful to oneself makes everyone aware of what harms others and this same knowledge is possessed by people in every age and nation. Murder, mayhem, assault and battery are universally condemned whether committed with a bow and arrow or a gun; human bondage consists of the forcible deprivation of liberty and is recognized as such by all people; deceit consists of the intentional misrepresentation of what one believes to be true whether undertaken by an educated man or an illiterate; and theft is regarded as such whether the object taken is a string of beads or an aeroplane.

It is also true that those motives which prompt men to take and injure the elements of freedom—hate, envy, pride, lust, revenge, etc. are the same whether found in the civilized man or the savage.

In this universal desire for freedom and the common knowledge of those acts and intentions which destroy its elements, we have a moral standard to which all men can be expected to conform. Anyone who deviates from this standard and, without justification, intentionally deprives another of some freedom element, has violated his own standard of right conduct. He has done to another that which the actor knows would be wrong and harmful if done to him. One who commits such an act realizes that he deserves to be punished. He knows that it would be a miscarriage of justice if he were not made to suffer for his intentional wrongdoing. Man's intelligence tells him that if there is a rule or a law of right conduct, there must be a punishment for violation of that law for by very definition there can be no law unless there is a penalty or loss for disobedience.

It will be our principal objective throughout the remainder of this book to determine what government should and should not do to enforce but not violate this universal standard of morality. We shall first undertake to specifically identify those laws of nature which must be obeyed by government in order to protect freedom. Since, as has been noted, the need and desire for freedom is common to all people; and since those possessions essential to its exercise are identical for every person; and finally since those acts and intentions which destroy these possessions never vary, then those man-made laws necessary for their protection should be the same in every age and nation. Once identified they may be adopted and relied upon to serve the needs of people in every country.

CHAPTER III

THE NATURAL LAWS GOVERNING FREEDOM

3.1 THE RIGHTS OF MAN AND THE ELEMENTS OF FREEDOM

Having shown that individual freedom is the overriding need and desire of all men and should therefore be regarded as the controlling purpose of government, we will now undertake to formulate those natural laws which must be obeyed to reach this universal goal. It is believed that such laws will be more readily recognized as such if stated as rules which must be followed to protect human rights. The doctrine that men have a set of unalienable natural rights provides a familiar and sound basis upon which to erect a political structure.

We shall build on this foundation by first pointing out that these celebrated rights of man are nothing more and nothing less than his rights to the four elements of freedom-life, liberty, property and knowledge. We shall then demonstrate that such rights exist only when the duties which correspond and relate thereto are enforced. And finally we shall show that by enforcing such duties (but no others) the natural laws governing freedom are complied with.

Those who established the American Constitutional system of government did so under the assumption that each individual possesses certain unalienable rights and that governments are formed to secure them. The essence of this "rights of man" philosophy is expressed in the Declaration of Independence in these words:

> We hold these truths to be self-evident, that all men are created equal, that they are endowed by their Creator with certain unalienable rights, that among these are Life, Liberty and the pursuit of Happiness. That to secure these rights, governments are instituted among men. . .

While this statement specifically identifies some of man's rights, by its very wording it does not presume to list them all. However, the fact that life and liberty are named necessarily implies that the other two elements of freedom—knowledge and property—are among them. This is so because the four elements are indivisible and inseparable. Not one of them is usable unless the other three are also present. Since the main arguments supporting this conclusion were advanced earlier, they will not be repeated here. However, additional evidence of its truth lies in the fact that it is impossible for government to protect one of these rights without protecting the other three. This is particularly true with respect to life, liberty and property. Affording protection to liberty and property is of no value if life goes unprotected. Nor can one derive much benefit from the protection of life and property without his liberty. And finally, even though there is a current political philosophy which pretends that mankind can enjoy the protection of life and liberty while being denied the right of private property, this is one of the most easily exposed of all falsehoods. Let us observe why life and liberty are largely unusable unless the right of private property is protected.

The primary purpose for which men use life and liberty is to obtain and dispose of property as they desire. When left free to do so, they spend their entire productive lives in acquiring property so that they may use it to sustain themselves and exercise freedom by carrying out other purposes. Therefore, unless men are free to enter the occupation of their choice so that they may obtain property, and unless they are free to utilize the fruits of their labors to sustain life and achieve their goals, neither life nor liberty is protected. These latter two elements of freedom are denied to the same extent that the right of private property is denied. Moral man has always regarded the protection of property as one of the most important functions of government. The English philosopher, John Locke, took the position that this is its primary purpose. According to him:

> The great and chief end, therefore, of men uniting into commonwealths, and putting themselves under government, is the preservation of their property. . . (2nd Essay on Govt., Par. 124)

That those who founded the American system of government regarded the protection of property equally as important as the protection of life and liberty seems apparent from the following provision in the Constitution:

> No person shall be . . . deprived of life, liberty or property
> without due process of law; nor shall private property be taken for
> public use, without just compensation. (5th Am.)

It should be apparent to all that if a person has a right to life, he
of necessity must have a right to acquire that property without which
life cannot be sustained. If he has a right to liberty, he must have a
corresponding right to obtain and utilize that property without which
liberty cannot be exercised. And if he has a right to knowledge, he
has a right to acquire property with which to gain and utilize knowledge. The unalienable rights of man which the American system of
government was formed to protect consist then of the right to the
four elements of freedom—life, liberty, knowledge and property.

3.2 RIGHTS EXIST ONLY IF REPRESENTED BY DUTIES

If it is assumed that all men are endowed by their Creator with a
set of unalienable rights to the four elements of freedom, it must also
be assumed that all men are burdened with a corresponding set of
undelegable duties respecting those rights. Basic to an understanding
of a right is the realization that it cannot exist without a matching
duty; for what can a right consist of other than the enforcement of a
duty concerning it? By very definition a right cannot exist in one
person unless there is a corresponding duty in another. Unless there
is someone who can be compelled to do or refrain from doing something to give the right meaning, it has no substance.

Rights and duties are as inseparable as are the concepts of light
and darkness, positive and negative, good and evil. One term standing alone is meaningless because it can neither be comprehended nor
explained without considering its opposite with which it must be
contrasted. Once this fact is recognized it becomes apparent that if
all men have been endowed with a right to the four elements of freedom, all men have had imposed upon them a set of duties concerning those rights. And what is the nature of these reciprocal rights and
duties? Each member of society is entitled to have all others refrain
from injuring or taking his life, liberty, property or knowledge and
each is obligated in turn to refrain from invading or violating these
endowments of his fellow men.

3.3 NATURAL RIGHTS AND DUTIES

Let us denominate the rights and duties just described as "natural" because we are born with them. They are conferred upon us and imposed upon us without any conscious action on our part. Every member of society is endowed with a set of natural rights and the corresponding duties are an indispensable part of them. We may regard the duties here described as being negative in nature because they obligate us to refrain from acting. We are required to abstain from that conduct which will cause harm to others. Only when we have violated this negative duty by committing a wrong are we obligated to take affirmative action and make amends for the injury inflicted.

3.4 ACQUIRED RIGHTS AND DUTIES

In addition to the "natural" rights and duties just described, there is another set which do not arise automatically but come into existence as a result of our voluntary action. These are acquired or assumed as a result of a deliberate and premeditated intent that they do so. The most common and familiar type of such rights and duties arises out of the business contract. In the typical case two parties enter into a binding agreement under the terms of which one party assumes an obligation to deliver goods or perform services in exchange for the right to receive money. The other party assumes the duty to pay the money and acquires the right to compel delivery of the goods or performance of the services.

Another type of acquired rights and duties arises out of the family relationship. Under the marriage contract each party acquires legally enforceable rights against the other and assumes obligations in exchange therefor. The rights and duties between parents and children are different in some respects from those created by the ordinary agreement but are nonetheless real. Even though no formal agreement is entered into between the parties, when parents bring a child into the world they voluntarily assume the duty to support and care for that helpless infant until he is able to fend for himself. In exchange for such benefits, the child owes the parents obedience and also the duty to provide for their needs if their positions become reversed with the parents becoming helpless and the child able to sustain them.

It is observed that the rights and duties which we acquire concern the elements of freedom just as do those we have called natural. The rights acquired under a business contract or because of a family relationship entitle the holder thereof to have his life or liberty maintained or his property or knowledge increased while the performance of the duty requires an expenditure or utilization of these possessions. Whether the right is natural or acquired the owner thereof is entitled to have others observe a duty respecting the elements of freedom—either refrain from injuring them or take some affirmative action concerning them.

In our discussion of natural duties we noted that they are negative in nature because the obligation imposed is to refrain from acting. The duty is to avoid committing any act which inflicts an injury. The corresponding right to compel action arises only after there has been affirmative conduct which violates it. But duties which are assumed or acquired are ordinarily affirmative in nature because the obligations here are to act rather than to refrain from acting. The right to compel action comes into existence when the business contract is entered into or the family relationship is formed. In these cases the right is denied and the injury caused by a failure to perform the duty assumed rather than by affirmative conduct which breaches the duty.

3.5 RIGHTS AND DUTIES WITHOUT SUBSTANCE UNLESS ENFORCED

Just as a right does not exist without a duty, neither rights nor duties exist unless enforced. Unless the person who violates a right is compelled to atone for the wrong and make restitution for the injury, it is a misuse of the term to call it a right. The substance of a right consists of the power to compel the wrongdoer to make restitution and the substance of a duty consists of being compelled to perform it. Unless the performance of the duty is enforced, the right is without a remedy and the failure to perform the duty without a penalty. It is the enforcement which brings both into existence and gives them substance.

The doctrine of the rights of man then necessarily includes the use of force on humans for without such violence and the threat thereof, they do not exist.

3.6 GOVERNMENT NECESSARY FOR THE ENFORCEMENT OF RIGHTS

> WE believe that governments were instituted of God for the benefit of man; and that he holds men accountable for their acts in relation to them, both in making laws and administering them, for the good and safety of society.
>
> We believe that no government can exist in peace, except such laws are framed and held inviolate as will secure to each individual the free exercise of conscience, the right and control of property, and the protection of life. *(D&C 134:1, 2)*

If it be true that rights do not exist unless enforced, it is also true that they exist incompletely or not at all in the absence of government; this being the only agency which is at once powerful enough and impartial enough to exercise the force required. Government is the supreme physical force in society. To perform its functions it must be supplied with sufficient manpower and means to enforce its will against all persons and groups whatsoever. Only with such power can it adequately enforce human rights. When government functions properly it enforces rights and duties in a just manner. It is not subject to bias and partisan pressure. It correctly appraises the character of the wrong committed, the restitution required and the punishment deserved. This combination of superior force and impartial judgment is indispensable if human rights are to be properly protected. It is most apparent that if each person had to rely on his own resources to enforce his rights, many would remain unenforced and would therefore not exist. The strong and cunning would prevail over the weak regardless of whose rights had been invaded. Thus, in the great majority of cases, rights and duties would disappear for want of enforcement. In those instances where the strongest happened to be in the wrong there would be little chance of justice since the natural bias of men makes them unfit to be judges in their own cases. In view of these facts we can conclude that the rights of man consist of the right to use the force of government to punish wrong and compel the performance of duties.

This is in harmony with the philosophy of the Declaration of Independence which says:

> To secure these rights, governments are instituted among men.

3.7 THE DUTY TO SUPPORT GOVERNMENT

> We believe that all men are bound to sustain and uphold the respective governments in which they reside, while protected in their inherent and inalienable rights by the laws of such governments; and that sedition and rebellion are unbecoming every citizen thus protected, and should be punished accordingly; and that all governments have a right to enact such laws as in their own judgments are best calculated to secure the public interest; at the same time, however, holding sacred the freedom of conscience. *(D&C 134:5)*

> And now, except ye do repent of that which ye have done, and begin to be up and doing, and send forth food and men unto us, and also unto Helaman, that he may support those parts of our country which he has regained, and that we may also recover the remainder of our possessions in these parts, behold it will be expedient that we contend no more with the Lamanites until we have first cleansed our inward vessel, yea, even the great head of our government.

> Ye know that ye do transgress the laws of God, and ye do know that ye do trample them under your feet. Behold, the Lord saith unto me: If those whom ye have appointed your governors do not repent of their sins and iniquities, ye shall go up to battle against them. *(Alma 60:24, 33)*

The list of man's rights and duties would be incomplete without noting his right to call upon government for protection and his duty to support it in performing this function. It has been seen that only the agency of government can properly protect rights. Once it is established and assumes this responsibility, each citizen is entitled to call upon it for his own protection. But no one can lay claim to this right without assuming a corresponding duty and the duty in this instance is to support government. Government cannot operate unless supported and such support must be provided by those it protects.

From this it must be concluded that the duty to support government is an integral and indispensable part of the doctrine of the rights of man. Human rights do not exist unless this duty is performed. And let it be recalled that a duty is without substance unless it is enforced; therefore, government must have the power to compel those it protects to pay taxes and perform other necessary duties such as serve in the armed forces.

As long as government restricts itself to the function of protecting the elements of freedom and as long as it apportions the taxes and other essential duties equitably, no one can justly complain about his own duties. Since everyone desires and needs to have his rights protected and since government is the only practical means by which this can be done, everyone should realize that for his own benefit it must be supported. Each should be able to see that it would be unjust and destructive of his own rights if others were permitted to withhold their support; therefore, if he fails to bear his fair share he knows he is shirking a duty which is rightfully his and, therefore, force may properly be used to compel him to perform.

3.8 THE NATURAL LAWS GOVERNING THE PROTECTION OF FREEDOM

In the foregoing discussion it has been shown that man has both natural and acquired rights to the four elements of freedom. Government protects freedom by protecting these rights to the elements of freedom. It protects man's rights to the elements of freedom by enforcing those duties which relate thereto. It enforces these duties in two ways:

(1) by punishing their violation;
(2) by compelling their performance.

These are the only two means government has of performing its functions. Consequently the natural laws which govern the protection of freedom are those rules government must obey in using these two methods. Those rules or natural laws which government must obey in enforcing duties may be stated as follows:

Government must,

(1) punish the intentional violation of duties;
(2) punish nothing except the intentional violation of duties;
(3) stand ready to compel the performance of all duties when petitioned to do so;
(4) compel the performance of no duties except those which are natural or acquired.

Let us briefly consider why the protection of freedom requires that government obey each of these four laws.

3.9 *LAW NUMBER ONE:* GOVERNMENT MUST PUNISH THE INTENTIONAL VIOLATION OF DUTIES

We believe that the commission of crime should be punished according to the nature of the offense; that murder, treason, robbery, theft, and the breach of the general peace, in all respects, should be punished according to their criminality and their tendency to evil among men, by the laws of that government in which the offense is committed; and for the public peace and tranquility all men should step forward and use their ability in bringing offenders against good laws to punishment. *(D&C 134:8)*

And now, behold, I speak unto the church. Thou shalt not kill; and he that kills shall not have forgiveness in this world, nor in the world to come.
And again, I say, thou shalt not kill; but he that killeth shall die.
Thou shalt not steal; and he that stealeth and will not repent shall be cast out.
Thou shalt not lie; he that lieth and will not repent shall be cast out. *(D&C 42:18-21)*

And it shall come to pass, that if any persons among you shall kill they shall be delivered up and dealt with according to the laws of the land; for remember that he hath no forgiveness; and it shall be proved according to the laws of the land.

And if a man or woman shall rob, he or she shall be delivered up unto the law of the land.

And if he or she shall lie, he or she shall be delivered up unto the law of the land.

And if he or she do any manner of iniquity, he or she shall be delivered up unto the law, even that of God. *(D&C 42:79, 84, 86, 87)*

Nevertheless, they durst not lie, if it were known, for fear of the law, for liars were punished; therefore they pretended to preach according to their belief; and now the law could have no power on any man for his belief.
And they durst not steal, for fear of the law, for such were punished; neither durst they rob, nor murder, for he that murdered was punished unto death.

But if he murdered he was punished unto death; and if he robbed he was also punished; and if he stole he was also punished; and if he committed adultery he was also punished; yea, for all this wickedness they were punished.
For there was a law that men should be judged according to their crimes. Nevertheless, there was no law against a man's belief; therefore, a man was punished only for the crimes which he had done; therefore all men were on equal grounds. *(Alma 1:17-18; 30:10-11; See Also: Exodus Ch. 21, 22)*

The experience of mankind has uniformly demonstrated that the intentional violation of duties must be punished or human freedom is forfeited. This has been found to be the only effective means of protecting life, liberty, property and knowledge against criminals who would otherwise injure and destroy them. Unless those who deliberately destroy the rights of their fellow man are jailed, fined and executed, violence goes unrestrained and the exercise of freedom is largely denied. Throughout history moral man has regarded the intentional and unjustified denial of the elements of freedom as an evil which must be punished.

The necessity of punishing crime is more apparent when it is realized that even though the criminal element in society may be relatively small, the capacity of this minority to destroy freedom is all out of proportion to their number. A person's ability to tear down is many times greater than his ability to create. While it takes years of tender care to nurture a child to the maturity of a full-grown man, it takes only a few seconds of crude violence to extinguish that life. And property which has required many lifetimes of ingenuity, skill and painstaking effort to construct, can be destroyed almost instantaneously by a criminal who has no more knowledge or skill than that required to light a match or explode a bomb. Only when government seeks out, punishes, and thereby restrains such intentionally destructive acts can the members of society pursue their activities without fear and in an atmosphere of freedom.

Not only must government protect its citizens from criminals within the nation but from foreign aggressor nations as well. It must maintain an army and navy sufficiently strong to prevent destruction by foreign criminals. The protection of life, liberty and property by punishing those who would otherwise intentionally destroy these possessions is the first and most fundamental law which government must obey to protect freedom.

3.10 <u>LAW NUMBER TWO</u>: GOVERNMENT MUST PUNISH NOTHING EXCEPT THE INTENTIONAL VIOLATION OF DUTIES

We believe that religion is instituted of God; and that men are amenable to him, and to him only, for the exercise of it, unless their religious opinions prompt them to infringe upon the rights and liberties of others; but we do not believe that human law has a right to interfere in prescribing rules of worship to bind the consciences of men, nor dictate forms for public or private devotion; that the civil magistrate should restrain crime, but never control conscience; should punish guilt, but never suppress the freedom of the soul. *(D&C 134:4)*

Behold, there are many called, but few are chosen. And why are they not chosen?

Because their hearts are set so much upon the things of this world, and aspire to the honors of men, that they do not learn this one lesson—

That the rights of the priesthood are inseparably connected with the powers of heaven, and that the powers of heaven cannot be controlled nor handled only upon the principles of righteousness.

That they may be conferred upon us, it is true; but when we undertake to cover our sins, or to gratify our pride, our vain ambition, or to exercise control or dominion or compulsion upon the souls·of the children of men, in any degree of unrighteousness, behold, the heavens withdraw themselves; the Spirit of the Lord is grieved; and when it is withdrawn, Amen to the priesthood or the authority of that man.

Behold, ere he is aware, he is left unto himself, to kick against the pricks, to persecute the saints, and to fight against God.

We have learned by sad experience that it is the nature and disposition of almost all men, as soon as they get a little authority, as they suppose, they will immediately begin to exercise unrighteous dominion.

Hence many are called, but few are chosen. *(D&C 121:34-40)*

Now there was no law against a man's belief; for it was strictly contrary to the commands of God that there should be a law which should bring men on to unequal grounds.

For thus saith the scripture: Choose ye this day, whom ye will serve.

Now if a man desired to serve God, it was his privilege; or rather, if he believed in God it was his privilege to serve him; but if he did not believe in him there was no law to punish him. *(Alma 30:7-9)*

Judge not unrighteously, that ye be not judged; but judge righteous judgment.

For with what judgment ye shall judge, ye shall be judged; and with what measure ye mete, it shall be measured to you again.

And again, ye shall shall say unto them, Why is it that thou beholdest the mote that is in thy brother's eye, but considerest not the beam that is in thine own eye? *(Matt. 7:2-4 JST)*

The same considerations which require that the elements of freedom be protected from unjustified destruction by men outside of government require that they be protected from those within its framework. History is replete with instances where those in control of government have murdered, plundered and enslaved the citizens of their own nation. While governments are most essential for the protection of freedom, they can be, and ofttimes are, prostituted and used to destroy that which they were established to protect. Having been supplied with means and manpower for the specific purpose of using physical violence, they are horribly efficient in destroying the elements of freedom when used for this purpose.

Therefore, it is of the utmost importance that a precise limit be placed upon the power of government to deprive its citizens of their lives, liberties and properties for the purpose of punishing them. According to this second natural law, that limit has been reached when intentional violations of duty have been punished. Unless a person has undertaken without justification to destroy or injure an element of freedom, he should not be subjected to a penalty. Or to state the matter otherwise, innocent conduct, or conduct motivated by a desire to increase or preserve the elements of freedom should never be punished.

Both humanity and justice dictate obedience to such a law. Logic also requires its observance. The purpose of punishment is to restrain and prevent the evil which almost invariably arises from the attempt to commit evil, not to prevent the good which almost always results from an attempt to do good. When a person undertakes to do good, or in other words increase the elements of freedom, he ordinarily accomplishes this purpose. At least he seldom achieves the opposite result. Therefore, punishing such conduct deprives society of the good which otherwise results when people are left free to engage in beneficial activities. It also destroys freedom by taking from the person punished one of the elements of freedom—either his life, his liberty or his property.

Even though a person who undertakes to do good, inadvertently causes harm, it is still illogical to punish him. A well-meaning person need not be punished to induce him to try to avoid injuring others. This he does voluntarily. And if he has unintentionally caused harm and has failed to make restitution, the injured party may recover in a civil suit. A criminal action is not brought for that purpose. Punishment in this, as in every other case where there is no intent to violate a duty, is not only unnecessary, but is cruel, barbarous and contrary to the plainest dictates of common sense. When a party who is innocent of an evil intent negligently causes harm, it is proper to compel him to make restitution, but this is all the force which is either necessary or proper to protect the right which has been denied.

3.11 LAW NUMBER THREE: A GOVERNMENT MUST STAND READY TO COMPEL THE PERFORMANCE OF ALL DUTIES WHEN PETITIONED TO DO SO

WE believe that governments were instituted of God for the benefit of man; and that he holds men accountable for their acts in relation to them, both in making laws and administering them, for the good and safety of society.

We believe that no government can exist in peace, except such laws are framed and held inviolate as will secure to each individual the free exercise of conscience, the right and control of property, and the protection of life. *(D&C 134:1, 2)*

> Now if a man owed another, and he would not pay that which
> he did owe, he was complained of to the judge; and the judge exe-
> cuted authority, and sent forth officers that the man should be
> brought before him; and he judged the man according to the law
> and the evidences which were brought against him, and thus the
> man was compelled to pay that which he owed, or be stripped, or
> be cast out from among the people as a thief and a robber. *(Alma
> 11:2; See also Exodus Ch. 21, 22)*

Having considered those natural laws which determine when a
violation of duty should and should not be punished, let us now
examine those which determine when government should use force
to compel performance of duties. Once it is assumed that an individual has a right to the elements of freedom, it is also assumed he has a
right to recover damages from anyone who injures those elements.
The one causing the injury has violated his duty to refrain from
doing so. But unless the duty can be enforced, the right which it represents does not exist. Therefore, government must be available to
compel the performance of every legally enforceable duty whether
natural or acquired and whether the breach is intentional or due to
negligence.

In the situation where the breach of the duty is intentional, compelling the criminal to make restitution is in addition to inflicting a
penalty on him under the criminal law. If government does no more
than punish such breaches, the victim suffers a loss which remains
unredressed. Therefore, he must be able to recover damages in the
case where the injury is intentional as well as where it is negligently
caused.

There are several types of laws under which government compels the performance of duties. They are as follows:

(1) tort laws;
(2) contract laws;
(3) family relations laws;
(4) tax laws and laws providing for military conscription.

The tort laws provide for restitution in the cases where the rights
violated and the duties breached are "natural" rather than
"acquired". The injuries inflicted in these instances are generally due
to the intentional or negligent conduct of the wrongdoer and the tort
laws provide for redress in either case.

If the rights injured and the duties breached are "acquired" rather than "natural", relief is available under either the law of contracts or that of family relations. In these cases the breach of the duty usually consists of a failure to act rather than affirmative conduct. If one fails to discharge the duties he has assumed under a business contract or a family relationship, the party injured may obtain the aid of government to compel performance or recover damages.

Duties owed to government are enforced under tax laws, and laws providing for military conscription, jury duty, etc.

In the foregoing discussion we have treated "punishment" and "compelling performance" as though they are two distinctly different methods of protecting the elements of freedom. While it is true that punishment is used almost exclusively in those cases where there has been an affirmative act causing injury, whereas compelling performance is usually limited to those instances where there has been a failure to perform, there are instances where punishment is appropriate in the latter situation. If a person who is obligated to perform deliberately refuses to do so even though able, punishment may be necessary. But let it be recognized that in such a case the violation of the duty is intentional and therefore properly punishable.

3.12 *LAW NUMBER FOUR: GOVERNMENT MUST COMPEL THE PERFORMANCE OF NO DUTIES EXCEPT THOSE WHICH ARE NATURAL OR ACQUIRED*

Thou shalt not be idle; for he that is idle shall not eat the bread nor wear the garments of the laborer.

It is wisdom in me; therefore, a commandment I give unto you, that ye shall organize yourselves and appoint every man his stewardship;

That every man may give an account unto me of the stewardship which is appointed unto him.

For it is expedient that I, the Lord, should make every man accountable, as a steward over earthly blessings, which I have made and prepared for my creatures.

I, the Lord, stretched out the heavens, and built the earth, my very handiwork; and all things therein are mine.

And it is my purpose to provide for my saints, for all things are mine.

> But it must needs be done in mine own way; and behold this
> is the way that I, the Lord, have decreed to provide for my saints,
> that the poor shall be exalted, in that the rich are made low. *(D&C
> 42:42; 104:11-16)*

> And it came to pass on the other hand, that the Nephites did
> build them up and support them, beginning at the more wicked
> part of them, until they had overspread all the land of the
> Nephites, and had seduced the more part of the righteous until
> they had come down to believe in their works and partake of their
> spoils, and to join with them in their secret murders and combina-
> tions. *(Hela. 6:38)*

If governments are established only to protect rights, they are established only to enforce duties because every right is represented by a duty. Therefore, when government has enforced all the duties of man whether natural or acquired, it has completed the entire purpose for which it is formed and reached the limit of its powers. This is to conclude that government has no power to either create new rights nor impose new duties, but only to protect those rights and enforce those duties which already exist.

This limit on the civil power is indispensable to the protection of freedom because if government can of its own volition create a right in one person which did not theretofore exist, it must needs have the power to impose a duty on another which theretofore did not exist. But it can enforce such a duty only by compelling the obligor to give up either his life, his liberty or his property, and this it cannot do without depriving him of his unalienable natural rights.

When government takes one of the elements of freedom only to the extent necessary to enforce existing duties, the one from whom it is taken loses nothing to which he is entitled for no one has a right to violate or refuse to perform his duties. The force used in such instances is unavoidably necessary for the very existence of rights—his as well as others.

But if force is used for any purpose other than the enforcement of duties, the effect is to destroy freedom rather than protect it. At that point government crosses that precise line which divides the protection of rights from their destruction and acts directly contrary to the purpose for which it is formed. Those in government have no more authority to arbitrarily impose new duties than do the citizens they represent. If an individual citizen undertook to impose and enforce a duty to which he had no right, his act would be regarded as a crime. It is no less a crime when performed by men acting in the name of government.

Men surrender none of their rights when they establish government. They merely delegate to that agency the power of enforcing their rights. Neither do they assume any new duties. In the absence of government, each man would be under the necessity of enforcing and protecting his own rights—and doubtless at great cost. Upon the formation of government this task is transferred to it along with the cost. Therefore, when we support government we do not perform a new duty. We only discharge in a more effective and economical manner an obligation which already existed—that of protecting our own rights. These fundamental principles underlie the American Constitutional System of Government and are expressed in the Declaration of Independence in the following words:

> That to secure these rights, governments are instituted among men . . . that, whenever any form of government becomes destructive of these ends, it is the right of the people to alter or to abolish it, and to institute new government . . .

Jefferson, who is generally regarded as the author of the above words, provided a more complete exposition of these views in a letter written to Francis Gilmer in 1816 which reads in part as follows:

> Our legislators are not sufficiently apprized of the rightful limits of their power; that their true office is to declare and enforce only our natural rights and duties, and to take none of them from us. No man has a natural right to commit aggression on the equal rights of another; and this all from which the laws ought to restrain him; every man is under the natural duty of contributing to the necessities of the society; and this is all the laws should enforce on him; and, no man having a natural right to be the judge between himself and another, it is his natural duty to submit to the umpirage of an impartial third. When the laws have declared and enforced all this, they have fulfilled their functions, and the idea is quite unfounded, that on entering into society we give up any natural right. The trial of every law by one of these texts, would lessen much the labors of our legislators, and lighten equally our municipal codes. (*Works of Thomas Jefferson*, Federal Edition, G.P. Putnam & Sons, (1905), Vol. XI, pp. 533-34)

It will be our purpose throughout the remainder of this work to show how the principles expressed in the four laws we have formulated were implemented under the American system of government.

Preliminary thereto we shall examine the nature, source and extent of political power under that system and also the constitutional framework within which that power is exercised.

Chapter *IV*

Justice According
To The Golden Rule

4.1 The Necessity Of A Standard For Determining Punishments And Restitution

Heretofore it has been concluded that since freedom is the paramount need and desire of mankind, and since, when attained, it makes possible the achievement of all other purposes to which men can aspire, it can be made not only the primary purpose of government, but also its exclusive purpose.

To achieve this universal goal we developed the following natural laws for government to obey:

(a) Inflict punishment for the intentional violation of duties but for no other purpose;
(b) Stand ready to enforce all existing rights and duties but never create rights nor enforce any except those which are natural or have been acquired with the consent of the obligor.

While these laws establish that line between those circumstances under which government should and should not take action, they fail to specify exactly what that action should be. While they state when a punishment should be inflicted and restitution should be compelled, they do not set up a standard for determining the nature of the punishment nor the amount of the restitution. Obviously such a standard is necessary if a government is to perform its duties properly.

Punishments can range from a slap on the wrist to death; from a day in prison to incarceration for life; from a fine of a dollar to one of a million or more. A similarly wide range of choices is open in granting restitution. To leave such matters to the whim or caprice of judges, juries and bureaucrats is to establish a government of men rather than one of laws. It is to introduce inconsistency, unpredictability and inequity into a system which should treat all men alike. People cannot be expected to respect nor voluntarily support a government with such infirmities.

The standard which is adopted must enable those who use it to obtain exact answers to the questions raised because whenever a case comes before a court or other tribunal for resolution, government is faced with the unavoidable task of giving precise answers to those questions. If it be a criminal case where the defendant has been convicted of a crime such as murder or robbery, an exact penalty must be imposed. If he is not sentenced to death then the precise number of years or days he must spend in prison or the exact amount of his fine must be determined. An accurate determination of the damages to be assessed in civil cases also must be made.

Difficult and disagreeable though the task may be, there is no escape from the necessity of giving precise answers in every case which arises. This being so, the standard which is established to guide judges and juries must provide exact answers. Does such a standard exist? With this question in mind, let us consider the principles of justice.

4.2 THE PRINCIPLES OF JUSTICE

According to the laws and constitution of the people, which I have suffered to be established, and should be maintained for the rights and protection of all flesh, according to just and holy principles;

WE believe that governments were instituted of God for the benefit of man; and that he holds men accountable for their acts in relation to them, both in making laws and administering them, for the good and safety of society. *(D&C 101:77; 134:1)*

When they have a matter, they come unto me; and I judge between one and another, and I do make [them] know the statutes of God, and his laws.

And Moses' father in law said unto him, The thing that thou doest [is] not good.

Thou wilt surely wear away, both thou, and this people that [is] with thee: for this thing [is] too heavy for thee; thou art not able to perform it thyself alone.

Hearken now unto my voice, I will give thee counsel, and God shall be with thee: Be thou for the people to God-ward, that thou mayest bring the causes unto God:

And thou shalt teach them ordinances and laws, and shalt shew them the way wherein they must walk, and the work that they must do.

Moreover thou shalt provide out of all the people able men, such as fear God, men of truth, hating covetousness; and place [such] over them, [to be] rulers of thousands, [and] rulers of hundreds, rulers of fifties, and rulers of tens:

And let them judge the people at all seasons: and it shall be, [that] every great matter they shall bring unto thee, but every small matter they shall judge: so shall it be easier for thyself, and they shall bear [the burden] with thee.

If thou shalt do this thing, and God command thee [so], then thou shalt be able to endure, and all this people shall also go to their place in peace.

So Moses hearkened to the voice of his father in law, and did all that he had said.

And Moses chose able men out of all Israel, and made them heads over the people, rulers of thousands, rulers of hundreds, rulers of fifties, and rulers of tens.

And they judged the people at all seasons: the hard causes they brought unto Moses, but every small matter they judged themselves.

And Moses let his father in law depart; and he went his way into his own land. *(Exodus 18:16-27; See also Mosiah Ch. 29)*

The need and desire for justice seems to be inherent in every person who believes in moral values and the distinction between good and evil. One who believes in good and evil also believes that the good should be rewarded and the evil punished. But in the final analysis, this is what justice consists of. Or to put the matter otherwise, when people believe there is a right and a wrong, they also believe that when a wrong is committed, it remains such until a proper punishment is imposed, a correct restitution is made or both. The situation can be made right and their sense of justice satisfied only when this occurs.

Furthermore the punishment must fit the crime and the restitution be equal to the injury. If the penalty is either too severe or too lenient or the restitution too great or too small, to this same extent justice has not been done.

To summarize, moral people possess an innate sense of justice which insists that there exists in nature an exactly deserved reward for every good, a fitting punishment of every evil, and a precisely correct restitution for every injury. Dictionaries confirm that this is the meaning people intend when they use the term. For example one dictionary definition reads:

Conformity to truth, fact or reason, correctness, rightfulness,
. . . to treat fairly or according to merit.

Another defines justice as:

The constant and perpetual disposition to render every man
his due.

It is this universal belief in good and evil and the accompanying
desire to see that justice is done which prompts men to establish
governments and confer upon them the power to punish evil, protect
good and make restitution for injuries. Justice is, indeed, the great
object of government. As was stated by Madison and Hamilton in
the Federalist Papers:

Justice is the end of government. It is the end of civil society.
It ever has and ever will be pursued until it be obtained, or until
liberty be lost in the pursuit. (Fed. Papers #51)

The various definitions given of the word justice do not ordinarily specify what punishments and rewards consist of. It is assumed
that everyone will understand that a reward always consists of an
increase in the elements of freedom while a punishment consists of a
denial or deprivation of one of those elements. Certainly when government acts to dispense justice it does so by granting or taking life,
liberty or property. With this fact in mind we might more completely
define justice as:

Allotting to each exactly the amount of freedom he deserves.

We will now turn to the "Golden Rule" of the Christian religion
to determine exactly how much freedom a court should take from or
award to an individual in any given case to achieve justice.

4.3 JUSTICE ACCORDING TO THE GOLDEN RULE

We believe that men should appeal to the civil law for redress
of all wrongs and grievances, where personal abuse is inflicted or
the right of property or character infringed, where such laws exist
as will protect the same; but we believe that all men are justified in
defending themselves, their friends, and property, and the government, from the unlawful assaults and encroachments of all persons

in times of exigency, where immediate appeal cannot be made to the laws, and relief afforded. *(D&C 134:11)*

The Golden Rule is stated in the book of Matthew in the Bible in these words:

> Therefore all things whatsoever ye would that men should do to you, do ye even so to them: For this is the law and the prophets. *(Matt. 7:12)*

As set forth in this quotation, the Golden Rule constitutes a commandment to treat others as we would be treated. But it also states that this is "the law and the prophets." In what way does it constitute a law? That is, if the Golden Rule is the law, what are the rewards for obedience and the penalties for disobedience? Simply this: as we do unto others, so shall it be done unto us. This was made plain by Christ in another statement in the Sermon on the Mount wherein He said:

> For with what judgment ye judge, ye shall be judged: and with what measure ye mete, it shall be measured to you again. *(Matt. 7:2)*

It might be assumed by some that the Golden Rule was intended to have application only in an afterlife but not here on earth. The teachings of the Bible do not justify such a conclusion. The "law" spoken of by Christ was, of course, the one given to the Israelites through Moses. In criminal cases there was a one to one correspondence between the injury inflicted and the penalty imposed as the following familiar quotation indicates:

> And thine eye shall not pity; but life shall go for life, eye for eye, tooth for tooth, hand for hand, foot for foot. *(Deut. 12:21)*

In the above quoted passage the fundamental rule of Christian justice which decrees that a criminal shall be treated as he treats his fellow man is set forth in simplicity and plainness. However the following explanations seem necessary to avoid unwarranted conclusions regarding its meaning.

(1) Except in cases such as murder where restitution is impossible, the wrongdoer in a criminal case was not required to suffer in the same manner as did his victim if he was able to atone for his

crime otherwise such as by paying a fine or rendering a service.

(2) The accused was judged by his intent to do evil rather than by the amount of harm he had caused. If the injury was inflicted accidentally or in justifiable self-defense for example, no punishment was imposed.

(3) In cases of theft or malicious destruction of property, the wrongdoer was required to pay his victim several times the value of the property taken. This was considered necessary for two reasons: (a) To effectively deter crimes of this nature; and (b) To adequately recompense the victim not only for his lost property, but also for his lost time, trouble and inconvenience.

In civil cases, that is in those situations where one person had caused harm negligently but without intending to do so, he was required to make restitution equal to the damage inflicted and thus suffer to the same extent as he had caused another to suffer.

4.4 LIMITATIONS ON GOVERNMENT POWER UNDER THE GOLDEN RULE

Not only does the Golden Rule provide government with a precise standard regarding what it should do, but it sets up an equally precise standard regarding what it should not do. It applies to all of the actions of men whether they are committed alone or while acting in concert with others and thus places the same restraints on governments as on individuals. This conclusion may seem novel to some since the rule is generally thought of as having application only to individual behavior. But there are compelling reasons why men should obey it when they act under the authority of the state. Before enumerating them, we desire to point out that when men act through government they use force and the threat of force on humans. This fact seems to be so little understood and so commonly overlooked that it deserves special attention.

No matter how governments may differ from one another otherwise, there is one feature common to all: they use force and the threat thereof to accomplish their purposes. This is the exclusive method by which they secure obedience to their decrees.

There are two methods of influencing human behavior: one is by compulsion, the other by persuasion. A distinct line separates these methods. Let us examine it. When compulsion is used the one being compelled is not allowed his choice in the matter. He is commanded or forbidden to act in a specified manner and if he fails to do so he is physically punished until he complies. If he resists he is overpowered or punished until his resistance ceases. Punishment consists of depriving him of one of those possessions which every person desires to retain—life, liberty or property.

When persuasion is used the one doing the persuading may use argument, pleading, logic or even the offer of a bribe. However, the one being influenced is left free to make his own decision as to whether or not he will comply. He knows that if he decides not to obey he may incur the displeasure of his persuader but nothing more. Neither his life, liberty, nor property are in jeopardy. No physical punishment is inflicted or even threatened, otherwise the case is one of compulsion.

When governments act they use the compulsion method. Every law which they adopt contains a penalty clause which directs the officers of government to take either the life, the liberty or the property of those who disobey. Unless a law provides for the loss of one of these possessions it cannot be properly termed a law. It is nothing more than a request or a recommendation which the people are as free to disregard after its enactment as they were before.

Some may imagine that certain types of government action are nothing more than voluntary cooperation with no compulsion being involved. This view is demonstrably false and cannot be held by those who understand the true nature of laws and government. The only reason we pass any law is to force those to obey it who would not do so unless threatened with death, imprisonment or fine. If we desire to use only voluntary means to influence others we either proceed alone or through some voluntary organization such as a club, a church, a lodge or some other non-governmental group. The only ones who conform and join such organizations are those who do so of their own free will. The only ones who pay dues and obey the rules are those who consent thereto. No one is threatened, compelled, or physically punished for non-conformance.

But when government is used every person must obey the laws whether he agrees with them or not. Every taxpayer must support government programs no matter how violently he may oppose them. Even those laws which merely provide for making "gifts" or hiring administrators to carry out so-called "optional programs" involve the use of force because no gift can be made nor administrator hired without collecting taxes under laws which compel their payment. If anyone refuses to pay his taxes, his property is taken from him by force; and anyone who attempts to obstruct a government program is physically prevented from doing so. Non-compliance is put down with any necessary force. Physical violence and the threat thereof lie behind every law and every government activity and anyone who does not realize this does not understand the true nature of this organization. With this fact clearly in mind let us observe why the Golden Rule should apply to government action.

4.5 THE EFFECT OF USING FORCE IS THE SAME WHETHER EMPLOYED BY THE STATE OR THE INDIVIDUAL

> We believe that religion is instituted of God; and that men are amenable to him, and to him only, for the exercise of it, unless their religious opinions prompt them to infringe upon the rights and liberties of others; but we do not believe that human law has a right to interfere in prescribing rules of worship to bind the consciences of men, nor dictate forms for public or private devotion; that the civil magistrate should restrain crime, but never control conscience; should punish guilt, but never suppress the freedom of the soul. *(D&C 134:4)*

> Now there was no law against a man's belief; for it was strictly contrary to the commands of God that there should be a law which should bring men on to unequal grounds.
> For thus saith the scripture: Choose ye this day, whom ye will serve.
> Now if a man desired to serve God, it was his privilege; or rather, if he believed in God it was his privilege to serve him; but if he did not believe in him there was no law to punish him. *(Alma 30:7-9)*

It cannot be denied that the nature and consequence of an act of force is not altered merely by changing the number engaged in its commission. The effect is the same whether done by one person or a million. The one against whom it is used is just as dead and just as surely bereft of his liberty or his property in the one case as in the other. Insofar as he is concerned it makes not the slightest difference from whence it proceeds. Furthermore the mere passing of a law which legalizes an act of violence has no effect either. Clothing force in the robes of legality may obscure or hide the naked fact from view but it does nothing to change its nature. Legislatures, monarchs and even democratic majorities are as powerless to alter the effect of an act of compulsion on a human as they are to alter the effect of the law of gravity on him.

Therefore if it would be wrong and a violation of a person's rights for him to suffer at the hands of an individual, it would be equally wrong and equally violative of his rights for him to suffer at the hands of the multitude. If the act is reprehensible, it remains so regardless of who does it. On the other hand, if the use of force is proper, that is, if the one against whom it is employed deserves to be punished or compelled to pay a debt the effect upon him is again the same regardless of its source. This being so, logic requires that we use the same standard to determine the propriety of its use in both cases. If the Golden Rule is a proper rule for individual action it is proper for government action.

4.6 GOVERNMENT DERIVES ITS POWER FROM THE PEOPLE AND THAT POWER CAN RISE NO HIGHER THAN ITS SOURCE

> Unto the day when the Lord shall come to recompense unto every man according to his work, and measure to every man according to the measure which he has measured to his fellow man. *(D&C 1:10)*

> JUDGE not, that ye be not judged.
> For with what judgment ye judge, ye shall be judged: and with what measure ye mete, it shall be measured to you again. *(Matthew 7:1-2; See also Alma Ch. 41)*

It is a basic and familiar tenet of American political philosophy that all power which the state possesses comes from the people. The fundamental documents of both the national and state governments acknowledge this fact and the writings of the founding fathers repeatedly refer to it. The Declaration of Independence asserts it in these words:

That to secure (our inalienable rights), . . . governments were instituted among men, deriving their just powers from the consent of the governed.

The United States Constitution recognizes the people as the source of its authority in the preamble which reads in part as follows:

We, the people of the United States . . . do ordain and establish this Constitution for the United States of America.

Virtually all state constitutions expressly affirm this truth with over half of them using words identical with, or similar to, the following:

All political power is inherent in the people.

The writings of the men who founded our nation are further evidence of how deeply this principle is imbedded in our American system. In his Farewell Address, Washington states that: "The basis of our political systems is the right of the people to alter their constitutions of government." Alexander Hamilton in arguing that the people themselves were the only ones competent to ratify the United States Constitution stated:

The fabric of American empire ought to rest on the solid basis of THE CONSENT OF THE PEOPLE. The streams of national power ought to flow immediately from that pure, original fountain of all legitimate authority. (Federalist Papers #22)

James Madison who is commonly referred to as "the father" of the United States Constitution expressed his belief in this doctrine in these words:

The genius of republican liberty seems to demand on one side, not only that all power should be derived from the people, but that those intrusted with it should be kept in dependence on the people, by a short duration of their appointments. . . . (Federalist Papers #37)

Since all political power comes from the people and since it is a fundamental axiom that a power can rise no higher than its source, the right of government to use force is coextensive with, and limited by, the right of the individual to do so in its absence.

People are unaccustomed to thinking about the right of individuals to use violence on one another since the need therefore so seldom arises. Nevertheless the right to do so exists and the laws of the various states recognize it. For example the laws of the state of New York contain this provision:

> A person may use physical force upon another person in defending himself or a third person, in defending property, in making an arrest or in preventing an escape. (New York Penal Law, Part 1, Sec. 35.10 (6))

Even the use of "deadly force" or force sufficient to cause death is authorized under some circumstances. As an illustration we cite the California Penal code which justifies homicide under these circumstances among others:

> Homicide is also justifiable when committed by any person in any of the following cases:
>
> 1. When resisting any attempt to murder any person, or to commit a felony, or to do some great bodily injury upon any person; or,
> 2. When committed in defense of habitation, property, or person, against one who manifestly intends or endeavors, by violence or surprise, to commit a felony, or against one who manifestly intends or endeavors, in a violent, riotous or tumultuous manner, to enter the habitation of another for the purpose of offering violence to any person therein . . . (California Penal Code, Title 8, Sec. 197)

The right of the individual to employ force is much more extensive than is generally thought. However when governments are formed, this right is delegated to it and may be exercised thereafter by the individual only in those cases where government is unavailable to perform its duties. But the right to do so in such cases is firmly and plainly established. And why should this not be so? If we take a contrary view, then the rights of man cease or become suspended whenever there is a failure of government. But this would be to deny the proposition that man's rights are inherent and unalienable. They existed before government came into being and will exist after it is destroyed. If such be not the case then men do not have within themselves the power to protect life, liberty and property; and if they lack this power, they cannot transfer it to government; and if they cannot do this, government is without any legitimate authority to use physical violence on humans.

But individuals do have the right to use force on one another and the extent of that right is limited by the Golden Rule. When they delegate that right to government, those same limitations are still attached since no one can delegate a power he does not possess.

And what are those limitations?

(1) We cannot authorize government to commit an act which would be evil or wrong for the individual to commit.
(2) We cannot authorize the use of force on another if, being in his position, we would consider it wrong to have that force used on us.

It is observed that these restrictions imposed upon government by the Golden Rule are identical with those imposed by the natural laws previously developed for the protection of human freedom. According to those laws, government was forbidden to punish anything except the intentional violation of duties and was restricted to enforcing only existing rights. Since it would be manifestly evil and a violation of the Golden Rule for the individual to use force for any purposes other than these, the restrictions are the same.

4.7 IS THE USE OF THE GOLDEN RULE AS A STANDARD OBJECTIONABLE BECAUSE IT MIXES RELIGION AND POLITICS?

I, the Lord God, make you free, therefore ye are free indeed; and the law also maketh you free.

According to the laws and constitution of the people, which I have suffered to be established, and should be maintained for the rights and protection of all flesh, according to just and holy principles;

That every man may act in doctrine and principle pertaining to futurity, according to the moral agency which I have given unto him, that every man may be accountable for his own sins in the day of judgment. *(D&C 98:8; 101:77, 78; See Also D&C 121:34-40)*

Some may object to the use of the Golden Rule as a standard of political justice on the ground that to do this would violate the principle of separation of church and state. They might feel that it would be contrary to the first amendment of the United States Constitution which says:

> Congress shall make no law respecting an establishment of religion nor prohibiting the free exercise thereof . . .

Does this restraint on government power prohibit the use of the moral teachings of religion as the basis for the laws of the land?

In response to this question we might ask why men form governments at all if not for the purpose of enforcing a moral code which is derived primarily from religious beliefs? If we do not use our religious or moral convictions as a guide in distinguishing between the good which government should protect and the evil which it should punish then what do we use?

It will be admitted that there are in the world today utterly amoral people such as the Communists who deny God, ridicule religion and reject the idea of moral law. They would use government, not as an agency to enforce justice, but as a means by which they, a self-anointed elite can dominate and control those they regard as the ignorant and deluded masses who are so foolish as to believe in God and moral law. Fortunately the overwhelming majority in the United States reject atheistic materialism as a political philosophy and subscribe to the view of the Founding Fathers that governments should not only enforce, but also obey moral law.

Another question which might be asked of those who object to the use of religious principles as a guide in political matters is this: Can the principles of justice professed by a person in his religion logically be in conflict with those professed by him in his politics? Can that which is evil and injurious according to his church be, at the same time, good and beneficial according to his government? Obviously not.

However, being consistent in religion and politics does not require that the code of justice taught by one's church must be coextensive with that taught by the state. A Church ofttimes teaches its members to obey rules with which the state has no concern. For example a religious denomination may instruct its members that they have a duty to support that organization with their funds and participate in its activities. It may tell them that according to the justice of God, their very salvation depends upon their doing so. But to make such church commandments a part of the laws of the land enforceable by the police power would be a direct violation of the First Amendment.

On the other hand, everything which government does should conform to the individual's code of private morality. The reason for this is most apparent. A moral person who believes that the taking of life, liberty and property always has moral consequences and who realizes that each man-made law has this effect, will recognize that every law is either good or evil. If there is sufficient moral justification for executing, jailing and fining those who violate the law and, for threatening violence to induce all men to obey it out of fear, then one's moral principles are not offended. However if such justification does not exist, then he must regard those who befriend such a law as murderers, slave masters and thieves. A just person cannot countenance the unjustified denial of life, liberty and property by the state any more than he can by the individual.

Thus while it is logically feasible for a person to believe in religious laws which should not be enforced by the state, it is not consistent for him to hold political beliefs which do not conform to his moral principles whether they are derived from his religion or elsewhere.

According to this analysis, every moral person should be intensely interested in seeing that the laws of the land conform to his moral beliefs. There is no violation of the First Amendment in doing this. On the other hand any law which would prevent a religious person from seeking to incorporate the moral principles of his church into the laws of the land would violate that amendment. Such a law would also contravene those other provisions of the First Amendment which provide that:

> Congress shall make no law . . . abridging the freedom of speech or of the press . . .

The people should have as much freedom to write and speak about religious principles and the desirability of having them made a part of the laws of the land as they have to write and speak on other subjects.

The First Amendment had for its purpose the placing of restraints only upon government and not at all upon the liberties of the citizens. Of course every citizen, as he writes, speaks and practices his religion, is obligated to obey the criminal and tort laws. If he makes fraudulent statements, commits perjury, defames or otherwise injures his fellow man, not only is he subject to punishment, but is civilly liable to those he has injured as well.

4.9 THE GOLDEN RULE: THE ONLY ACCEPTABLE STANDARD OF JUSTICE KNOWN

Granted that the enforcement of a code of justice derived from moral or religious convictions should be the object of government and that every person should strive to have his own moral beliefs enforced, which of the various codes should be adopted? It must be recognized that only one set of moral principles can be contained in the laws at any one time and that all people, regardless of the differences in their religions and beliefs must conform to that one set. Is there one standard which will satisfy everyone?

It is submitted that the Golden Rule is the only universal standard of justice known to man. It is the fundamental moral law of all great religions and the only code of justice upon which all men can agree. One who is punished or compelled to make restitution according to this standard has no grounds for complaint. By his actions toward others he has adopted a standard of behavior. Can he object when he is subjected to that same standard? Is this not what he would consider just if he were the injured party or the one administering justice?

The Golden Rule would appear to require that before justice is administered, the one doing so should mentally place himself in the position of the defendant and consider the propriety of the action being taken. This added precaution if done honestly, would help to insure that justice is being attained.

The Golden Rule is easily explained, understood and remembered even by the uneducated, the simple and the young. It has the indispensable virtue of being unchangeable and therefore predictable. It incorporates into the administration of justice those elements of certainty and stability so essential to the public tranquility. Let that person who would reject it as a standard, undertake to formulate another to take its place.

I reverence the Constitution of the United States as a sacred document. To me its words are akin to the revelations of God, for God has placed his stamp of approval on the Constitution of this land. I testify that the God of heaven sent some of His choices spirits to lay the foundation of this government, and He has sent other choice spirits—even you who read my words—to preserve it.

President Ezra Taft Benson,
(The Constitution: A Heavenly Banner p.31)

CHAPTER V

THE UNITED STATES CONSTITUTION

5.1 THE FUNCTIONS OF A CONSTITUTION

> Therefore, it is not right that any man should be in bondage one to another.
>
> And for this purpose have I established the Constitution of this land, by the hands of wise men whom I have up unto this very purpose, and redeemed the land by the shedding of blood.

> Have mercy, O Lord, upon all the nations of the earth; have mercy upon the rulers of our land; may those principles, which were so honorably and nobly defended, namely, the Constitution of our land, by our fathers, be established forever. *(D&C 101:79-80; 109:54; See also D&C 98:4-8)*

Constitutions of both the Federal and State governments serve the following purposes:

1. Establish the framework of government by setting up its branches, the various offices therein and how they are filled:
2. Delegate to each branch the powers it may exercise;
3. Specify the procedures which must be followed by the officers in the exercise of their powers; and
4. Place restraints on government power

We shall discuss each of these matters in turn commencing in this chapter with a brief review of the framework established by the United States Constitution.

One of the most novel and remarkable features of the political system established by this Constitution was the division of powers between the Federal and the State governments. Let us consider how these powers were divided. It is submitted that a correct understanding of this matter is best obtained by recognizing the purposes for which the Federal government was established and then noting the powers which were necessary for it to accomplish these purposes. A study of the conditions which existed among the thirteen states at the time the Constitution was adopted and the problems facing them which demanded solutions, discloses that there were three primary motives for uniting under a single government: (l) The threat of foreign aggressor nations; (2) The likelihood of civil strife between the states if they continued to be disunited; and (3) The trade barriers and other economic restrictions which existed between the states and would have continued in the absence of a Federal government. Let us consider what transfer or delegation of powers to a central government was required to solve these three problems.

5.2 POWERS NECESSARY TO COPE WITH THE THREAT OF FOREIGN NATIONS

> And it came to pass that I, Nephi, beheld that the Gentiles who had gone forth out of captivity did humble themselves before the Lord; and the power of the Lord was with them.
>
> And I beheld that their mother Gentiles were gathered together upon the waters, and upon the land also, to battle against them.
>
> And I beheld that the power of God was with them, and also that the wrath of God was upon all those that were gathered together against them to battle.
>
> And I, Nephi, beheld that the Gentiles that had gone out of captivity were delivered by the power of God out of the hands of all other nations.
>
> Nevertheless, thou beholdest that the Gentiles who have gone forth out of captivity, and have been lifted up by the power of God above all other nations, upon the face of the land which is choice above all other lands, which is the land that the Lord God hath covenanted with thy father that his seed should have for the land of their inheritance; wherefore, thou seest that the Lord God will not suffer that the Gentiles will utterly destroy the mixture of thy seed, which are among thy brethren.
>
> For it is wisdom in the Father that they should be established in this land, and be set up as a free people by the power of the Father, that these things might come forth from them unto a remnant of your seed, that the covenant of the Father may be fulfilled which he hath covenanted with his people, O house of Israel;
> *(1 Nephi 13:16-19, 30; 3 Nephi 21:4))*

The several states acting separately from one another were comparatively weak both economically and militarily and no match for the armed might of foreign countries. This weakness together with the fact that the vast fertile land areas of America offered great temptations to the empire-hungry nations of Europe, demanded that they unite for their very survival. That unity which had been so necessary for them to achieve independence was equally necessary to preserve it.

To provide this unity and combine their powers into one, it was necessary to make the central government responsible for the national defense and delegate to it those powers necessary to perform this vital function. To this end the Constitution authorized the Federal Congress "to declare war . . . to raise and support armies . . . to provide and maintain a navy" and, in short, to handle all matters concerning foreign nations. To enable it to obtain the means necessary to carry out this and other functions Congress was also empowered "to lay and collect taxes, duties, imposts and excises, to pay the debts and provide for the common defense and general welfare of the United States." (Art. I, sec. 8)

To insure that the power of the Federal government was exclusive in this field, the States were specifically prohibited from involving themselves in foreign and federal relations by such clauses as these:

> No State shall enter into any Treaty, Alliance, or Confederation; . . . No State shall, without the consent of Congress, lay any duty of tonnage, keep troops, or ships of war in time of peace, enter into any agreement or compact with another State, or with a foreign power, or engage in war, unless actually invaded, or in such imminent danger as will not admit of delay. (Art. I, Sec. 10)

5.3 POWERS NECESSARY TO PREVENT CIVIL STRIFE BETWEEN THE STATES

Unless the states had formed a national government, vested it with power to settle disputes between them and incorporate into the union the western territories, it is inconceivable that there would not have been armed conflict to resolve these matters. Boundary disputes, conflicting claims to the unsettled land, unredressed injuries both imagined and real would, in all likelihood, have kept the states in constant turmoil and embroiled them in a series of wars such as have racked the nations of Europe for centuries past.

To avoid such strife, it was necessary to establish a federal judiciary and give it jurisdiction over such matters as:

> controversies between two or more States; between a State and citizens of another State; —between citizens of different States;—between citizens of the same state claiming lands under grants of different states. . . (Art. 3, Sec. 2)

5.4 POWERS NECESSARY TO REMOVE TRADE BARRIERS AND ECONOMIC RESTRICTIONS

Tariff walls, diverse and unstable monetary systems, differing standards of weights and measures and similar economic impediments which invariably arise between sovereign nations, strongly influenced the colonists to vest the Federal government with power to prohibit such harmful legislation and otherwise unite the nation into a single economic entity. To insure the free flow of commerce and people across the state lines the Constitution provided that:

> The citizens of each state shall be entitled to all privileges and immunities of citizens in the several states. (Art. IV)
> No state shall, without the consent of the Congress, lay any imposts or duties on imports or exports, except what may be absolutely necessary for executing its inspection laws . . . (Art. I, Sec. 10)

The power to prevent such restrictions was placed in the Federal legislature by this clause:

> The Congress shall have power . . . to regulate commerce with foreign nations, and among the several states and with the Indian Tribes. (Art. I, Sec. 8)

To guarantee that every state would have a sound and redeemable monetary system it was provided that:

> No State shall . . . make anything but gold and silver coin a tender in payment of debts. (Art. I, Sec. 10)

Then to establish a uniform monetary system throughout the nation, Congress was given power:

To coin money, regulate the value thereof and of foreign coin.

The states were prohibited from either coining money or issuing paper money as legal tender by this clause:

No state shall . . . coin money; emit bills of credit . . . (Art. I, Sec. 10)

To give inventors and authors the benefit of their efforts throughout all the nation, the National government was authorized to issue patents and copyrights. It was also empowered to establish a uniform system of weights and measures and to handle bankruptcy cases thus insuring equitable treatment for all creditors. To overcome the jurisdictional limitations of state courts and to insure an impartial tribunal for litigants not resident in the same state, the federal judiciary was authorized to handle cases between citizens of different states.

5.5 *MISCELLANEOUS POWERS*

In addition to those powers necessary to accomplish the three main purposes discussed above, there were a few others necessary to enable the Federal government to function without hindrance or interference from state governments. That it might have a home base of operations over which it could exercise exclusive jurisdiction, and to enable it to establish and control military bases within state boundaries, Congress was given power:

To exercise exclusive legislation in all cases whatsoever, over such District (not exceeding ten miles square) as may, by cession of particular states, and acceptance of Congress, become the seat of the Government of the United States, and to exercise like authority over all places purchased by the consent of the legislature of the state in which the same shall be, for the erection of forts, magazines, arsenals, dockyards, and other needful buildings; . . . (Art I, Sec. 8)

As to land areas subject to jurisdiction of the United States and not a part of any State, Congress was given the power to:

Dispose of and make all needful rules and regulations respecting the territory or other property belonging to the United States. (Art. IV, Sec. 3)

In addition it could:

> Define and punish piracies and felonies committed on the
> high seas, and offenses against the law of nations. (Art. I, Sec. 8)

The Federal government was enabled to prevent its own destruction by being given the "power to declare the punishment of treason." (Art. III, Sec. 3) It was also authorized to provide for the punishment of counterfeiting the securities and current coin of the United States.

5.6 GOVERNMENTAL POWERS RESERVED TO THE STATES

While it would be necessary to examine the constitutions of the several states to determine the powers possessed by each of them, we can generalize about the division of power between them and the federal by stating that it was intended that they possess the great mass of the powers of government while the national government was to exercise relatively few of them. The following statement by James Madison who deserves, if anyone does, the title of "Father of the Constitution," is representative of the feelings of the founding fathers regarding this division:

> The powers delegated by the proposed Constitution to the
> Federal government are few and defined. Those which are to
> remain in the State governments are numerous and indefinite. The
> former will be exercised principally on external objects, as war,
> peace, negotiation, and foreign commerce; . . . The powers
> reserved to the several States will extend to all the objects which,
> in the ordinary course of affairs concern the lives, liberties, and
> properties of the people, and the internal order, improvement, and
> prosperity of the State. (Fed. Papers #45)

Under the federal system then the National government is assigned the duty and power of defending the nation against foreign aggression and of handling foreign and federal affairs. In performing these functions it is empowered to impose taxes on the people and establish military forces. But other than this, it was given very little power over the citizens of the various states. The power to punish crime, to adopt and enforce contract and tort laws, to determine the ownership of property and otherwise perform those functions necessary to protect the lives, liberties and properties of the people was left to the states. It is true that the Federal government was empowered to punish a few crimes such as treason and counterfeiting; to determine property rights in a few cases such as patents, copyrights and bankruptcies; and even to decide other cases when the litigants were citizens of different States. But other than those cases enumerated, it was not empowered to use force against the citizens. To make certain that it would neither claim nor exercise powers other than those granted, the following provision was adopted:

> The powers not delegated to the United States by the Constitution, nor prohibited by it to the States, are reserved to the States respectively, or to the people. (10th Amendment)

5.7 SEPARATION OF POWERS DOCTRINE

The Constitution divides the powers of government six different ways: First between the states and the Federal, and secondly between the legislative, executive and the judicial branches within each. While there is no mention in the Constitution of the necessity of these three departments within the state governments, this division was assumed to be a necessary attribute of the "republican form of government" which the Constitution guarantees to each state. The federal Constitution provides for these three departments as do the Constitutions of every state, and the separation of powers intended appears to be essentially the same in all American Constitutions even though the methods of choosing the officers vary.

The necessity of keeping the powers of government divided, and the danger of not doing so, was explained by Madison in the following passage:

> The accumulation of all powers, legislative, executive, and judiciary, in the same hands, whether of one, a few, or many, and whether hereditary, self-appointed, or elective, may justly be pronounced the very definition of tyranny. (Federalist Papers #47)

In the same number from which the above was taken, Madison quotes with approval these words from the celebrated French authority, Montesquieu, on this subject:

> When the legislative and executive powers are united in the
> same person or body, there can be no liberty, because apprehen-
> sions may arise lest the same monarch or senate should enact
> tyrannical laws to execute them in a tyrannical manner . . . Were
> the power of judging joined with the legislative, the life and liber-
> ty of the subject would be exposed to arbitrary control, for the
> judge would then be the legislator. Were it joined to the executive
> power, the judge might behave with all the violence of an oppres-
> sor. (Id.)

According to the following provision, the power of passing laws
is vested exclusively and solely in the Congress:

> All legislative powers herein granted shall be vested in a
> Congress of the United States, which shall consist of a Senate and
> a House of Representatives. (Art. I, Sec. I)

Since "all legislative powers herein granted" are vested in
Congress, it would be patently wrong for the executive, the judicial
or any other agency to exercise law-making powers. Such a power,
where held, is vested exclusively in the Senate and House.
Legislation from any other source would be unconstitutional.

According to the original plan of the Constitution the people
elected the members of the House of Representatives directly while
the State legislatures chose the members of the Senate. Since all proposed legislation which becomes law must pass both houses, this
system theoretically gave the people a veto power over all laws
through their representatives, and it also gave the State governments
the power to prevent the Federal Government from destroying the
rights of the States through the control they exercised over the
Senate. However, in 1913 the 17th Amendment was adopted which
made Senators subject to popular vote. This left the state governments without any voice in the Federal.

The executive power of the United States government is vested
in a President. He is the Commander-in-chief of the army and navy
and has the power, by and with the consent of the Senate, to make
treaties, appoint ambassadors, federal judges and other public ministers. He has the power to veto legislation which may then be passed
over his veto by a two-thirds majority of both houses. The President
together with the Vice-President, who serves as president of the
Senate, are elected by electors who are in turn elected by the people.

The third branch of government, the judiciary, is established by
the following provision:

The judicial power of the United States shall be vested in one Supreme Court, and in such inferior courts as the Congress may from time to time ordain and establish. (Art. III, Sec. I)

In addition to its power to try cases arising between States and the citizens of different States, the judicial power extends to all cases:

1. Arising under the Constitution, the laws of the United States, and treaties made under their authority;
2. Affecting ambassadors and other public ministers;
3. Of admiralty and maritime jurisdiction;

Federal Court judges are not subject to the vote of the people but are appointed by the President by and with the consent of the Senate. They have lifetime tenure, hold their offices during good behavior, and their compensation cannot be diminished while in office. These provisions make them independent of the influence and control of the other branches of government and leave them free to pass judgment on the constitutionality of laws without fear of reprisal.

5.8 A System Of Checks And Balances

The central problem which men face in forming a government was succinctly stated by James Madison in these words:

In framing a government which is to be administered by men over men, the great difficulty lies in this: You must first enable the government to control the governed; and in the next place oblige it to control itself. (Federalist Papers, #51)

Those who established the United States Constitution solved this problem with unmatched skill. They accurately perceived that while government is essential for the protection of human rights, it is also their greatest danger. The real genius of their accomplishment lay not in conveying to government sufficient power to protect these rights, for that requires little statesmanship. Their consummate wisdom and art was displayed in devising a structure which, while adequate to its task, contained a system of checks and balances skillfully designed to prevent the concentration and abuse of power.

To avoid the concentration of power they divided it between the states and the federal and then between the three branches within each. The legislature being the strongest of the three and the most likely to exceed its authority was again divided.

A series of hurdles were erected to prevent the passage of ill-considered legislation with each branch of government empowered either to prevent or render difficult its adoption. Since all laws require the approval of both houses of Congress, the people, through their elected representatives, could obstruct the passage of laws inimical to their interests. Under the original plan the State legislatures appointed the members of the Senate and could preserve their rights through the control they exercised over that body. The President, while not having an absolute negative, could, through the veto power, prevent the passage of any measure not receiving the approval of a two-thirds majority of both houses. And finally, even though a bill had received the approval of the other two branches, the Supreme Court could declare it unconstitutional if they found that it provided for the exercise of powers not granted by the people.

5.9 THE PRINCIPLE OF SELF-GOVERNMENT

Under the American political system, not only are the people the source of all power, but they have a continuing right to govern themselves. To do this they must have an effective voice in determining the regulations to which they are subject, the taxes they are compelled to pay and how those taxes are spent. To have an effective voice in these matters, it is necessary that the individual voter be able to influence those who pass laws.

But the individual's ability to influence a lawmaker varies inversely with the number of voters in the lawmaker's district. The greater the number of voters, the smaller the influence. While a voter might be able to have substantial influence on his county commissioner or city councilman, his influence on a national congressman—especially one from another state or district—would be virtually nil.

Therefore, to make the principle of self-government a reality, the taxing and spending powers must be kept as close to home as possible. Government functions must be assigned to the lowest level of government which can perform them. To the extent this rule is violated, to this same extent the right of self-government is denied.

The men who established our National and State governments adopted this rule. To the Federal they delegated only those powers of national defense and foreign and federal relations which state and local governments could not perform. State governments were assigned only those functions which the local could not handle. This principle was succinctly expressed by Thomas Jefferson in the following words:

> . . .The way to have good and safe government is not to trust it all to one; but to divide it among the many, distributing to every-one exactly the functions he is competent to. Let the National Government be entrusted with the defense of the nation, and its foreign and federal relations; the State governments with the civil rights, laws, police and administration of what concerns the state generally; the counties with the local concerns of the counties and each ward direct the interests within itself. It is by dividing and subdividing these republics, from the great national one down through all its subordinations, until it ends in the administration of every man's farm and affairs by himself; by placing under every one what his own eye may superintend, that all will be done for the best. What has destroyed liberty and the rights of man in every government which has ever existed under the sun? The generaliz-ing and concentrating all cares and powers into one body, no mat-ter whether of the autocrats of Russia or France, or the aristocrats of a Venetian Senate.

There have been many tributes paid the United States Constitution. The most sincere praise is found in the fact that it has been emulated and its principles incorporated into the political systems of so many other nations. The British statesman, Gladstone, said of it:

> The American Constitution is the most wonderful work ever struck off at a given time by the brain and purpose of man.

And the historian, John Fiske, praised it in these words:

> It was one of the longest reaches of statesmanship ever known in the world.

5.10 THE MORAL CODE OF THE CONSTITUTION

Probably no one has more succinctly and accurately stated the moral code upon which our American Constitutional system is based than did Washington when he said in his first inaugural address:

> . . .(T)he foundation of our national policy will be laid in the pure and immutable principles of private morality.

Those principles were derived, of course, from the Christian religion to which the Founding Fathers subscribed. To them the Bible was the word of God and was the only reliable source of moral law upon which to erect a political structure. And so they turned to that source for guidance.

In the Ten Commandments and the rules given in connection therewith, they found listed that conduct which was so evil that it should be discouraged with physical punishment. Also, the penalties (or judgments as they were called) which should be inflicted were given. These laws were tempered with the fundamental concept of Christian justice which decrees that punishment shall never be inflicted unless the accused has violated his conscience—unless he has done to another that which he would believe wrong and harmful if done to him. In the laws given to Moses, it was also provided that those who either intentionally or negligently injured their neighbor should make restitution. These principles of justice formed the basis of the private code of morality which was incorporated into the Constitution and laws of this nation.

The Common Law of England which the colonists adopted provided for punishing evil and making restitution for injuries. But the part of the laws of England which they refused to accept were those which violated the Christian moral code. It was their position that governments themselves must obey the moral law; that their powers are limited to punishing evil and providing restitution, and anything more than this is evil; that anything which is evil or unjust for the individual to do, is equally wrong for men to do in the name of government.

It was because the English had undertaken to impose upon them laws which violated this moral code that the Revolutionary War was fought. It was because the nations of Europe had enacted such laws that the Pilgrims had come here seeking freedom in the first place.

And so, in the Declaration of Independence the point was made:

> That whenever any form of Government becomes destructive of these ends, (securing man's rights) it is the Right of the People to alter or to abolish it, and to institute new Government. . . .

The concept that governments are themselves obligated to obey the moral code they are established to enforce was truly a revolutionary idea. No government at that time was so confined. And yet this was a very vital part of the moral code of the Christian religion. The Bible clearly teaches that rulers should confine themselves to punishing only that which is evil. It instructs them to be just; to observe the Golden Rule; to never do to another that which they would consider wrong if done to themselves. There is no principle of Christian justice more firmly established than this: that an innocent person shall not be punished.

And so the Founders built into the system they established protection against violation of this vital principle. Those safeguards were of two kinds: (1) Procedural, and (2) Substantive. The procedural defenses against injustice were largely contained in the Common Law of England which guaranteed the accused the right to a jury trial, the privilege against self-incrimination, the right to be faced by his accusers, the right to counsel, etc. But they wanted to provide against a danger which was, if anything, even greater: the adoption of unjust laws. To them it was as much a violation of the moral law to convict and punish a person who was guilty of violating an unjust law, as it was to convict and punish one who was not guilty of violating a just law. And so great care was taken to limit the power of government accordingly. This principle is strictly in harmony with the natural law developed in Chapter III which decrees that: "Government shall punish nothing except the intentional violation of duties." It also conforms to the thought developed in Chapter IV that since government is a derived power, it can do nothing which would be wrong for the individual to do for himself.

In the succeeding chapters we shall discuss how the moral code of the Constitution was implemented. In the chapter on crimes we will discuss the punishment of evil. The chapters on torts and contracts will consider the principle that governments should be available for compelling restitution for injuries to the elements of freedom. We shall also point out the natural limits on the power of government as it performs these functions.

We believe in being subject to kings, presidents, rulers, and magistrates, in obeying, honoring, and sustaining the law.

(Articles of Faith No. 12)

And if a man or woman shall rob, he or she shall be delivered up unto the law of the land.

And if he or she shall steal, he or she shall be delivered up unto the law of the land.

And if he or she shall lie, he or she shall be delivered up unto the law of the land.

(D&C 42:84-86)

CHAPTER VI

CRIMINAL LAWS

6.1 CRIMINAL LAW DEFINED

One of the natural laws discussed in Chapter III decrees that government must punish the intentional violation of duties in order to protect human rights. This function is performed under the criminal laws and we shall use the term "criminal law" to mean every law, ordinance, regulation or court decree which commands or forbids human conduct and provides a punishment for disobedience. It is the provision for a penalty which distinguishes a criminal law from laws of other types.

When a person violates a criminal law, the officers of government are duty bound to prosecute him, prove his guilt and inflict the punishment provided. On the other hand, when a person fails to perform a duty set forth in the civil laws, no penalty is imposed. The one to whom the duty is owed may bring a lawsuit against the debtor, prove the obligation and use the machinery of government to enforce its payment. However, this is the extent to which force may be used in a civil case.

It should be recognized that government can, and sometimes does, punish the non-performance of civil duty. But before doing so it must make the violation a criminal offense. It cannot impose a penalty unless a law, or a court decree provides therefor. When this is done, failure to perform becomes a crime as well as a breach of a civil duty. According to the foregoing analysis, we may formally define a criminal law as:

> A decree or enactment by the state which commands or forbids certain conduct and provides an adequate penalty for disobedience.

The only penalties which have been found to be adequate are: (1) Death or bodily injury; (2) Imprisonment or some other denial of liberty; (3) A fine or some other deprivation of property or property rights.

6.2 COMMON LAW DEFINITION OF A CRIME

Sir William Blackstone (1723-1780), an English judge and author, is generally conceded to be the greatest authority and exponent of the Common Law who ever lived. It is not improbable that his famous treatise, *Commentaries on the Laws of England*, wielded a greater influence on the development of the Common Law in America than any other work. Certainly he has been quoted more frequently by the various courts of the United States than any other writer. Therefore, his definition of a common law crime should be authoritative. We quote it below.

> To make a complete crime cognizable by human laws, there must be both a will and an act. For though . . . a fixed design or will to do an unlawful act is almost as heinous as the commission of it, yet, as no temporal tribunal can search the heart, or fathom the intentions of the mind, otherwise than as they are demonstrated by outward actions, it therefore cannot punish for what it cannot know. For which reason in all temporal jurisdictions an overt act, or some open evidence of an intended crime, is necessary in order to demonstrate the depravity of the will, before the man is liable to punishment. And, as a vicious will, without a vicious act is no civil crime, so, on the other hand, an unwarrantable act without a vicious will is no crime at all. So that to constitute a crime against human laws, there must be, first, a vicious will; and, secondly, an unlawful act consequent upon such a vicious will. (4 Blackstone, *Commentaries on the English Law*, p. 21)

According to this statement, there are two essential elements to every crime: (1) A vicious will, and (2) An act committed to accomplish it. Let us now define a crime according to the natural laws developed in Chapter III and then compare it with Blackstone's Common Law definition.

The first two natural laws stated that government must, (1) Punish the intentional violation of duties; (2) Punish nothing except the intentional violation of duties. If these laws are obeyed, government can inflict punishment for a crime only where there is both an intent to violate a duty and an act to accomplish it. But if an "intent to violate a duty" means the same as "a vicious will," then the definition of a crime according to our natural laws is the same as that at common law. In any event a wrongful intent is required in both cases.

But over the years this fundamental requirement of a criminal intent has been dispensed with in some areas so that today under statutory laws it is no longer required in many instances. Current textbooks and dictionaries define a crime somewhat as follows:

> An act committed or omitted in violation of a public law forbidding it. (*Bouvier's Law Dictionary*, 1934 Ed.)

According to the theory expressed here, the state is free to forbid and punish any conduct it chooses. It is not limited to punishing those acts which are motivated by an evil intent.

Since the relaxation of the requirement of a criminal intent, the number of laws which provide for punishing good and innocent behavior have grown until today they are far more numerous than those which punish evil or harmful conduct.

6.3 THE CRIMINAL INTENT

There is no problem of government of greater importance than that of deciding whether proof of an evil intent is required before punishment can be imposed under a criminal law. Freedom of contract, and indeed all other freedoms largely depend upon how this question is answered. In prior chapters we have briefly considered the problem of the criminal intent and have concluded that it is equivalent to the intentional violation of that duty which every rational person recognizes—the duty to avoid injuring the elements of freedom. It is appropriate that we now recapitulate and elaborate our discussion of this vital matter.

There are two opposing views which can be taken regarding the punishment of a crime. One is that the powers of government are unlimited so that it has the unrestricted right to define what a crime is and inflict any punishment it desires. The other is that the powers of government are limited; that there is a precise line between good and evil; that it may punish the evil but nothing else.

Those who subscribe to the first view either contend that there is no fixed line between good and evil or, if there is, those in control of government are free to ignore it. Their position is that the rulers, whether they be kings, dictators or a democratic majority, have, by virtue of the fact that they are rulers, the sole power to specify what conduct is punishable and the penalty for disobedience. In other words they are at liberty to punish any act or omission whatsoever and without regard to the intent with which it is committed.

Those of the second view contend that governments exist to enforce an immutable code of private morality; that when those in control formulate criminal laws, they are confined to punishing that conduct which that code defines as evil. This places a limit on their authority.

These two views are irreconcilable. Either the powers of government are limited or they are not. There is no intermediate position. Some may contend that there are limits but no one knows what those limits are; that there is a line between the good which should not be punished and the evil which should, but they cannot tell where that line is. Such people, whether they are aware of it or not, have accepted the view of unlimited power.

To say that there are limits but that those limits cannot be established has the same consequence as saying there are none. To contend that men have rights which government cannot invade, but to be unable to discern when that happens, is tantamount to admitting they do not exist. One who knows not what his rights are can never know when they are taken and is unable to defend them. He is like a man who believes he owns a piece of ground which his neighbor also claims, but he doesn't know its boundaries. The neighbor continues to encroach further and further onto land he suspects is his, but since he is never certain where the boundary is, he cannot check the advance. Until he takes a firm position and says: "this far and no further," there is no line.

The position taken herein is that the powers of government to punish are limited, and those limits are clearly discernible. It is submitted that no other view is possible to one who believes in the American Constitutional system. There is no principle of that system which is more basic and more clearly proclaimed than that men have certain unalienable rights which public officers cannot deny.

Those men who framed the Declaration of Independence, the United States Constitution and the constitutions of the various states placed in those documents more restraints on government power than grants. The entire Bill of Rights of the Federal Charter, whose main provisions are also contained in state constitutions, is nothing more than an enumeration of restraints. These limitations have one purpose and one effect: They place restrictions on the power to pass and enforce criminal laws. They prohibit the taking of life, liberty and property except for certain offenses. They establish procedures which must be followed in proving that those offenses have been committed.

Granted that the powers of government are limited, what are those limits? Unless they are known, for all practical purposes they do not exist. The natural tendency of men to abuse authority is so strong that those in government will always expand and enlarge their powers unless restrained. They will continually adopt laws making the exercise of freedom a crime until no freedom remains. They will, if permitted to do so, suspend procedural guarantees until they can convict and punish without inconvenience and without proof of guilt.

The limits of the power to punish are determined by the purpose for which that power is given. Under the American political system, governments are established to protect human freedom. The power to punish must be used then to promote this purpose but never defeat it. By punishing those who undertake to destroy freedom this purpose is served. Those who would otherwise engage in freedom-destroying conduct are deterred from doing so. But the punishment of conduct other than this destroys freedom. For example, if a law is adopted which makes it a crime to enter a legitimate business and produce goods and services, freedom is destroyed in two ways: (1) People are denied freedom to engage in the prohibited activity, and (2) The production of those goods and services which otherwise would have been used in the exercise of freedom is prevented.

If then we define an "evil intent" as the intent to destroy or deny the elements of freedom, and if we forbid government the power to punish without first proving an evil intent, we have placed that limit on this power which is required to accomplish its purpose.

Furthermore, this definition of an evil intent is the only one upon which everyone can agree. We all love our own freedom and regard it as wrong and harmful when others injure it. From this we are all aware that when we violate the Golden Rule and undertake to do to others that which we would consider wrong if done to us, we are guilty of an evil intent.

6.4 THE PURPOSES OF ENFORCING CRIMINAL LAWS

We believe that the commission of crime should be punished according to the nature of the offense; that murder, treason, robbery, theft, and the breach of the general peace, in all respects, should be punished according to their criminality and their tendency to evil among men, by the laws of that government in which the offense is committed; and for the public peace and tranquility all men should step forward and use their ability in bringing offenders against good laws to punishment. *(D&C 134:8)*

And Moses came and told the people all the words of the LORD, and all the judgments: and all the people answered with one voice, and said, All the words which the LORD hath said will we do.

And Moses wrote all the words of the LORD, and rose up early in the morning, and builded an altar under the hill, and twelve pillars, according to the twelve tribes of Israel.

And he took the book of the covenant, and read in the audience of the people: and they said, All that the LORD hath said will we do, and be obedient.

And Moses took the blood, and sprinkled [it] on the people, and said, Behold the blood of the covenant, which the LORD hath made with you concerning all these words. *(Exodus 24:3-4, 7-8)*

AND Moses called all Israel, and said unto them, Hear, O Israel, the statutes and judgments which I speak in your ears this day, that ye may learn them, and keep, and do them.

The LORD our God made a covenant with us in Horeb.

The secret [things belong] unto the LORD our God: but those [things which are] revealed [belong] unto us and to our children for ever, that [we] may do all the words of this law. *(Deuteronomy 5:1-2; 29:29)*

Remember ye the law of Moses my servant, which I commanded unto him in Horeb for all Israel, [with] the statutes and judgments. *(Malachi 4:4)*

Remember ye the law of Moses, my servant, which I commanded unto him in Horeb for all Israel, with the statutes and judgments. *(3 Nephi 25:4)*

Criminal laws are enforced to protect freedom by punishing

those who destroy its elements for selfish purposes. By doing so governments fulfill that natural law which decrees that, for the protection of freedom, the intentional violation of duties must be punished.

When only those criminal laws which punish the intentional violation of duties are enforced, society is benefitted in a number of important ways: (1) Evil is suppressed; (2) Freedom is protected; (3) Peace is maintained; and (4) The members of society are taught to distinguish accurately between good and evil. Punishment may also benefit the criminal by: (1) Enabling him to pay his debt to society to the extent this is possible; and (2) Causing him to reform.

There are those who favor the enforcement of criminal laws because they believe that in so doing, they are obeying the commandments of God. This was true of the Israelites in Moses' time and of their descendants for centuries thereafter. In their view, omniscient Deity had, through revelation, identified that conduct which was so evil it should be physically punished and had commanded them to inflict the punishment. The Ten Commandments and the other laws given in connection therewith formed the basis of their entire religion and they were directed to compel obedience to this code by punishing those who disobeyed it. Those who accept the Bible as the word of God and understand its teachings will enforce criminal laws for the same reason.

6.5 PUNISHMENT DETERMINED BY CRIMINALITY OF THE INTENT

One of the most difficult problems in criminal law is to determine the punishment which fits the crime. While it should be severe enough to deter future offenses, it should not be more severe than justice to the offender requires. These two standards should coincide. In our criminal laws today, except where proof of a criminal intent is not required at all, there is a direct relationship between the amount of injury intended by the criminal and the penalty imposed. It is generally assumed that the greater the harm, the more vicious the will; and the more vicious the will, the greater should be the punishment. But there is sometimes a great disparity between the severity of the harm and the punishment. This is explained by noting that the punishment imposed for a crime is determined almost entirely by the criminality of the intent rather than by the actual amount of harm done. This point is well illustrated by the criminal laws covering homicide.

For example, the laws of the state of Utah, which are fairly typical, define murder as, "the unlawful killing of a human being with malice aforethought," and they make it punishable by death or life imprisonment. In contrast to this, manslaughter which is also the unlawful killing of a human being, but without malice, is punishable by imprisonment in the state prison from one to ten years if it is "voluntary," and by imprisonment in the county jail for not exceeding one year if it is "involuntary." And finally there is "justifiable" and "excusable" homicide which are not punishable at all. Thus, depending upon the intent of the actor, a homicide may be punishable by death or may carry no penalty whatsoever. The same harm—death—has been caused in each instance. But the extent to which it is punishable is determined entirely by the intent of the actor.

The Israelites at the time of Moses were largely relieved of the problem of deciding upon a correct punishment because the penalty to be imposed was ofttimes given along with the law. In the case of injuries to the body, there was a one-to-one correspondence between the injury and the penalty as the following familiar scripture indicates.

> And he that killeth any man shall surely be put to death. . . .
> And if a man cause a blemish in his neighbor; as he hath done, so
> shall it be done to him; Breach for breach, eye for eye, tooth for
> tooth. . . . *(Lev. 24:17-20)*

This same penalty rule was followed in punishing one guilty of bearing false witness. One who testified falsely was given the same punishment which the one falsely accused would have suffered had he been found guilty. *(Deut. 19:19)*

In the case of theft, the wrongdoer was required to restore to the victim several-fold the value of the property stolen. The effect of this rule was to impose a fine upon the criminal but rather than giving it to the state, as is done today, it was given to the one who sustained the loss and experienced all of the inconvenience and wasted time resulting therefrom.

From what has been said regarding the criminal laws of the Israelites, it should not be assumed that their judges administered penalties mechanically and without mercy. The criminality of the intent was the determining factor then as, under the rules of Christian justice, it should always be. While today it might seem unjust to enforce some of the laws they were punished for disobeying, the Bible explains that those people had been given physical evidence that their laws came from God and therefore they could not disobey any of them with a clear conscience.

6.6 *Capacity To Form The Criminal Intent*

Since an evil intent is a necessary part of every crime, if the accused lacks the capacity to form such an intent, it would be logically impossible to convict him. It is for this reason that infants of a tender age and mental incompetents who cannot distinguish between right and wrong are not punishable under criminal law.

At common law, a child under seven was conclusively presumed to be incapable of committing a crime. Children from seven to fourteen were presumed to be unable to form the criminal intent, but this presumption could be rebutted. That is, the state was allowed to attempt to prove the existence of sufficient mental capacity and if it succeeded, a conviction was possible. Anyone fourteen or older was treated as an adult and presumed to be competent. State statutes have largely followed these common law rules.

Even though a person fourteen or older is presumed to be sane, this presumption can be rebutted. If it can be shown that the accused was unable to distinguish between right and wrong at the time the alleged criminal act was committed, he cannot be convicted.

A person who has deliberately diminished his mental capacity with drink or drugs cannot thereby escape responsibility for acts committed during a state of intoxication. His offense is not diminished when, by yielding to his vices, he deprives himself of reason and moral self-restraint. No one has a right to make a dangerous animal of himself thereby jeopardizing the welfare and safety of others.

Although there is a trend today to hold corporations liable for certain criminal acts, since it is manifestly impossible for them to form a criminal intent this is contrary to the most elementary principles of justice. Corporate officers and other agents are, of course, capable of committing crimes. And when they do they should be punished. But to charge their misdeeds to the corporate entity has the effect of punishing stockholders who may be completely innocent. This is as illogical as punishing an employer for the crimes of his employees or the voters for the crimes of their elected representative.

6.7 TYPES OF CRIMES

Crimes may be classified, according to their seriousness, into two broad categories: (1) Felonies which are punishable by death or imprisonment in the state prison; and (2) Misdemeanors which include all crimes other than felonies.

Another classification which is commonly made is based upon the element of freedom injured. Crimes against life and liberty are usually grouped together and called "crimes against the person." These include murder, mayhem, assault, battery, kidnapping, false imprisonment and the sex crimes.

Crimes against property are probably more numerous than any other type. Some of the more important ones are: robbery, burglary, arson, larceny, embezzlement, extortion, forgery and obtaining money by false pretenses.

Crimes against knowledge are variously called lying, deceit, misrepresentation, false advertising and false personation.

In another category we may place crimes against government. While they may not adversely affect the elements of freedom directly, they do so indirectly since their effect is to defeat the administration of justice. Such offenses as treason, perjury, bribery and abuse of process are placed under this heading.

6.8 ATTEMPTED CRIMES

An attempted crime is an act done with an intent to commit the crime, but, through circumstances independent of the will of the actor, not completed. This constitutes a punishable offense at common law and under the statutory laws of the various states. Mere preparation which, according to the calculations of the actor is insufficient and actually does fail to complete the offense, would not constitute an attempt to commit that particular crime even though those preparations may be indictable on some other ground.

For example, if a person purchases a pick lock and a crowbar with the intent to use them to commit a burglary but is apprehended before doing so, he is not guilty of the crime of "attempted burglary," but probably is guilty of the crime of "possession of burglarious tools." On the other hand if he took an article intending to steal it, but discovered later he had taken his own property, he would not be guilty of larceny, but would be guilty of "attempted larceny."

6.9 DEGREE OF PROOF REQUIRED TO CONVICT

A people whose moral convictions constrain them to be concerned about justice and the well-being of their fellowmen have a strong repugnance against punishing the innocent. If they have a choice, they would prefer that some of the guilty escape punishment rather than that any who are innocent would be subjected to it.

This kind of a choice is available in establishing the rules which must be followed in the administration of the criminal laws. In the United States it is uniformly agreed that the guilt of one accused of a crime must be established "beyond a reasonable doubt" before he may be punished. Adherence to this rule has doubtless allowed many who have been guilty to escape punishment. But on the other hand it has greatly reduced the chance that one who is innocent will be convicted.

Under the Constitution of the United States, "The trial of all crimes, except in cases of impeachment, shall be by jury." (Art. III, Sec. 2) The effect of this provision and the rule of evidence stated above is that no person can be convicted of a crime under the Constitution unless the government has convinced a jury "beyond a reasonable doubt" that he committed a criminal act with a criminal intent.

The importance of this rule might be better appreciated by comparing it with the one applicable in civil cases. In a civil suit where the court is asked to determine the rights and liabilities of private parties, the person who wins must establish his case merely by "a preponderance of the evidence." That is, he must present evidence which weighs more heavily in his favor than that which is against him. This is a much lighter burden than the prosecutor has in the criminal case.

6.10 SHOULD PROOF OF AN EVIL INTENT BE REQUIRED AS AN ELEMENT OF EVERY CRIME?

> Yea, well did Mosiah say, who was our last king, when he was about to deliver up the kingdom, having no one to confer it upon, causing that this people should be governed by their own voices—yea, well did he say that if the time should come that the voice of this people should choose iniquity, that is, if the time should come that this people should fall into transgression, they would be ripe for destruction.
>
> And now behold, I say unto you, that the foundation of the destruction of this people is beginning to be laid by the unrighteousness of your lawyers and your judges.
>
> And it came to pass that they took Alma and Amulek, and carried them forth to the place of martyrdom, that they might witness the destruction of those who were consumed by fire.
> And when Amulek saw the pains of the women and children who were consuming in the fire, he also was pained; and he said unto Alma: How can we witness this awful scene? Therefore let us stretch forth our hands, and exercise the power of God which is in us, and save them from the flames.
> But Alma said unto him: The Spirit constraineth me that I must not stretch forth mine hand; for behold the Lord receiveth them up unto himself, in glory; and he doth suffer that they may do this thing, or that the people may do this thing unto them, according to the hardness of their hearts, that the judgments which he shall exercise upon them in his wrath may be just; and the blood of the innocent shall stand as a witness against them, yea, and cry mightily against them at the last day. *(Alma 10:19, 27; 14:9-11)*

We have seen that under the Common Law, as interpreted by Blackstone, an evil intent was an essential element of every crime. We also observed that under the laws of today, proof of such an intent is dispensed with in a great many cases. Let us consider whether it should be.

The most obvious reason for requiring proof of an evil intent is that it violates our sense of justice not to do so. No rational person will agree that he should be punished for doing an act with a clear conscience. If he is just, he will apply the same rule to others. It is cruel and inhumane to punish one who is innocent. The criminal laws have always excused mental incompetents and infants who lacked the capacity to form an evil intent. But logically it is equally unjust to punish a sane person who has intended no evil, as to punish a mental incompetent who has intended none.

But aside from the moral issue, the practice has a deplorable effect upon the victim as well as society. The effect of punishing the innocent will likely be just the opposite of punishing the guilty. Rather than causing him to reform, it is apt to provoke him to retaliate for the unjust treatment. Instead of incapacitating him to commit further evil, it will prevent him from doing the good he would otherwise do.

The effect upon society is also opposite to that which is desired. As in the case of the accused, rather than being deterred from evil, they are deterred from good. Rather than promoting peace, the more likely result is to cause unrest and turmoil.

> Yea, wo be unto you because of that great abomination which has come among you; and ye have united yourselves unto it, yea, to that secret band which was established by Gadianton!

> AND now it came to pass that when Nephi had said these words, behold, there were men who were judges, who also belonged to the secret band of Gadianton, and they were angry, and they cried out against him, saying unto the people: Why do ye not seize upon this man and bring him forth, that he may be condemned according to the crime which he has done?
> Why seest thou this man, and hearest him revile against this people and against our law?
> For behold, Nephi had spoken unto them concerning the corruptness of their law; yea, many things did Nephi speak which cannot be written; and nothing did he speak which was contrary to the commandments of God.
> And those judges were angry with him because he spake plainly unto them concerning their secret works of darkness; nevertheless, they durst not lay their own hands upon him, for they feared the people lest they should cry out against them. *(Helaman 7:25; 8:1-4)*

But the most pernicious effect of unjust laws is to corrupt the morals of the people. There is a pronounced tendency for the citizens of a nation to conform their private moral code to the laws of the land; to condemn what the laws condemn and to consider as innocent, if not virtuous, that which they condone. And why should this result not be expected? Criminal laws are for the express purpose of punishing evil. Theoretically, they allow that which is good or innocent to go unpunished. If those laws which the people are taught to respect and obey condemn and punish certain behavior, what is more natural than for the citizens to view the matter in the same light? And if the laws fail to condemn other conduct, be it good or evil, it can only be expected that they will assume that such practices are authorized and they are free to engage in them without censure from anyone.

> And there began to be men inspired from heaven and sent forth, standing among the people in all the land, preaching and testifying boldly of the sins and iniquities of the people, and testifying unto them concerning the redemption which the Lord would make for his people, or in other words, the resurrection of Christ; and they did testify boldly of his death and sufferings.
>
> Now there were many of the people who were exceedingly angry because of those who testified of these things; and those who were angry were chiefly the chief judges, and they who had been high priests and lawyers; yea, all those who were lawyers were angry with those who testified of these things.
>
> Now there was no lawyer nor judge nor high priest that could have power to condemn any one to death save their condemnation was signed by the governor of the land.
>
> Now there were many of those who testified of the things pertaining to Christ who testified boldly, who were taken and put to death secretly by the judges, that the knowledge of their death came not unto the governor of the land until after their death. *(3 Nephi 6:20-23)*

> They were innocent of any crime, as they had often been proved before, and were only confined in jail by the conspiracy of traitors and wicked men; and their innocent blood on the floor of Carthage jail is a broad seal affixed to "Mormonism" that cannot be rejected by any court on earth, and their innocent blood on the escutcheon of the State of Illinois, with the broken faith of the State as pledged by the governor, is a witness to the truth of the everlasting gospel that all the world cannot impeach; and their innocent blood on the banner of liberty, and on the magna charta of the United States, is an ambassador for the religion of Jesus Christ, that will touch the hearts of honest men among all nations; and their innocent blood, with the innocent blood of all the martyrs under the altar that John saw, will cry unto the Lord of Hosts till he avenges that blood on the earth. Amen. *(D&C 135:7; See Also Matt. Ch. 23; 27)*

The tendency of the people to conform their ideas of right and wrong to the laws of the land is clearly evident in their reaction to criticisms levelled at their own laws as compared to their reaction to criticisms offered to them against the laws of another nation. When the laws of their own country are condemned as evil, they are apt to become deeply offended at the critic. He may even be in danger of physical violence. But when a group hears the laws of another nation criticized, they will usually accept what is said with no emotion at all. And it is not merely a sense of loyalty and patriotism which rouses people to anger when the laws of their nation are censured. Their feelings go much deeper than this. Their own moral beliefs have been challenged and they are usually willing to argue at great length in defense of their position.

The subjection of private morals to public laws can have the most evil consequences. When the laws become corrupt, the fathers pass on to their children a false moral code which leads them to believe evil is good and good is evil and this is one of the greatest tragedies which can befall them. Not only do they willingly accept those laws which enslave them, but their individual moral fiber is weakened and destroyed. Former Supreme Court justice, Louis D. Brandeis, once commented upon the influence of government in these words:

> Our government is the potent, the omnipresent teacher. For good or for ill, it teaches the whole people by its example. If the government becomes a lawbreaker, it breeds contempt for the law; it invites every man to become a law unto himself.

6.11 THE NATURAL LIMITS OF THE POWER TO INFLICT PUNISHMENT

> We believe that religion is instituted of God; and that men are amenable to him, and to him only, for the exercise of it, unless their religious opinions prompt them to infringe upon the rights and liberties of others; but we do not believe that human law has a right to interfere in prescribing rules of worship to bind the con-sciences of men, nor dictate forms for public or private devotion; that the civil magistrate should restrain crime, but never control conscience; should punish guilt, but never suppress the freedom of the soul. *(D&C 134:4)*

If men establish governments for the purpose of punishing and preventing crime, they do not authorize them to commit crime. This implied prohibition marks the natural limits of the power to punish. If it inflicts a penalty for any purpose other than to punish a crime, it commits a crime.

All human conduct may be divided into two categories: (1) Those acts committed or omitted with an intent to do evil—to injure or destroy the elements of freedom without justification; and (2) Those committed or omitted without such an intent. All criminal laws may be divided into two categories: (1) Those which provide for punishing only conduct of the first type; and (2) Those which provide for punishing conduct of the second type. When a government adopts laws which provide for punishing conduct of the first type, it has reached the natural limits of its power to punish. All criminal laws other than these provide for punishing the innocent and this is a crime. In fact, the threat to enforce laws which punish innocent behavior is a crime because those who obey them out of fear are denied a rightful freedom. While men should not be free to do evil without fear of punishment, their freedom to do good should be unrestricted. When this is taken from them by the passage of an unjust law, a crime is committed.

Throughout history, men have committed a hundredfold more crimes when acting in the name and by the authority of government than when acting outside its framework. This is obvious if we consider only the death, destruction and suffering caused by those who used this agency to wage aggressive international warfare. But when we add to this the millions upon millions who have been murdered, plundered and enslaved by the officers of their own government, it is clear beyond any doubt that government is the great criminal of the ages. The unjustified loss of life, liberty and property chargeable to its account staggers the imagination.

While governments are established to protect freedom, they constitute the greatest threat to freedom which exists. Whether they act in the role of a protector or a destroyer is determined by the extent to which they respect the natural limit of their powers to punish. The greatest problem mankind faces is to keep governments within those limits.

(Note: All of Chapter 7 and 8, through section 8.5 inclusive, deal with tort and contract law. The reader not concerned with definitions of various types of tort and contract violations may wish to skip these parts.)

CHAPTER VII

TORT LAWS

7.1 DEFINITION OF A TORT

(See Exodus Ch. 21, 22)

A tort is a wrong arising from the violation of a natural duty. It is an unwarranted injury to a natural, as contrasted with an acquired, right. The law imposes upon each individual the duty to refrain from damaging others either intentionally or negligently. A tort is committed when this duty is breached.

A tort may arise from either an act or an omission. While the great majority of them are caused by affirmative conduct, a few result from a failure to act when a duty exists to do so.

The coverage of the tort law is extremely broad in that it provides restitution for injuries which are intended as well as for those resulting from negligence. However, it does not extend to injuries arising from breach of agreements. This is the province of the law of contracts and family relations. But except for these, the law of torts covers essentially every injury which one person may inflict upon another which is considered compensable.

7.2 THE DISTINCTION BETWEEN TORT AND CRIMINAL LAWS

While the tort and criminal laws both serve the broad purpose of protecting our natural rights, the tort law does so by permitting the injured party to obtain restitution for injuries, whereas the criminal law does so by punishing those who undertake to inflict injuries.

A tort action is brought by the injured party, whereas a criminal case is prosecuted by the state. In a tort case, the plaintiff must prove his case merely by a preponderance of the evidence. In other words, proof of his injuries and the defendant's responsibility for them must preponderate over any evidence to the contrary. However, in the criminal case the state must prove its case with sufficient evidence to convince the jury beyond a reasonable doubt. The rules of evidence used in a criminal case are much more strict and limiting than those used in the tort case.

Nearly all crimes are also torts because when a crime is committed, the result is usually to inflict harm on a victim who then has a right to obtain restitution from the criminal. However, all torts are not crimes. The great majority of them are caused by negligence and thus a criminal intent is lacking.

7.3 THE PURPOSES OF ENFORCING TORT LAWS

Broadly speaking, tort laws permit one who has suffered harm at the hands of another to go into court, prove the extent and cause of his injuries and collect damages from the one who caused them. Thus, they provide for enforcing that universally accepted principle of justice which demands that a person who has either intentionally or negligently injured another make restitution. By enforcing tort laws, governments partially fulfill that natural law discussed in Chapter III which requires them to be available to compel the performance of duties.

In another view, tort laws are for the purpose of protecting man's unalienable rights to the elements of freedom by providing that one who has suffered a loss through the fault of another can recover for that loss.

Tort laws are also enforced to prevent those breaches of the peace which would otherwise occur. So strong is the feeling that one who causes an injury should pay for it, that if the law did not provide a means of recovery, some would doubtless take matters into their own hands and use violence to obtain that which they believed to be rightfully theirs. Only by having available an impartial arbitrator with the power to enforce its decrees can this be avoided.

The enforcement of tort laws has another beneficial effect: it causes people to be more careful than they otherwise would be, thus reducing the number and severity of injuries. When one knows that he must pay for any damages he causes, he will tend to exercise greater caution.

Some may favor the enforcement of tort laws for the same reason they might favor the punishment of crime: the Bible commands it be done. The Mosaic Code specifically instructed the judges to permit one who had been either intentionally or negligently injured by another to recover from the wrongdoer. The amount of the damages to be awarded was also given in many instances. It is of peculiar interest that when an intentional tort had been committed and a crime was also involved, the criminal and tort aspects of the matter were handled in the same judicial proceeding rather than separately as is the custom today. Furthermore, the fine imposed for the crime was given to the victim rather than to the judges. *(See Ex. Ch. 22)*

7.4 ELEMENTS OF TORT LIABILITY

Three elements are necessary to fix legal responsibility under tort law: (1) A voluntary act or omission by the defendant; (2) Injury to the plaintiff; and (3) The act or omission must be the legal cause of the injury.

7.5 VOLUNTARY ACT OF OMISSION

Conduct is voluntary only when it arises from the will of the actor. Acts which are committed or omitted by one acting under duress are not voluntary, and, therefore, the one being compelled would not be liable for any resulting harm. Also, when a person who is faced with a sudden peril causes a lesser injury while trying to avoid one even greater, he may not be held liable.

7.6 INJURY TO THE PLAINTIFF

Unless the plaintiff has sustained injury or harm, he cannot recover under tort law. This does not mean, however, that he must always prove that physical harm was inflicted or even that he sustained an economic loss. The terms injury and harm cover such things as mental distress, invasion of privacy and interference with family relationships.

7.7 LEGAL CAUSE

In most tort cases, the injury sustained is so immediately and directly related to the defendant's conduct that there is little difficulty in establishing the element of legal cause. In others, however, where the harm is so far removed from the act complained of, or where the defendant's conduct was only one of several causative factors, it becomes difficult to determine whether this particular defendant should be held responsible.

Courts are not in complete agreement regarding what constitutes legal cause; however, they usually require that the defendant's act be a "substantial factor." Some courts hold that the defendant is not liable unless the injury is the natural and probable consequence of his acts and thus foreseeable. The question of legal cause is one of fact to be determined by the fact-finding body in the court which is usually the jury.

7.8 TYPES OF TORTS

Since tort law has for its purpose the protection of the elements of freedom, it seems logical that we should classify torts according to the element injured. However, a broader system of classification based upon the nature of the liability of the wrongdoer has been developed by the courts over the years. Under this system torts are divided into these three divisions: (1) Intentional, (2) Negligent, and (3) Strict liability. Liability is imposed under the first type because the actor intended harm; under the second because of his negligence or carelessness; and under the third, it is imposed arbitrarily even though there is no blameworthy conduct. Recovery for injuries to the four elements of freedom is possible under each of these three types.

7.9 INTENTIONAL TORTS AGAINST THE PERSON— ASSAULT, BATTERY, AND EMOTIONAL DISTRESS

The most common types of torts against the body are assault and battery. Assault consists of intentionally putting another in immediate apprehension of harmful or offensive physical contact. Actual physical harm or even contact is unnecessary to constitute an assault. The essence of the tort is intentionally causing apprehension.

Battery does require harmful or offensive physical contact. Obviously under crowded conditions today there are innumerable physical contacts which do not constitute battery either because they are harmless, inoffensive or unintended.

Closely related to the tort of assault is that of inflicting emotional distress. One who by extreme or outrageous conduct causes severe emotional disturbance in another may be liable for any bodily harm resulting from such distress. Before permitting recovery for this tort, the courts ordinarily require evidence that the conduct complained of was outrageous, intentional (or at least reckless) and that actual physical harm resulted.

7.10 Intentional Tort Against Liberty—False Imprisonment

The tort against a person's liberty is called false imprisonment. This consists of intentionally confining another for an appreciable length of time within boundaries fixed by the wrongdoer. It is the restricting of the freedom of another through fear or force.

7.11 Intentional Torts Against Property— Trespass And Conversion

The two intentional torts against property are trespass and conversion. Trespass may be either against land or personal property. In the former case, it consists of any unpermitted or unprivileged entry on land or wrongfully causing an object to enter thereon. Physical damage to the premises is not an essential element of the tort. However, in the absence of injury, only nominal damages may be recovered. If a defendant persists in committing trespass, the plaintiff may secure a court injunction against such, violation of which may be punishable by fine or imprisonment.

Trespass to personal property consists of an intentional and unprivileged interference with the possession or use of property rightfully in the hands of another. If no harm is caused to the property and if the possessor suffers no loss or inconvenience, recovery will be denied.

Conversion is the wrongful dominion over, or the unlawful appropriation of the personal property of another. Obviously, the crime of theft is also the tort of conversion. However, the tort is broader than the crime since it covers those cases where there is no criminal intent. If the wrongdoer takes the property of another, sells, leases or otherwise deals with it under the mistaken impression that he owns it, he is still liable for damages to the true owner under the tort law even though he is not subject to criminal prosecution.

7.12 TORTS AGAINST KNOWLEDGE—DECEIT, DEFAMATION, MALICIOUS PROSECUTION, ABUSE OF PROCESS

The essence of the tort of deceit is the intentional perversion of the truth for the purpose of causing harm. In order for a plaintiff to recover for the tort of deceit, he must prove the following five elements: (1) A false misrepresentation of a material fact; (2) Made with the intent to deceive; (3) Made with the intention to induce the plaintiff to rely upon the false statement; (4) Justifiable reliance by the plaintiff; (5) Damage to the plaintiff.

The misrepresentation must be of a fact which is past or existing. The prediction of a future event or the mere expression of an opinion is insufficient in the ordinary case. Furthermore, the fact must be material. It must be of sufficient importance that if known the plaintiff would not have taken the action which caused him injury.

Proof of an intent to deceive is essential. However, if it be shown that the defendant acted with a reckless disregard for the truth and under the realization that he lacked sufficient knowledge to make a positive statement, this is usually sufficient.

The plaintiff must have reasonably relied on the misrepresentation. If, from all the surrounding circumstances he either knew or should have known the statement to be false, he cannot recover.

And, finally, the plaintiff must prove that he suffered a loss and that the loss was caused by his reliance.

The tort of defamation consists of wrongfully subjecting another to public ridicule, contempt or shame. It is a false statement which injures a reputation. There are two forms of defamation. The written, printed or caricature form is called libel. That which is oral is called slander. One of the natural rights of a person is that false defamatory information not be published against him. When this right is invaded, the injured party may recover from the one responsible.

If the derogatory statements are true, this is a good defense against a tort action. It should be recognized that even though the person publishing the defamatory statements believes them to be true, this does not excuse him from liability if they are indeed false. Also, the statements must be published to a third party. Making false statements to the plaintiff out of the hearing of others, or writing him a personal letter containing defamatory material will not subject one to liability for this tort.

Under certain circumstances the person making the defamatory statements has either an absolute or a conditional privilege to do so and is not subject to liability. For example, Congressmen while speaking before a legislature, judges, attorneys, jurors and witnesses while performing their functions during a court trial, and certain other public officials in the performance of their duties may have an absolute privilege.

A conditional privilege is usually granted to credit bureaus in making credit reports and to corporate officials in making intercompany communications in connection with their jobs. Of course these privileges may be lost if the disclosures are made maliciously or the privilege otherwise abused. It should also be noted that false and defamatory statements made about public figures, or concerning matters of public interest, are usually privileged provided the statements are made without malice. By becoming a public figure, one loses a certain amount of the protection against false statements to which he would otherwise be entitled.

The torts of malicious prosecution and abuse of process are closely related in that they both consist of subjecting a person to unjustifiable litigation. When one maliciously institutes or continues a criminal prosecution against a person without probable cause, which proceeding terminates in favor of the accused, he has committed the tort of malicious prosecution.

Abuse of process exists when a person institutes a civil action or lawsuit with improper motives. While each person who sincerely believes he has a good cause of action against another should feel perfectly free to bring his case before the court, if he files such a suit for the purpose of harassing or injuring the defendant rather than for the relief asked, he may be liable for abuse of process.

7.13 THE TORT OF NEGLIGENCE

Man's rights to the elements of freedom are protected not only from intentional injuries but from those caused by negligence as well. The basis for liability here is that each person owes a duty to exercise a certain degree of caution in the conduct of his affairs to avoid injuring others and that when he breaches that duty, he is liable for the resulting damages.

To recover damages for negligence the plaintiff must prove that: (1) The defendant owed a duty of due care to the plaintiff which the defendant breached and (2) The breach of the duty caused the plaintiff to suffer.

The duty of due care which each person owes to all others is that he act as a reasonable man of ordinary prudence would do under the circumstances to avoid causing injury. This is called the "reasonable man standard" of conduct. The meaning of this is that if a man of reasonable prudence would have foreseen the injury which occurred and refrained from the action which caused it, then the defendant who failed to do so acted unreasonably and is liable.

7.14 DEFENSES—CONTRIBUTORY NEGLIGENCE AND ASSUMPTION OF RISK

Even though a defendant's negligence may have been a contributing cause of the plaintiff's injury, if the plaintiff was also negligent, and if this was a partial cause of his injuries, under the doctrine of "contributory negligence" he cannot recover. If both parties have suffered injuries from their combined negligence, neither may recover from the other. The courts adopted this contributory negligence rule because of the difficulty of apportioning damages. To fairly allocate a certain portion of the injury to the negligence of either in such cases seems an almost impossible task. Today, however, there is a growing trend on the part of the courts to undertake this very thing. Under the doctrine of "comparative negligence," the jury is asked to estimate what portion or percentage of the total fault is attributable to each and to apportion the damages accordingly.

In some instances a party whose negligence has caused injury may not be liable because the injured party had previously agreed not to hold him. If they have entered into an agreement under the terms of which the injured party agreed either expressly or impliedly that he had no right to recover even though the other caused him injury, then he may not do so. As an example of implied assumption of risk, let us consider the case of a person who enters a baseball park and is hit by a ball. He probably cannot recover from those responsible because he assumed the risk of being hit.

7.15 NUISANCE

Some torts are neither wholly intentional nor wholly the result of negligence, but somewhat a combination of both. Of such a nature is the tort of nuisance. There are two types of nuisances: (1) Private, and (2) Public.

A public nuisance is an act or omission which interferes with the interests of the community at large or some sizeable portion thereof. Activities injurious to public safety, morals or health constitute nuisances and may be abated by the police power. Public nuisances are also crimes and are punishable as such.

7.16 BUSINESS TORTS

Other torts which cannot be properly classified as either intentional or negligent are those which protect certain economic or business relations from improper interference. One of these is called "unfair competition." This consists of palming off one's goods onto the public as being those of another. If a merchant packages, labels, or otherwise represents his product in such a way as to deceive the public into believing that it is the same as that sold by a competitor, he may be liable for having committed the tort of unfair competition.

However, copying a competitor's product is not tortious unless in doing so there is an infringement of the competitor's rights to patents, copyrights, trademarks or trade secrets. The invasion of these rights is tortious and the injured party may secure both damages as well as an injunction.

The tort laws also protect contract rights from unreasonable interference by outsiders. If an outsider maliciously induces one of two contracting parties not to perform his obligations thereunder, the other party who was thereby deprived of his contract rights may recover damages from the one inducing the breach. Of course, he may have rights against the breaching party also but may prefer not to pursue them.

Closely related to the tort of defamation of the person is that of disparagement of goods. Not only does the tort law permit one to recover damages for false and defamatory statements made concerning himself, but also for those made against the products and services he sells.

7.17 STRICT LIABILITY

Under some circumstances the tort laws of today hold a person liable for injuries suffered by others even though he neither intended them nor did they result from his negligence. This imposition of "strict liability," or liability without fault may seem unjust, and strong arguments can be made for that point of view. Nonetheless, in a growing number of cases courts and legislatures are making defendants liable for injuries for which they are not to blame.

One instance of this is found in the laws relating to employment relations. Under workmen's compensation acts and similar legislation, employers are held liable for all injuries suffered by employees except those which are self-inflicted or which result from drunkenness.

Strict liability is imposed upon merchants and manufacturers who sell defective products, upon those who spray crops from aircraft, engage in blasting operations or who keep wild animals on their premises. To recover for injuries sustained as a result of these activities it is unnecessary to prove negligence. Furthermore, contributory negligence is not a defense in cases of strict liability.

7.18 WHO MAY BE HELD LIABLE FOR TORTS?

Generally speaking, each person is liable for those torts he commits and no others. There are certain exceptions to this rule which we will now consider.

As under the criminal law, infants under the age of seven and people who are totally incompetent mentally, are generally not held liable for injuries they cause. Since they lack the capacity to intend harm or to act negligently, the only basis for holding them would be to impose strict liability, and this is not done. Minors between the ages of seven and fourteen are presumed to have the capacity to commit a tort but this presumption may be rebutted. If it can be shown that a mentally deficient person is capable of negligence, he can be held liable.

At common law, parents were not liable for the torts of their child unless they had failed to exercise proper parental supervision or unless they had placed in the child's hands an instrumentality which he would likely use to cause harm. Today the statutes of some states impose a limited liability upon parents for property damage caused by their children.

Under common law as well as under the statutory laws today, employers are held liable for torts committed by their employees while acting within the scope of employment. The imposition of this vicarious liability does not relieve the employee from liability. Furthermore, the employer may recover from the employee when the former is compelled to pay for injuries caused by the latter.

Governments have generally held themselves immune from liability for injuries caused by their employees; however, recent court decisions as well as certain statutes, such as the Federal Tort Claims Act, have altered this rule to an undetermined extent. Public officers are generally accorded immunity from liability for torts committed while discharging their duties.

7.19 NATURAL LIMITS OF THE POWER TO GRANT RESTITUTION UNDER TORT LAW

The usual consequence of enforcing a tort law is to compel the wrongdoer to transfer to the other party money or property estimated to have a value equal to the amount of the loss. It is immediately apparent that if the loss sustained is not properly chargeable against the one compelled to pay, or if the amount of damages awarded exceeds the amount of the injury, an injustice has been committed. This then is the natural limit of the power to grant restitution under tort law: the defendant shall not be compelled to pay more than is sufficient to make restitution for the loss he has caused.

This is not to say that the plaintiff should not be able to recover for injuries other than those directly traceable to defendant's tortious conduct. It may be entirely proper to reimburse him for indirect injuries such as inconvenience, loss of time and expense in enforcing his claim. But whatever the amount which is properly recoverable, if the award exceeds this, the defendant has suffered an injustice. As is the case with inflicting punishment under criminal law, when governments undertake to dispense justice they walk a fine line. They either do justice or commit an injustice in the process.

7.20 COMPREHENSIVE SCOPE OF TORT LAWS

A brief examination of the torts discussed herein reveals that they cover virtually every conceivable wrong or injury of a non-contractual nature. It is difficult to think of a harm which one person can do to another which is not compensable. Each one of the elements of freedom is quite fully protected. It is admittedly true that there are a great many tortious injuries which go unredressed either because the injured party finds it too expensive to enforce his remedies or because he is otherwise reluctant to file a lawsuit. But for every injury of any consequence, government stands ready to compel the performance of the duty to make restitution if the aggrieved party petitions it to do so.

CHAPTER VIII
CONTRACT LAWS

8.1 DEFINITION OF A CONTRACT

Thou shalt not take thy brother's garment; thou shalt pay for that which thou shalt receive of thy brother. *(D&C 42:54)*

Now if a man owed another, and he would not pay that which he did owe, he was complained of to the judge; and the judge executed authority, and sent forth officers that the man should be brought before him; and he judged the man according to the law and the evidences which were brought against him, and thus the man was compelled to pay that which he owed, or be stripped, or be cast out from among the people as a thief and a robber. *(Alma 11:2)*

A contract is a promise or a set of promises which courts will enforce. It is an agreement which government will either compel the parties to perform or pay damages if they fail to do so.

When a party claims that the agreement he has made is enforceable, he has the burden of proving first of all that it is of the kind which society considers legally binding. In many instances we do not intend that our agreements have legal consequences; therefore, the courts refuse to give them this effect. Social engagements are of this nature. The plaintiff must also show that he gave, or promised to give, some legal right in exchange for the promise he is trying to enforce. Unless he gave what is termed "consideration," or "legal detriment," to the other party, he cannot recover. Courts will not enforce the mere promise to make a gift.

But even though plaintiff proves the existence of the agreement, that it is of the type which is enforceable and that he gave consideration, he still may not be able to enforce the promise made to him. The defendant may raise any one of the following defenses: (1) That the agreement was the result of a mistake, misrepresentation or duress; (2) That he, the defendant, is excused from liability by the law because he was a minor or a mental incompetent at the time the agreement was formed; (3) That the contract is of the type which the law demands be written and this one is not; (4) That the purpose of the agreement is to commit a crime and is therefore illegal and unenforceable.

8.2 PURPOSE OF ENFORCING CONTRACTS

Man's unalienable rights to the elements of freedom may be divided into two categories: (1) Natural, and (2) Acquired. Natural rights are those with which we are born. They entitle us to protection by imposing upon all others the duty to refrain from injuring our life, liberty, property and knowledge. These rights are protected by the criminal and tort laws. Acquired rights are those we obtain by making agreements with others. They are protected primarily by the law of contracts.

We enter into contracts for the purpose of acquiring from another the right to compel him to give us something which will enable us to accomplish our purposes or exercise our freedom. To acquire such a right, we must in turn give him the right to compel us to do something which will aid him in the exercise of his freedom.

Contracts are enforced to give these reciprocal rights substance. Were this not done the rights would not exist. The promises made by the parties would depend entirely upon the whim of the promisor. It is their enforcement which turns them into acquired rights.

8.3 THE IMPORTANCE OF RIGHTS ACQUIRED UNDER CONTRACT

Contracts are so common in our lives that it is easy to fail to see their importance. Virtually the entire time we spend in our occupations is devoted to fulfilling contractual obligations owed to others. The balance of our time is largely spent enjoying the benefits of contractual rights acquired from others. If we are employed, our productive time is used discharging the duties assumed under the employment contract. If we are self-employed we are engaged in producing goods and services we have contracted, or will contract, to sell. Upon receiving our wages or the selling price of what we produce, we use the money to make contracts for the purchase of goods and services produced by others. There are very few activities which are not directed toward the discharging of contractual obligations or the enjoyment of contractual rights.

This situation is a consequence of the very extensive division of labor in our well-developed economy wherein we consume very little of what we produce and produce very little of what we consume. Each man specializes. He learns a particular vocation, develops his skill, acquired the facilities necessary for mass production and then produces in quantity for sale.

But let it be observed that this division of labor with the enormous advantages and benefits derived therefrom, depend entirely upon freedom of contract. Take that away and each man is under the necessity of building his own home with materials prepared by himself, weaving his own cloth and making his own clothing, raising and preparing his own food and building his own automobile.

The importance of contractual freedom is better seen if we consider what other freedoms would remain if this one were denied. The right of private property lies at the foundation of all other freedoms and under circumstances which prevail today, freedom of contract is the very heart and soul of the right of private property. To the extent it is restricted the freedom to acquire from others those goods and services we need to accomplish our purposes is restricted. The necessity of this freedom was stated by George Jessel in these words:

> If there is one thing more than any other which public policy requires, it is that men of full age and competent understanding shall have the utmost liberty of contracting, and that contracts when entered into freely and voluntarily, shall be held good and shall be enforced by the courts of justice. (Printing and Numerical Registering Co. v. Sampson, 19 L.R. Eq. 462, 465)

The importance attached to the contract obligation by the Founding Fathers is indicated by the following Constitutional limitation which they placed on the power of state governments to deny the rights represented by such obligations:

> No state shall . . . pass any . . . law impairing the obligation of contracts. (Art. I, Sec. 10)

8.4 THE LIMIT ON FREEDOM OF CONTRACT

The limit on the freedom to make contracts and act jointly towards a common purpose is the same as the limit on the freedom to act alone: It shall not be used to commit crimes. Projects undertaken by two or more people with an evil intent are obviously more dangerous and harmful to society than those undertaken by the individual and must be forbidden and punished. The test as to what constitutes an evil intent is the same for those who act in concert as for the man who acts alone: Was it their design to injure the elements of freedom by doing to others that which they knew would be wrong and harmful if done to them?

8.5 NATURAL LIMITS ON THE POWER TO DENY FREEDOM OF CONTRACT

Just as it is wrong for the citizens to abuse their freedom of contract by committing crimes, even so it is wrong for government to abuse its power to deny freedom of contract by committing crimes. The limit of the power of government to punish group behavior is identical with its power to punish individual behavior: It shall not punish any acts except those committed with an evil intent. When it does so, rather than punishing a crime it commits one.

When people act in concert either for good or evil, their capability to accomplish their purposes is increased immeasurably over the sum total of their capabilities when acting alone. Therefore just as it is imperative for government to forbid its citizens to enter contracts to do evil, it is equally needful that it leave them free to enter contracts to accomplish good. To prevent men from entering into agreements to promote their mutual interests is to deny them that freedom which is the most effective of all—the freedom to cooperate. They can achieve their respective goals with infinitely greater ease and promptness if left free to make exchanges and coordinate their efforts. Unfortunately, governments are continually adopting laws which deny their citizens this freedom. Let us consider some of them.

8.6 DENIAL OF FREEDOM OF CONTRACT BY PUNISHING ONLY ONE OF THE CONTRACTING PARTIES

Except for those which forbid evil conduct, virtually all laws which deny freedom of contract permit only one of the two contracting parties to be punished for violating them. The party singled out for condemnation is always the one against whom there exists a prejudice in our society today. He is the capitalist, the employer, the manufacturer, the seller, the lender. He also just happens to belong to the economic interest with the least number of votes. Whenever he makes an agreement, his motives are presumed to be evil. He wants to pay the lowest wage for the most work; charge the highest price for the cheapest product; obtain the largest return on the smallest investment. The motives of the other party to the contract are always above reproach. All he wants is the highest wage for the least effort; the best product for the cheapest price; the biggest loan at the lowest interest rate. These feelings are common to all of us and so they cannot possibly be evil and punishable. To see clearly the injustice of laws which destroy freedom of contract, and to correctly appraise the enormous harm they cause, it is necessary to remove this prejudice which obscures our vision.

Let us do so by assuming that such laws provide for punishing the employee rather than the employer; the buyer rather than the seller, etc. Or we might assume that the law provides for punishing both parties. It is perfectly safe to do this because it doesn't alter the effect of the laws to any appreciable degree. They will be obeyed and no one will be punished in the overwhelming majority of cases no matter which party is made the criminal.

Let us assume then a minimum wage law which makes only the employee the offender in case of violation; that he violates the law by entering into a contract with his employer providing for less wages than the law permits; that he is being prosecuted before a jury. Can anyone imagine he will be convicted? His defense is that he could not obtain employment for a higher wage or he would have done so. He accepted this job in lieu of public welfare or permitting his family to go hungry and why should he be punished for that? He has saved the public the cost of feeding him, has accommodated the employer who needed his services and has produced goods which the public wants. How can the law make such conduct a crime, he wants to know?

In answer to the argument that low wages hurt the cause of the working man, he points out that higher wages are always passed on to the consumer in the form of higher prices and since the great majority of the consumers are laborers, the benefits from higher wages are illusory. The real effect of the law is to injure labor because the price of the product must be raised by more than the raise in wages to cover the additional taxes levied to support the regulatory agency.

He admits that he broke the law but he claims the law to be unjust. It denies him his right to make a living. It punishes him for innocent behavior. It increases taxes and prevents the production of goods and services which the public needs and wants.

For a second illustration, let us assume there is a licensing law which provides for punishing both of the contracting parties in case of violation, that an unlicensed seller has sold some goods to a buyer and both are now being prosecuted. The government admits that there is no evidence that the transaction harmed anyone. There was no deception involved; the seller owned the merchandise, represented it fairly and the price was below that being charged by sellers with licenses. Nevertheless, says the prosecutor, these men entered into a contract in violation of a law, this makes them criminals and they should be punished.

The defense used by the buyer and seller is that the law is unconstitutional in that it violates their unalienable rights to deal with private property. Their position is that the Constitution places a limit on the power of government to pass laws and that limit has been exceeded in this case; that it is the function of government to protect the right of private property and to uphold and enforce contracts but this law is in direct opposition to both of these purposes. They further contend that it provides for punishing people who have intended no evil and caused no harm and it is therefore contrary to the elementary principles of justice upon which our Constitutional system is founded. Their final argument is that if anyone should be punished in this case, it should be the licensees and the legislators who are responsible for the law and who are committing extortion by forcibly restraining competition and causing a rise in prices.

The two laws discussed in the above cases are fairly typical of an enormous number of administrative laws now in force on both the national and the state level—except for the fact that legislators would never provide for punishing the laborer and the consumer. But the important point to be gathered from these cases is that the effect of the laws is virtually the same as if they did. Laborers and consumers are denied their freedom of contract no matter which party the law condemns. It is impossible for government to deny freedom to one party to a contract without denying freedom to the other to the same extent. If one cannot make an agreement contrary to the law neither can the other.

The effect on the public is the same in either case. When freedom of contract is interfered with the inevitable result is to reduce the amount of goods and services available for consumption and raise both taxes and prices.

And finally, even though prejudice may prevent us from recognizing the fact as clearly as we should, when criminal laws are passed which deny freedom to enter into legitimate contracts, the unavoidable consequence is to punish the innocent who have intended no evil nor committed harm.

8.7 LICENSING LAWS

The most common method used by government to suppress freedom of contract is by adopting licensing laws which deny people the right to enter the occupation of their choice and to patronize the business of their choice. There are two types of licensing laws: (1) Those adopted for revenue-raising purposes where the only requirement to obtain the license is to pay a fee; (2) Those of the regulatory type which make it a criminal offense to engage in the licensed activity without the consent of the state. We are here concerned only with the latter type.

Regulatory licensing laws may be divided into three main categories:

(1) Those making the prohibition against competition complete by denying a license to all except one or two businesses. Illustrative of this type are those which grant an exclusive franchise to a utility, transportation or communication business to operate in a certain area.

(2) Those which prevent an applicant from obtaining a license unless he owns certain facilities for carrying on the business. Of this type are

laws which make it a crime to produce farm or dairy products without a "base" or a "quota"; those which require a minimum of capital such as is demanded for entry into banking or insurance; zoning laws which dictate the type of activity which may be conducted on land in a certain area.

(3) Those which restrict entry into the trades and professions by requiring that the practitioner have a specified minimum amount of education or experience, or have passed an examination. The professions of law, medicine and engineering, and the plumbing, electrical and construction trades are protected from competition by such laws.

In each of these cases the law either flatly prohibits entry into the licensed field or imposes conditions which the overwhelming majority cannot meet without spending years of time and thousands of dollars. Thus the practical effect of licensing laws is to create a government enforced monopoly which controls the number of licensees merely by raising or lowering the entry requirements. Let us examine the purpose and effect of such laws.

8.8 DO LICENSING LAWS RESTRAIN CRIME?

Some claim that licensing laws serve to restrain crime. But how can they have this effect when existing criminal laws cover every type of criminal activity conceivable? The particular crime which people seem to fear most is that of false advertising. They assume that except for such laws, a great many criminals would enter the monopolized occupations and deceive the public with false claims.

There seems to be no historical evidence to support this assumption and logic refutes it. Why should it be assumed that unlicensed people are more criminally inclined than those who are licensed? Anyone who desires to make a living at a particular trade or profession cannot afford to jeopardize his reputation by engaging in criminal activity. Nor can he risk dealing falsely with his customers, thereby inviting expensive lawsuits. But even though it were true that those without licenses are more prone to deceive, existing criminal laws such as the following typical statute provide all of the protection against this threat which the law can give:

76-4-1. Sales to be made or service furnished—False representations. —Every person, whether acting on his own behalf or on behalf of another, who, with intent to sell or in any way dispose of real or personal property, choses in action, merchandise, service or anything of any nature whatsoever offered by such person, directly or indirectly, to the public for sale, use or distribution, or with intent to increase the consumption thereof, or to induce any member of the public to enter into any obligation relating thereto, or to acquire title thereto, or any interest therein, publishes, disseminates, circulates, or causes to be published, disseminated or circulated, or who in any manner places, or causes to be placed, before the public in this state, by any newspaper, magazine, book, pamphlet, circular, letter, handbill, placard, poster or other publication, or by any billboard, sign, card, label or window sign, showcase or window display, or by any other advertising device, or by public outcry or proclamation, or by telephone or radio, or in any other manner whatever, an advertisement regarding such property or service so offered to the public, which advertisement shall contain any statement, representation or assertion concerning such property or service, or concerning any circumstance or matter of fact connected in any way, directly or indirectly, with a proposed sale, performance or disposition thereof, which is deceptive or misleading, and which is known, or by the exercise of reasonable care could be known to be false, deceptive or misleading, to the person publishing, disseminating, circulating or placing before the public such advertisement, is guilty of a misdemeanor. (Utah Code Annotated, 76-4-1)

8.9 DO LICENSING LAWS PROTECT THE PUBLIC AGAINST INCOMPETENCE?

Another argument used to justify licensing laws is that they serve to protect the public against incompetence and inexperience. The feeling seems to be that only those who are the most qualified have a right to serve the people. Let us examine this argument.

We will commence with the trite observation that no one is free from error. No matter how old or young, how educated or ignorant, how experienced or untried, everyone is subject to making mistakes. Each person who lives a full and ordinary life, commences in a state of utter helplessness at birth, increases in ability until he reaches his prime, which is always short of perfection, and then returns again to utter incompetence at death. While some may largely retain their mental faculties until the end, physical deterioration is as certain as death itself.

Since all men are imperfect and prone to make mistakes,

virtually every act of any consequence which we perform might possibly injure someone. No matter how careful, how well-trained or how well-intentioned we may be, the possibility of human error is always present to threaten the life, liberty, property or knowledge of others.

No physician, nurse or other practitioner of the healing arts ever becomes so skillful and wise that he is free from the danger of taking the life he is trying to save. No mechanic, builder, machine operator or craftsman ever becomes so proficient that he can claim that his efforts will always be constructive but never destructive; or that the product of his work will be free from dangerous defects. No producer of food or clothing ever reaches that state of perfection that the consumer is always benefitted but never harmed. No teacher ever becomes so knowledgeable and wise that he can be certain that he will always teach truth and never falsehood.

Being the humans that we are, we are forever subject to failure of mind and body; to malfunction of brain and muscle; to heart attack, lapse of memory and mistake of judgment. Especially is this true in view of man's inability to fully understand and control the elements around him. Who can erect a structure which will withstand every earthquake or storm? Who can construct a piece of machinery so perfectly that it might not fail because of mental fatigue or some other unknown and unpredictable defect? Who understands the diversity of human minds and bodies well enough that he can foresee the effect of a given medicine or piece of information upon any particular person?

Furthermore, everyone is in a constant state of change. We are continually learning and forgetting; acquiring a skill only to lose it again; gaining vigor and health during one period and losing them in another.

Now is it possible for any licensing agency (who are erring humans themselves) to classify this infinite and ever-changing diversity of human imperfection into two groups—the qualified and the unqualified—and be just to everyone? Any line which is drawn must be purely arbitrary with nothing more to support it than the prejudice or selfish interest of the one who drew it because all he has to choose between is varying degrees of constantly changing ignorance, incompetence and inexperience. And even though it were possible to distinguish between the "fit" and the "unfit," due to the constant changes taking place in people, this classification would not be valid for more than a brief period. There would be those close to the line who would be constantly crossing over it going both ways.

Even admitting all of this to be true, argues the licensing advocate, still we must allow only those who are the "best" qualified to serve the public.

But who are the "best" qualified? If there is a sound reason why only the most superior should be entitled to make a living at law, medicine, engineering, banking or plumbing, then why don't we permit only the top ten percent of those now engaged in these various activities to have licenses? If the public is entitled to have only the "best" why allow this other ninety percent who are inferior to sell to the public their "inferior" goods and services?

The obvious answer to this proposal is that it would have the effect of eliminating approximately ninety percent of the goods and services now being produced. That which they are providing is needed even though it is somewhat inferior, and it would be most ill-advised to prevent them from working just because they are less skillful and more apt to make mistakes than the superior ten percent.

But where does this argument lead to? If we follow this logic through the next step we must conclude that existing licensing laws are now denying the public an untold amount of goods and services which otherwise would be available. If they were changed so that twice as many people could enter into a given trade or occupation we might find approximately twice as much being produced in that area. The demand for goods and services is literally unlimited. There are millions of people who now need dental, medical, legal, engineering and other professional assistance who cannot afford to pay the fees charged by those who have been compelled to spend a substantial portion of their lives and tens of thousands of dollars of their money obtaining a license. The same can be said of trades, occupations and businesses of all kinds. If the bars were removed, people would flood into these areas, become proficient and begin exchanging goods and services with each other to the economic benefit of everyone—except possibly the present licensees and the bureaucrats.

When we deny men their freedom to be productive because they might possibly cause harm, we act foolishly and unjustly. If a person intends to do good, he does infinitely more good than harm. One who enters a business or a profession is well aware that he must serve the public or go bankrupt. No sensible person will undertake a job which he knows he cannot do even if he could find a customer who would permit him to try. He knows that he must produce what is needed and wanted or subject himself to lawsuits for breach of contract, tortious conduct and even criminal negligence.

Licensing laws are passed for one reason: to deny the public their freedom of contract; to prevent them from patronizing those who would enter the field and serve them if it were open. Rather than saying that such laws keep out the unqualified, it is more accurate to say that they keep the unqualified in. Were it not for such laws, existing licensees would lose many of their customers to newcomers who would provide the public with goods and services of a quality and at a price they would prefer over what is now available.

In a free economy the only ones in business are those who have customers who come to them voluntarily and in preference to anyone else. They are producing goods and services which the public want and are willing to pay for. What other test is there for being qualified? This is the only one which is relevant and many there have been who have failed it. The consuming public is discriminating and demanding. They are also merciless. They can be counted upon to keep the "unqualified" from serving them. No licensing board or government agency is needed for this purpose.

If those who consider themselves better "qualified" want to prove their excellence, they may do so in the open market. But why should they be allowed to establish a government-enforced monopoly which compels customers to patronize them or go without? If they are fearful that buyers might not be able to distinguish between them and those less skilled, they should be free to form themselves into exclusive associations and advertise their superior talents. But at the same time why should the public be denied their freedom to reject their claims or purchase products and services of an inferior quality and at a cheaper price if they desire? In other words, why should we continue to allow licensing laws to deny people their freedom of contract?

8.10 REGULATORY LAWS AND FREEDOM OF CONTRACT

While licensing laws are the chief offenders in restricting economic freedom, every regulatory measure has this effect.

Businessmen are striving continually to perform a service or produce a product which satisfies their patrons. Their continuance in business demands this as do their profits. They must offer something which their customers want and at a price they can afford to pay. Every regulatory law interferes with their performance of this function and forces them to do things they consider inadvisable. The inevitable result is either to alter their products, raise their costs, or both. It is rare indeed when a regulatory measure has any different effect because the operators know far better than any legislator or bureaucrat how best to operate their businesses.

But if the producer's product is altered, the customer is no longer able to purchase that which he prefers. With every increase in price some buyers who would otherwise have made a purchase, are no longer able to do so and those who do buy cannot afford as much. In this manner every regulatory law denies freedom of contract.

8.11 WELFARE-STATE LAWS AND FREEDOM OF CONTRACT

The term "welfare-state laws" as used herein means those measures by which governments practice compulsory charity and otherwise dictate the purposes for which people may spend their money. Under such laws the state takes property from its rightful owners and makes a gift thereof to those to whom it does not belong. Thus rather than allowing the owners to determine how much of their property shall be used for charity and to whom it shall be given, their servants in government perform this function for them. Also under these laws, governments impose such levies as social security taxes, medicare and unemployment insurance contributions rather than allowing the people to choose their own retirement, unemployment and health-care plans.

Every welfare-state law takes property from its owner and transfers either ownership or control to government. But when government has ownership and control, the people do not and their freedom to contract with or about such funds is taken from them.

For it is expedient that I, the Lord, should make every man accountable, as a steward over earthly blessings, which I have made and prepared for my creatures.

I, the Lord, stretched out the heavens, and built the earth, my very handiwork; and all things therein are mine.

And it is my purpose to provide for my saints, for all things are mine.

But it must needs be done in mine own way; and behold this is the way that I, the Lord, have decreed to provide for my saints, that the poor shall be exalted, in that the rich are made low.

For the earth is full, and there is enough and to spare; yea, I prepared all things, and have given unto the children of men to be agents unto themselves.

(D&C 104:13-17)

CHAPTER IX

THE NATURE OF WEALTH

9.1 DEFINITION OF WEALTH

Wealth may be defined in a variety of ways; however, the following definition might properly be used to cover all classes:

> Wealth consists of raw materials and energy so organized that we may use it to accomplish our purposes.

9.2 THE EARTH A VAST STOREHOUSE OF RAW MATERIALS AND ENERGY

The earth together with other heavenly bodies constitutes a vast storehouse of raw materials and energy from which we may draw to create wealth. The elements of which the earth is composed (hydrogen, oxygen, carbon, iron, etc.) exist in an almost endless variety of substances, compounds and mixtures. They appear as gases, liquids and solids; as organic and inorganic matter.

When man organizes wealth, he selects from this enormous supply those items he considers best adapted to fill his needs and by using energy which is also available in a wide variety of forms, fashions these into consumable products which he calls wealth. Thus food, clothing, shelter, machinery and other products are nothing but the atoms and molecules of the earth so arranged and organized that they may be used to serve our purposes.

9.3 THE INDESTRUCTIBILITY OF RAW MATERIALS

As we consume our wealth we disorganize those atoms and molecules of which our possessions are composed and thus render them temporarily unusable for those purposes they have been serving.

But let it be recognized that these units of matter are, for all practical purposes indestructible so that they may be taken and organized again to serve as wealth the second time, the third time—yes a million times and never show the slightest sign of deterioration. When wealth is consumed all that is lost is the organizing effort and energy which made it wealth in the first instance. But the raw materials are still available and may be used over and over again for as long as intelligent man is around and has energy available to repeat the process.

It is entirely feasible to take the disorganized wealth which leaves the home and factory in the form of garbage, refuse and sewage, and reprocess these materials and organize them once again into the same usable products they represented originally. As a matter of fact this is what has been happening to some extent all along. No one will ever know how many times the same water molecule has appeared as tissue or fiber in plant or animal life or how many times a particular hydrogen, carbon, or iron atom has served our purposes. The recycling of waste products is going on all of the time and promises to become much more common in the future.

9.4 THE EXHAUSTION OF NATURAL RESOURCES AND THE RETRIEVAL OF RAW MATERIALS

It is to be recognized that nature by concentrating large stocks of homogeneous substances in one locality has made the acquisition and use of raw materials much easier than it otherwise would have been. Large deposits of ore, fossil fuels and other substances have facilitated the organizing process enormously. As these deposits or natural resources are exhausted and organized into consumable products and consumed, they are usually scattered abroad on the face of the earth. This makes it expensive to gather them up again and sort them out for re-use. However our ability to retrieve and utilize what has been thus scattered is developing substantially faster than the reserves are being depleted. Also as the necessity therefor increases we will doubtless be more cautious with our waste products so that the retrieval task will not be so difficult.

9.5 Loss Of Wealth Through Entropy And Obsolescence

It is undoubtedly true that most wealth is disorganized by consumption. However, another extremely important cause for the loss of wealth is entropy or the innate tendency of matter to reach the highest state of disorganization. Even if we do not consume our products but allow them to lie unused, the mere passage of time causes them to lose their utility. Someone has said that everything is on an irresistible march to the junk heap. The natural processes of deterioration and decay render much of what we produce unfit before it can be worn out or otherwise consumed.

Still a third factor adversely affecting the utilization of wealth is obsolescence. Some articles which we regard as adequate for our use at one time may be replaced by superior or more fashionable products and the old is then scrapped to make way for the new.

All of these factors conspire to render most forms of wealth unfit for use within a relatively short period of time after being produced, and thus condemn man to a life of ceaseless toil. We have had the sentence of labor for life passed upon us with no visible means of escaping therefrom. If we are to keep ourselves supplied with food, clothing and other products we must be continually engaged in the organizing process. Fortunately we need never fear that the raw materials necessary for the creation of wealth will become unusable. Matter is virtually indestructible and should serve us throughout eternity.

Before considering whether or not man is apt to be faced with a shortage of these indestructible elements, let us discuss the supply of energy without which the creation of wealth is impossible.

9.6 The Availability Of Energy

The sun has been the source of most of the energy man has used up to this point and from all we know it will continue to pour onto the earth all of the energy we can use for several hundred billion years or so if we will but learn to capture even a small fraction of the total amount available. During recent years the energy which the sun has stored in the form of coal, natural gas and oil deposits has been used at an ever-increasing rate. We have looked forward with fear to the time when these deposits might be exhausted because they have provided such a convenient and cheap source of energy.

However, the possible exhaustion of fossil fuels is no longer of really critical concern because of recent discoveries which makes available to us an almost limitless supply of nuclear energy. The physics books of today contain statements such as the following:

> The modern world is built around an abundant supply of energy. This energy may be converted from one form to another to perform tasks for man. It may truly be said that an abundant source of energy is a country's greatest national asset. The most useful supplies of stored energy in the past have been gravitational and electrical potential energy. Thus water stored behind a dam constitutes gravitational potential energy, while coal, oil, or the chemicals in a battery contain electrical potential energy in the arrangement of the electrically charged particles in the molecules. These sources are rapidly being depleted as world demands for energy become greater. Conversion of part of the mass of a nucleus to an equivalent amount of energy, however, promises to furnish an almost inexhaustible supply. (Fowler & Meyer, *Physics for Engineers and Scientists*, [1958] p. 496)

9.7 THE WEALTH CYCLE

Let us summarize the main points discussed above concerning man's creation and utilization of wealth. We take the indestructible raw materials with which the earth has been most generously supplied and then drawing from the inexhaustible sources of energy, we organize these raw materials into consumable products. This organized wealth then becomes disorganized either by being consumed or by deterioration accompanying the passage of time. But we can take these disorganized units of matter and utilize them to repeat the process again and again. Let us call this repetitive process the "wealth cycle" and note that it may be continued for as long as the supply of energy lasts. For all practical purposes the wealth cycle may be continued forever.

9.8 IS A SHORTAGE OF RAW MATERIALS LIKELY?

> For it is expedient that I, the Lord, should make every man accountable, as a steward over earthly blessings, which I have made and prepared for my creatures.
>
> I, the Lord, stretched out the heavens, and built the earth, my very handiwork; and all things therein are mine.
>
> And it is my purpose to provide for my saints, for all things are mine.
>
> But it must needs be done in mine own way; and behold this is the way that I, the Lord, have decreed to provide for my saints, that the poor shall be exalted, in that the rich are made low.
>
> For the earth is full, and there is enough and to spare; yea, I prepared all things, and have given unto the children of men to be agents unto themselves. *(D&C 104:13-17)*

With this understanding of the nature of wealth we are now ready to consider whether or not there is likely to be a shortage due to a scarcity of raw materials. Such a shortage cannot occur until there is a shortage of available atoms and molecules with which to construct consumable products. Until so much of the earth's surface is at one time incorporated into plant and animal life or into such things as food, clothing and shelter that difficulty is encountered in finding additional elements, compounds and substances with which to organize other products, there will be no shortage.

Such an eventuality is inconceivable within the foreseeable future. It is most obvious that at the present time we do not have even a millionth part of the available atoms and molecules incorporated into usable wealth. As an illustration of this fact let us consider the extremely vital compound, water, of which plant and animal life is mainly composed and which has an endless variety of other uses. When we compare the amount of water which is currently incorporated into usable products or being put to other beneficial use, with the oceans of it which are available, it is most apparent that we have not even begun to make full use of this resource. The same conclusion must be drawn regarding other compounds and elements which are vital to life and the exercise of freedom.

Furthermore since the wealth cycle is relatively short in most instances, and since the atoms and molecules of which it is composed are immediately available for re-use upon completion of the cycle, fears of a shortage of raw materials are quite groundless. When we speak of a shortage of natural resources what we really mean is that the most fertile soils are limited and already being tilled; the most accessible mineral deposits have been or are being mined; the water in a particular stream or location is currently being claimed or used by someone else. Everyone is aware there is an almost endless number of less favorable opportunities to produce wealth still open.

Therefore, a shortage, if it can be said to exist at all, amounts to no more than that there is a limit to the most advantageous opportunities and favorable locations. But this is unavoidable whenever, as is the situation on earth, there is a wide variation in resources, with a best at one extreme, a worst at the other, and numerous possibilities of varying desirability lying in between. It is most apparent that the earth could be made to produce millions of times more wealth than it now does without taxing its capacity in the least degree if men applied even their present technology to the task. Additional scientific discoveries can only expand this potential productivity further.

From this we must conclude that any shortage of consumable products which has occurred in the past or which will occur in the foreseeable future has been and will be caused by a lack of organizing effort on the part of man rather than from any shortage of raw materials and energy. Man's inherently selfish nature may blind him to this fact and cause him to squabble over who has the right to consume the wealth presently being produced. But a true appraisal of the situation will convince the logical mind that there is plenty for all if men will address themselves to the task of creating new wealth rather than worrying about shortages.

The earth's population has doubled within the past few years and threatens to double again in the near future unless nuclear war or some other catastrophe prevents it. But available figures demonstrate that with the increase in population there has been no increase in death from starvation but rather a decrease. This means that 3 billion people are having less difficulty obtaining the necessities of life than did 1.5 billion. This is true because the production of food, clothing and shelter is accomplished with much less human effort today than has ever been the case in recorded history. As power-driven machinery and cheap energy come into increasing use, the need for physical labor decreases correspondingly. People spend far less time and energy producing the necessities of life today than ever before and additional scientific advancement and technological progress promises to continue this trend.

There is no need to fear that the death rate from starvation will increase appreciably with 10 or 20 billion on the earth. Until the population approaches somewhere near the absolute physical limits of the earth to sustain life there is no reason to anticipate much change in the death rate from famine because of shortages of raw materials and energy. We have shown that such a shortage does not now exist and it will not exist during the foreseeable future.

9.9 SUPPOSE WE REACH THE PHYSICAL LIMITS OF THE EARTH'S SIZE?

Wherefore, men are free according to the flesh; and all things are given them which are expedient unto man. And they are free to choose liberty and eternal life, through the great Mediator of all men, or to choose captivity and death, according to the captivity and power of the devil; for he seeketh that all men might be miserable like unto himself. *(2 Nephi 2:27)*

But suppose the population approaches the finite limits of the earth's physical size. For those who choose to worry about such an eventuality, we submit the following observations made by Frederic Bastiat over one hundred years ago on this question:

Nature's relatively infinite prodigality with her forces keeps him (man) from being anything more than a mere custodian over some of them. Now, what will happen when men will have reached the limits of this bounty? It will no longer be possible for anything more to be hoped for in that direction. Inevitably the trend toward increased population will then come to a halt. No economic system can prevent this from necessarily happening.

Granted the tendency of the race to multiply, what will happen when there is no more room on the earth for new inhabitants? Is God holding back, for that epoch, some cataclysm of creation, some marvelous manifestation of His infinite power? Or in keeping with Christian dogma, must we believe in the destruction of this world? Obviously, these are no longer economic problems, but are analogous to the difficulties eventually reached by all sciences. The physicists are well aware that every moving body on earth goes downward and never rises again. Accordingly, the day must come when the mountains will have filled the valleys, when rivers will be high at their mouth as at their source, when their waters will no longer flow, etc., etc. What will happen then?

Should the physical sciences cease to observe and admire the harmony of the world as it now is, because they cannot foresee by what other harmony God will make provision for a state of things that is far in the future but none-the-less inevitable? It seems to me that this is indeed a case in which the economist, like the physicist, should respond by an act of faith, not by an act of idle curiosity. He who has so marvelously arranged the abode where we now dwell will surely be able to prepare a different one for different circumstances. (Bastiat, *Economic Harmonies*, Van Nostrand 1964, pp. 264-265)

9.10 THOSE FACTORS WHICH DETERMINE HOW MUCH WEALTH A SOCIETY WILL PRODUCE

The amount of wealth produced varies dramatically from society to society and from one period of time to another. Those factors which determine how much will be produced by any given society might be classified under the following headings:

1. The natural resources of the country such as the soil, climate, mineral deposits, rainfall, water sources and forests.
2. The capital equipment available such as machinery, tools, equipment and power production facilities.
3. The intelligence, knowledge and ability of the people.
4. The amount of freedom from coercion and restraint.
5. The incentive of the people to produce.

It would be difficult to measure the relative importance of each of these factors; however, there are certain general observations upon which agreement might be reached.

9.11 NATURAL RESOURCES

While it cannot be claimed that there is any shortage of either raw materials or energy with which to construct wealth, it certainly is true that the amount of labor and expense required in the production process in some areas is much greater than in others. Nature has rendered it relatively easy for the people in some countries to obtain sustenance while others have had to strive much harder to reach the same standard of living.

However, a rapidly advancing technology is tending to diminish these location advantages. The lack of fertile soil, adequate rainfall, rich ore deposits and cheap power can to a great extent be remedied with fertilizers, improved farming practices, irrigation systems, cheap transportation and nuclear fuel. Scientific advancement has enabled a "poor country" to produce many times more wealth today than a "rich country" could have produced only one hundred years ago.

9.12 CAPITAL EQUIPMENT OR SAVED LABOR

As technological advances have made available cheap power and power equipment, the relative importance of human and animal physical labor has declined almost to the vanishing point in some countries. Investment capital on the other hand has become a factor of great importance. For example, a man with a tractor and farm equipment can produce a hundred times more food than one working with his bare hands or a stick; a man with a truck, an airplane or railroad facilities can transport thousands of times more weight much faster than without such equipment; and one person operating a computer can make computations more rapidly than a large number of mathematicians working without such facilities.

Of course, we must recognize that the equipment and machinery which contributes so overwhelmingly to the production of goods and services is itself the product of labor. Furthermore, this equipment is constantly depreciating and becoming obsolete so that there is a continuing need to keep it in repair and replace it with new units from time to time. But let us note that these tools represent saved labor. They constitute work done and wealth produced by an individual over and above the amount he consumes. Unless a person saves a portion of what he earns and plows it back into labor saving equipment, research, and development, these capital goods cannot be had. In the production process this "saved labor" is many times more effective and efficient in the creation of most forms of wealth than is the labor which operates the machines.

Therefore, those nations with a large stock of labor saving equipment and cheap power will produce much more than the nation without such facilities. Any nation which desires to enjoy such advantages must have laws which allow the individual to benefit from his own "saved labor."

9.13 THE INTELLIGENCE, KNOWLEDGE, AND ABILITY OF THE PEOPLE

Without a group of people possessing technical knowledge and skill, an industrial revolution can neither commence nor continue. Not only is such learning and ability essential for the invention and manufacture of capital equipment, but also for its operation, replacement and repair. Therefore before the miracles of production which are brought about by the use of cheap power and power tools can occur, there must be inventors and technicians with the ability to produce and use them. That nation whose people are intelligent and educated in the production and use of capital equipment and who are willing and able to spend time and money in research and development can truly produce a cornucopia of wealth in this age of great scientific advancement.

Let it be recognized, however, that the great discoveries which have made this electro-mechanical age possible have been made by merely a handful of men and that mass production and assembly line techniques demand much less skill and thought on the part of those who operate such lines than was demanded of those who manufactured their products with cruder methods. The operators of the machines are so often little more than automatons whose function is largely mechanical and repetitious. For such people little skill, ability, or learning is required.

9.14 FREEDOM AND INCENTIVE

Freedom and incentive are so directly related to one another that it seems advisable to discuss their effect upon the production of wealth at the same time. Intelligent man loves freedom and he is intensely aware that its exercise is utterly dependent upon the ownership and control of property. When he is permitted to enjoy the fruits of his labor and use the wealth which he produces to achieve his own objectives (or, in other words, exercise his freedom) the incentive to produce wealth is guaranteed and will exist somewhat in proportion to his love of freedom.

On the other hand if he is denied the right to own that wealth which he produces, or is so regulated in its use that he is owner in name only, the powerful freedom incentive is destroyed and with it all of that wealth which it could otherwise bring into existence.

Therefore, no matter how abundant the natural resources of a nation, how plentiful the capital equipment, or how able the people, unless the other two factors—freedom and incentive—are present, no wealth will be produced. Not only will freedom and incentive determine how much labor will be expended in producing consumer goods, but it will also determine how much "saved labor" will be invested in machinery, equipment and other capital goods.

Whenever government uses its power to prohibit the people from entering legitimate economic activities wherein they can produce wealth for themselves, or when it regulates the citizens in the use of their property or forcibly deprives them of what they have earned, it is to this same extent reducing the amount of wealth produced in that nation. The only alternative to the freedom incentive is forced labor. The truth of this assertion is painfully apparent when one compares the economic well-being of the people in a country where the right of private property is protected with the extreme want present in those nations who use the police power to deny this right.

9.15 THE OWNERSHIP OF WEALTH (OR THE RIGHT OF PRIVATE PROPERTY)

Since wealth arises from the organizing efforts of the individual, moral people have always taken the view that it belongs to that person whose efforts created it. To deny the right of ownership and control of property to one who endured the pain of physical and mental toil to organize it is contrary to the rules of justice and common sense. Therefore, throughout history moral man has recognized and undertaken to protect the right of private property. In the succeeding chapter we shall discuss the nature and importance of this right and why it must be protected if freedom is to be preserved.

I believe in honest money, the gold and silver coinage of the Constitution, and a circulating medium convertible into such money without loss.
(Ezra Taft Benson, *An Enemy Hath Done This,* p. 145)

I have examined the Constitution upon this subject and find my doubts removed. . . The Constitution tells us what shall not be a lawful tender. The 10th section declares that nothing else except gold and silver shall be lawful tender. . . .
(Joseph Smith, *DHC* Vol. V, p. 289)

CHAPTER X

THE NATURE OF PROPERTY RIGHTS

10.1 THE DISTINCTION BETWEEN PROPERTY AND PROPERTY RIGHTS

There is a difference between property or wealth as we have defined it and property rights, which must be recognized if we are to have a correct understanding of the function of government in the protection of the right of private property. Whereas property consists of tangible organized raw materials and energy, a property right is always intangible and relates to one's rights against other people.

Property arises from the organizing efforts of individuals and its ownership is vested in the one who expended the necessary physical and mental energy to bring it into existence or obtained title to it otherwise. But what rights does this title give? The only rights one can possibly have as a result of ownership are against people rather than against the property. A property right is the right to use the police power to compel another to do something about property—either to leave it alone or take some affirmative action concerning it.

When a person asserts a property right he goes to court and induces the judge to issue a decree or a judgment against other individuals. The police power is then used to compel those named in the judgment (which may be everyone) either to refrain from some activity which affects the property in question or to take some positive action with respect thereto such as delivering possession of it. A property right is meaningless unless it enables its owner to use force against other people.

The right of a person to be left undisturbed in the possession and control of his property is protected by the criminal laws which provide for the punishment of any who cause intentional damage, and also by the tort laws which permit recovery from those who cause injury either intentionally or negligently. The right here protected is in the nature of a negative right—the right to be left alone in the possession and use of property. It is accompanied by a corresponding duty to leave others undisturbed in the ownership of their property.

But the affirmative right to compel others to take some positive action concerning property is ordinarily acquired by means of a voluntary agreement and is protected under contract law. When a person enters into a binding agreement he acquires the right to receive the payment of money, the delivery of goods or the rendering of service. The subject of business law is concerned with the acquisition and enforcement of such property rights.

10.2 THE IMPORTANCE OF PROPERTY RIGHTS

In a society where labor is highly specialized and a person consumes very little or none of what he produces, property rights are of great importance. In such a society, the great majority of those who produce goods and services are employees. Before they are paid each pay day, their entire income is in the form of a property right against their employer. It is the right to receive the money from him. But even those who are in business for themselves sell practically all they produce in exchange for property rights against their buyers. These buyers may sell to others who may in turn sell once again.

Thus it is seen that almost all goods and services are exchanged for property rights at least once, and usually several times, before they are eventually consumed. Almost everything a person owns has been acquired pursuant to a contract which gave rise to the right to receive that property. In an industrialized nation, a substantial portion of those possessions which have value consist of claims or property rights emanating from agreements.

Nearly every person is both a debtor and a creditor under a number of contracts all the time. We are continually striving to discharge business obligations to others and to induce others to fulfill their obligations to us. Most of what we do in the economic field is done to satisfy or discharge a property right owned by someone else against us and almost everything we receive is in satisfaction of a property right due us. We rely upon the fulfillment of obligations due us to live and to achieve our goals. Thus it is seen that property rights are of the greatest importance in an economically developed nation where there is a marked division of labor.

10.3 A PROPERTY RIGHT IS ORDINARILY THE RIGHT TO RECEIVE MONEY

In nearly every instance a property right is the right to receive money. When an employee enters a contract to work, his wages usually are paid in money. In contracts for the sale of merchandise, land, machinery, professional services, etc., the payment of money is bargained for in almost every instance.

But even where the property right which one obtains by contract is to receive other goods or services, if there is a default and the defaulting party is sued in court for damages, the award is almost always in terms of money. There are a few cases in which the courts give specific performance and order delivery of the thing bargained for. But this is relatively rare. Therefore, in the great majority of instances, when a person enforces a property right acquired under contract, his right turns out to be the right to receive a payment of money. This is generally true in the enforcement of tort claims also. This means that money is, for all practical purposes as important in our economic affairs as property rights. In most instances they are one and the same. To understand the nature of property rights then, it is necessary to understand the nature of money. Let us briefly examine this subject.

10.4 THE NATURE OF MONEY

There is a great deal of dispute (and therefore misunderstanding) about the subject of money and this extends to a correct definition of the term. Money has been variously defined as "a medium of exchange"; "a common measure of value"; "a store of value;" and as "a tender in payment of debts" among other things. It is not our purpose here to analyze or even criticize these various definitions except to point out that nothing can serve as money in a nation unless the government of that nation has decreed that it must be accepted in satisfaction of a debt. This is the critical test. Money amounts to nothing more and nothing less than that which the law declares will discharge a legal obligation which is payable in terms of money. If it does not do this, it cannot constitute money even though it may serve as a medium of exchange or a common measure of value, etc.

This point is of the utmost importance in the study of property rights because as we have seen a property right is in nearly every instance the right to use the police power to compel the payment of money in satisfaction of a debt. Money then is usually that which a person is forced to accept in discharge of his property rights. It is that which government decrees will fulfill contract obligations. It is also that which satisfies most obligations which arise under tort laws.

If the money used in a nation is a commodity such as gold or silver, the value of which does not diminish in relation to the value of other commodities, then the property rights which it satisfies will remain equally valuable. If, however, the money used is an irredeemable piece of paper which is worthless except as government invests it with the power to discharge debts, then the property rights which it satisfies are worthless to the same extent.

A government may decree that several different commodities shall serve as money for the payment of debts in the area under its jurisdiction. However, only one of those commodities can be used as a standard of value for the monetary system. As an illustration of this fact let us assume that the three commodities, gold, silver, and copper are all declared to constitute a tender in payment of debts. Now before the size of a debt or the value of property right can be stated in terms of money, one of these three metals must be selected as a standard or measure of value. It would be just as impossible to state the size of a debt or the amount of a property right without a standard of value, as it would be to state the weight and size of an object without a standard of weights and measures.

Let us assume that silver is chosen as the standard and that so many grains of that metal (a grain is a measure of weight equal to the weight of a grain of wheat) are set equal to the unit value of money such as the dollar, the franc, the peso, etc. The value of every other item in the nation is then measured in terms of the value set for that quantity of silver. Even the value of the other commodities used as money—gold and copper—must be measured by this standard and before a debtor can pay a debt with these other metals, the government must decree how many grains of each are equal in value to the value of the number of grains of silver chosen as the standard. Only when this is done can the debtor know the quantity necessary to discharge his money obligation.

It is observed that unless the values decreed for gold and copper are very near their actual market value, the people will be selective in which metal they use for the payment of debts. If they have a choice and there is a disparity between the market and the declared value, they will choose that metal which is the cheapest in terms of the other metals. It is seen that government must use great care to value the metals accurately otherwise the cheaper metal will drive the others out of circulation. Furthermore, as the supply and demand of the three metals varies relative to one another, government must recognize this by changing the money values of the two non-standard metals. Of course, the value of the number of grains of silver used as the standard will never be changed. This is fixed for all time just as the distance represented by a meter, a foot, or an inch remains constant. When a government "coins" money it takes so many grains of the money metal and alloys, shapes, and stamps it with markings so that one may see at a glance the value it has been declared to possess. That value will always be in terms of the standard chosen.

10.5 MONEY IN THE UNITED STATES

> Now these are the names of the different pieces of their gold, and of their silver, according to their value. And the names are given by the Nephites, for they did not reckon after the manner of the Jews who were at Jerusalem; neither did they measure after the manner of the Jews; but they altered their reckoning and their measure, according to the minds and the circumstances of the people, in every generation, until the reign of the judges, they having been established by king Mosiah.
>
> Now the reckoning is thus—a senine of gold, a seon of gold, a shum of gold, and a limnah of gold. *(Alma 11:4-5)*

When the framers of the U.S. Constitution made provision therein for a monetary system, they decreed that only "gold and silver coin" could be used as money. During their deliberations in the convention a proposal was made to allow the states to use either gold, or silver, or copper as money at their discretion. *(Madison's Debates May 29, 1787)* This idea was rejected. Later on, another proposal was made to permit the states to use either gold or silver as money and this was also turned down. The provision finally adopted remains unaltered in the Constitution today and reads as follows:

> No State shall . . . make anything but gold and silver coin a tender in payment of debts. (Art.1, Sec. 10)

This provision requires the states to use both gold and silver coin as money and nothing else. They were permitted no discretion in the matter whatsoever. They could not use gold alone or silver alone. Both must be recognized as money with the power to discharge debts.

To avoid the many problems which would have arisen had each state been permitted to coin its own money thereby setting up a variety of standards of value to impede and confuse the free flow of commerce across state lines, it was decided to give the Federal government the exclusive power to coin money. This would create a uniform system throughout the nation. To insure against diverse monetary systems, the states were specifically forbidden by the Constitution to "coin money". (Art. 1, Sec. 10) The power of the Federal government to coin money was granted by the following clause:

> The Congress shall have power . . . to coin money, regulate the value thereof, and of foreign coin. (Art. 1, Sec. 8)

The power to regulate the value was necessary because, as we have seen, only one of the two metals used as money could be the standard of value, and the value of the metal not chosen would necessarily have to be regulated from time to time as the relative value of the two metals varied in the market place.

By the first Coinage Act passed in 1792, Congress chose silver rather than gold as the standard for money in the United States and made 371.25 grains of pure silver the basic unit of our entire monetary system. They called it the "dollar" or the "unit." The value of gold was originally set at fifteen times the value of an equal weight of silver and the 1792 Act authorized the minting of both gold and silver coins and declared them both to "be a lawful tender in all payments whatsoever". (1 Stat. at Large, p. 250) In 1834 due to an increase in the value of gold relative to silver and the consequent disappearance of gold money in the United States, Congress regulated the value of gold as the Constitution authorized by decreeing that 23.4 grains of pure gold would henceforth (until further changed) be equal in value to the silver dollar standard of 371.25 grains of pure silver. According to this regulation, gold was declared to have a value almost 16 times that of silver rather than the 15 to 1 ratio originally established. It is not our purpose here to examine the various Acts of Congress which have had such a profound effect upon our monetary system since that date. Let us merely note that today because of such enactments, neither gold nor silver coin is used by the states as legal tender in payment of debts and the only money now in use consists of irredeemable paper and a debased coinage.

10.6 CAN IRREDEEMABLE PAPER CONSTITUTE MONEY IN THE UNITED STATES?

> I have examined the Constitution upon this subject and find my doubts removed. . . The Constitution tells us what shall not be a lawful tender. The 10th section declares that nothing else except gold and silver shall be lawful tender. . . . (Joseph Smith, *DHC* Vol. V, p. 289)

> I believe in honest money, the gold and silver coinage of the Constitution, and a circulating medium convertible into such money without loss. I regard it as a flagrant violation of the explicit provisions of the Constitution for the Federal Government to make it a criminal offense to use gold or silver coin as legal tender or to issue irredeemable paper money. (Ezra Taft Benson, *An Enemy Hath Done This*, Parliament Publishers, Salt Lake City, Utah, 1969, p. 145)

Since the Constitution specifically forbids the states to declare a debt paid unless paid in gold or silver coin, this clause alone should be sufficient to convince anyone that irredeemable paper money cannot constitute legal tender in the United States. But there is additional evidence of this fact both within the Constitution itself and also in the debates of the Convention which adopted it. In the following clause the Constitution forbids the States to issue paper money.

> No State shall . . . emit bills of credit. (Art. 1, Sec. 100)

When the framers used the words "emit bills of credit" they were referring to the issue of paper money. The above provision denies the States this power.

A similar provision against the issue of paper money by the Federal government is not found in the Constitution but this fact cannot be construed to mean that it was ever intended that such a power be held. Since the national government holds only those powers delegated to it by the Constitution and this power was not granted, it cannot be assumed that it is possessed. In fact the very opposite of this conclusion must be reached because there was a proposal made in the Convention to invest the Federal government with this power and the proposal was rejected by a majority of 9 to 2.

The reasons for denying this power are perhaps best explained by the comments made by the members of the Convention as they debated the issue. Following is a record of those comments as made by James Madison: (The clause being debated read— "The legislature of the United States shall have the power . . . to . . . emit bills, on the credit of the United States.")

MR. GOVERNEUR MORRIS moved to strike out "and emit bills on the credit of the United States". If the United States had credit, such bills would be unnecessary; if they had not, unjust and useless.

MR. BUTLER seconds the motion.

MR. MADISON. Will it not be sufficient to prohibit the making them a *tender*? This will remove the temptation to emit them with unjust views; and promissory notes, in that shape, may in some emergencies be best.

MR. GOVERNEUR MORRIS. Striking out the words will leave room still for notes of a responsible minister, which will do all the good without the mischief, The moneyed interest will oppose the plan of government, if paper emissions be not prohibited.

MR. GORHAM was for striking out without inserting any prohibition. If the words stand, they may suggest and lead to the measure.

MR. MASON had doubts on the subject. Congress, he thought, would not have the power, unless it were expressed. Though he had a mortal hatred of paper money, yet, as he could not foresee all emergencies, he was unwilling to tie the hands of the legislature. He observed that the late war could not have been carried on, had such a prohibition existed.

MR. GORHAM. The power, as far as it will be necessary or safe is involved in that of borrowing.

MR. MERCER was a friend to paper money, though, in the present state and temper of America, he should neither propose nor approve of such a measure. He was consequently opposed to a prohibition of it altogether. It will stamp suspicion on the government, to deny it a discretion on this point. It was impolitic, also, to excite the opposition of all those who were friends to paper money. The people of property would be sure to be on the side of the plan, and it was impolitic to purchase their further attachment with the loss of the opposite class of citizens.

MR. ELLSWORTH thought this a favorable moment to shut and bar the door against paper money. The mischiefs of the various experiments which had been made were now fresh in the public mind, and had excited the disgust of all the respectable part of America. By withholding the power from the new government, more friends of influence would be gained to it than by almost anything else. Paper money can in no case be necessary. Give the government credit, and other resources will offer. The power may do harm, never good.

MR RANDOLPH, notwithstanding his antipathy to paper money, could not agree to strike out the words, as he could not foresee all the occasions that might arise.

MR. WILSON. It will have a most salutary influence on the credit of the United States, to remove the possibility of paper money. This expedient can never succeed whilst its mischiefs are remembered; and, as long as it can be resorted to, it will be a bar to other resources.

MR. BUTLER remarked, that paper was a legal tender in no country in Europe. He was urgent for disarming the government of such a power.

MR. MASON was still averse to tying the hands of the legislature *altogether*. If there was no example in Europe, as just remarked, it might be observed, on other side, that there was none in which the government was restrained on this head.

MR. READ thought the words, if not struck out, would be as alarming as the mark of the beast in Revelation.

MR. LANGDON had rather reject the whole plan, than retain the three words, "and emit bills."

On the motion for striking out, —New Hampshire, Mass., Conn., Penn., Dela., Va., No. Caro., So. Caro., Georgia, ay, 9: New Jersey, Maryland, no, 2. (Madison's Notes, August 16, 1787)

In a footnote explaining his vote in favor of denying the power, Mr. Madison says:

This vote in the affirmative by Virginia was occasioned by the acquiescence of Mr. Madison, who became satisfied that striking out the words would not disable the government from the use of public notes, as far as they could be safe and proper, and would only cut off the pretext for a PAPER CURRENCY, and particularly for making the bills a TENDER either for public or private debts. (Madison's notes August 16, 1787)

From the above nothing can be clearer than this: The power to issue paper money as legal tender was never given to the Federal government but on the other hand was specifically denied to it by the Founding Fathers.

10.7 THE LOSS OF PROPERTY RIGHTS THROUGH THE USE OF PAPER MONEY

Most unquestionably there is no legal tender, and there can be no legal tender in this country, under the authority of this government or any other, but gold and silver, either the coinage of our own mints, or foreign coins, at rates regulated by Congress. This is a constitutional principle, perfectly plain, and of the very highest importance. The States are expressly prohibited from making anything but gold and silver a tender in payment of debts; and, although no such express prohibition is applied to Congress, yet, as Congress has no power granted to it, in this respect, but to coin money, and to regulate the value of foreign coins, it clearly has no power to substitute paper, or anything else, for coin, as a tender in payment of debts and in discharge of contracts. (Daniel Webster, *Great Debates In American History*, Vol. 13, p. 113)

By our original Articles of Confederation, the Congress have power to borrow money and emit bills of credit on the credit of the United States; agreeable to which was the report on this system, as made by the committee of detail. When we came to this part of the report, a motion was made to strike out the words "to EMIT BILLS OF CREDIT." . . .

But, sir, a majority of the Convention, being wise beyond every event, and being willing to risk any political evil rather than admit the idea of a paper emission in any possible case, refused to trust this authority to a government to which they were lavishing the most unlimited powers of taxation, and to the mercy of which they were willing blindly to trust the liberty and property of the citizens of every state in the Union; and they erased that clause from the system. (Luther Martin, delegate to the Constitutional

Convention from Maryland, *Elliot's Debates*, Vol. 1, pp. 369, 370)

It is apparent from the whole context of the Constitution as well as the history of the times which gave birth to it, that it was the purpose of the Convention to establish a currency consisting of the precious metals. These, from their peculiar properties which rendered them the standard of value in all other countries, were adopted in this as well to establish its commercial standard in reference to foreign countries by a permanent rule as to exclude the use of a mutable medium of exchange, such as of certain agricultural commodities recognized by the statutes of some states as tender for debts, or the still more pernicious expedient of a paper currency. The last, from the experience of the evils of the issues of paper during the Revolution, had become so justly obnoxious as not only to suggest the clause in the Constitution forbidding the emission of bills of credit by the States, but also to produce that vote in the Convention which negatived the proposition to grant power to Congress to charter corporations. (Andrew Jackson, *Messages and Papers of the Presidents*, Vol. 3, p. 246)

If creditors can demand that their property rights be paid with precious metals, it is impossible for a government to destroy the value of their claims through inflation. This conclusion does not deny the possibility of a fluctuation in the relative value of gold and wheat or of silver and steel. If the demand for wheat and steel suddenly increases and the supply diminishes this will tend to increase their value relative to other commodities including gold and silver. On the other hand the reverse of these same factors could operate to increase the value of the precious metals with respect to other products. But the important point is that gold and silver have retained their relative value throughout history and there is every reason to assume that they will not lose it in the future. On the other hand there has never been an issue of irredeemable paper money which has not suffered a loss in value. The only value such paper ever has is the power to pay debts and when this value is lost as always happens, it is utterly worthless except as a sad reminder of the foolishness of men. Since a property right is nearly always the right to receive money, when money loses its value, there is a corresponding loss in the value of the property right.

A great principle is involved in this money question. The Constitution of the United States undoubtedly contemplated the use of both gold and silver as coin and as tender in the payment of debts. The framers of that instrument held the views which were then current as to the necessity of having both metals in circulation as money. . . .

We have been led to expect that there would be attempts made to infringe upon the Constitution. . . . It is well for us who reside in these mountains to divest ourselves of prejudice and look upon these questions as free from passion as possible, and cultivate a conservative feeling. It certainly would be, in my opinion, a violation of the Constitution for silver advocates to attempt to strike down gold and to deprive it of its function as money and as a tender in payment of debts. So also is it a violation of the Constitution to attempt to make gold the only metal that possesses the function as a tender in payment of debts. Gold and silver should both be upheld and used, and any attempt to deprive either of these metals of its value as a tender in payment of debts seems to me a clear violation of the spirit of the Constitution. (George Q. Cannon, 1896, *Juvenile Instructor*, 31: 523-4)

Inflation inflicts the greatest harm on those who own property rights which take a long time to mature. Rights such as those represented by insurance policies, bonds, mortgage notes, pensions, and retirement benefits can be and are largely destroyed by inflation. But even more tragic than this is the loss of confidence between men and the destruction of the incentive to save. As men observe the destruction of property rights represented by long-term investments, they cease to make such investments. As inflation becomes more rapid, they cease to make any investments at all. To the extent that property rights become worthless merely by the passage of time, men refuse to enter into agreements which create such rights. No one will invest; no one will save; no one will loan, and no one will build. Thus all business comes to a standstill eventually and anarchy results. The late John Maynard Keynes regarded the corruption of the currency and inflation as the surest method of destroying the capitalistic system. Note his words:

> Lenin is said to have declared that the best way to destroy the Capitalist System was to debauch the currency. By a continuing process of inflation, governments can confiscate, secretly and unobserved, an important part of the wealth of their citizens . . . Lenin was certainly right. There is no subtler, no surer means of over-turning the existing basis of society than to debauch the currency. The process engages all the hidden forces of economic law on the side of destruction, and does it in a manner which not one man in a million is able to diagnose. (*Economic Consequences of the Peace*, pp. 235, 236, [1920])

The effect of inflation on property rights can be dramatically illustrated by comparing the buying power of the U.S. dollar before the nation went off the gold standard with its current buying power (1974) some 40 years later. The United States officially adopted the gold standard by "The Gold Standard Act" of March 14, 1900. That act declared the dollar containing 25.8 grains of gold, 0.900 fine to be "the standard unit of value." (U. S. Stat. at L. Vol. 31, pp. 45-50)

In effect this established the price of gold in terms of dollars at $20.66 per ounce. In 1974 according to the newspapers gold was being traded on the London, England exchange at between $150.00 and $160.00 per ounce. (There was no gold market in the U.S. at that time, such trading being forbidden by law.) This represents a decline in the purchasing power of the dollar of more than eighty percent during this period. Or to state the matter another way, before the gold standard was abandoned the U.S. dollar would purchase approximately 23 grains of gold . Today it will purchase less than four. Assuming that the value of gold relative to other commodities remained about the same during that 40-year period, the overall purchasing power of the dollar decreased eighty percent. Thus a property right such as a $1,000 insurance policy which was paid for prior to 1933 and which matured today would be worth no more than $200 of the $1,000 paid for it.

It is noted that to the extent the policy holder suffered from inflation, the debtor insurance company benefited because eighty percent of the real value of the debt was cancelled during the time it remained outstanding. But while non-government debtors benefit only to the extent that inflation discharges the real value of their obligation during the time it remains unpaid the debts of a government whose paper becomes completely worthless is entirely discharged in this manner. As an instance of this let us observe what will happen to the approximately four trillion dollar debt the U.S. government now owes to banks, insurance companies, individuals and other investors if inflation continues until the dollar declines to zero value.

The Federal government today claims the right to print any amount of paper money it needs for the payment of its debts. In other words it now asserts the power to completely discharge its enormous obligation with printing press money and assumes it can never be required to give to its creditors (at least those under its jurisdiction) either gold, silver or any other commodity of value in payment of their loans. However, this does not mean that any single set of creditors will be required to suffer a 100% loss of their investment. The identity of government creditors changes from time to time all throughout the period during which the dollar is losing its value. But amongst all such creditors they will eventually suffer a combined loss of four trillion dollars in property rights if inflation continues until the currency is worthless.

It is easy to understand that when inflation becomes a way of life in a nation and the community perceives that it is destroying their property rights, they refuse to become creditors under contracts which take a long time to mature. Then as inflation becomes more rapid, the time period during which credit will be extended, or for which property rights will be allowed to remain unsatisfied, becomes shorter and shorter until virtually all business ceases. This causes extreme want and suffering until finally the people in their extremity come to a full realization of the fact that it was the debauchery of their currency by government officials which caused the disaster. At this point the overturning of the existing basis of society can be expected.

Other than returning to a sound money system, there is one alternative which a government can pursue to prevent the above described chain of events from running their full course and that is to pass laws which deny the people their freedom to express a loss of confidence in the currency. This is done by imposing wage and price controls. Such laws make it a criminal offense for people to evaluate the dollar in terms of goods and services. Of course such controls lead inevitably to rationing and when such measures are added to the licensing, regulatory, and welfare state laws which are already on the books, the combined effect is to destroy freedom of contract. But the destruction of freedom of contract is tantamount to the destruction of the right of private property and all of the other basic freedoms which are dependent thereon. However, the imposition of wage and price controls does tend to keep hidden from the majority of the people the fact that it was the corruption of the monetary system in the first instance which led to a destruction of private property rights.

CHAPTER XI

LIMITATIONS ON GOVERNMENT POWER

11.1 THE ALTERNATIVES—LIMITED OR UNLIMITED GOVERNMENT

Up to this point we have been discussing the powers which have been delegated to government. We now turn our attention to limitations on those powers. We have already examined this problem to some extent as we considered the extent of delegated power. However, its transcendent importance justifies separate treatment.

The proposition, that there are limits to the power of government is not accepted by all people. The contrary view that those in control are answerable only to themselves and that the citizen possesses no rights which are immune from seizure has been and still is quite common. During certain periods in the past a belief in the "divine right of kings" was almost universal. According to that doctrine the king or potentate could do no wrong. He could deprive his subjects of their lives, liberties and property for any purpose his sovereign will might dictate and no one could properly question either his authority or his motives. He was regarded with superstitious and reverential awe—as a personage of superior, if not infallible, wisdom, virtue and judgment. His right to reign and the corresponding duty of all to obey were not matters for debate.

Today those who contend that there are no limits to government power have generally rejected the "divine right of kings" philosophy and have substituted in its place a belief in the "divine right of the majority." To such people the majority can do no wrong. As long as the police power is being used to do the will of the most numerous part of society, the act is proper regardless of its nature. This is the sole test of right and wrong in government action.

Those who believe in unlimited government power must reject the doctrine of the unalienable rights of man because the two positions are inconsistent. Once it is concluded that those who control government may use its power for any purpose they choose, it is also

135

concluded that the citizens have no rights which are beyond its reach. If the ruling sovereign or majority are at liberty to pass any law they desire, and if under that law they can punish any who disobey, the people have no possessions or rights which cannot be taken. Their lives, liberties and property are at the disposal of those who govern.

11.2 LIMITATIONS ON GOVERNMENT POWER UNDER THE CONSTITUTIONAL SYSTEM

Those who adopted the United States Constitution and established the American system rejected the idea of unlimited state power. Their underlying philosophy, as expressed in the Declaration of Independence, was that men possess certain unalienable rights which governments are to protect but never deny. They asserted that whenever any form of government becomes destructive of these rights, the citizens may alter or abolish it. The Revolutionary War was fought to affirm this basic principle.

But the Constitution itself is the best evidence of their belief in limited government. By actual count it contains more restrictions and denials of power than it does grants. The Bill of Rights consists entirely of such restraints. Not only does the national charter limit the Federal, but the state governments as well. State constitutions contain additional limitations. Evidence that these restrictions are real is found in the fact that since the beginning of our Republic the courts have been engaged in deciding cases in which it was alleged that government had exceeded its limitations.

11.3 THE CONTROVERSY OVER THE MEANING OF THE CONSTITUTION

Have mercy, O Lord, upon all the nations of the earth; have mercy upon the rulers of our land; may those principles, which were so honorably and nobly defended, namely, the Constitution of our land, by our fathers, be established forever. *(D&C 109:54)*

In these days when there is a special trend among certain

groups, including members of faculties of universities, to challenge the principles upon which our country has been founded and the philosophy of our Founding Fathers, I hope that Brigham Young University will stand as a bulwark in support of the principles of government as vouchsafed to us by our Constitutional Fathers. (Letter from President David O. McKay to Administration and Faculty of BYU, 1967)

Even though our constitutions were drafted with great care, much diversity of opinion has developed over their meaning. While there may have been substantial agreement regarding the meaning of power-granting and withholding clauses in the Federal Constitution during the lives of the Founding Fathers, today there is widespread controversy.

For example, there are now those who contend that the power given to Congress in Article 1, Section 8, "To lay and collect taxes . . . to . . . provide for the . . . general welfare of the United States" gives it the authority to redistribute the wealth of its citizens and even to make of America a fully socialized nation if those in office desire this to happen.

Another clause in this same section says that, "The Congress shall have power . . . to regulate commerce . . . among the several states. . . ." According to some, this provision authorizes the national government to regulate and control every phase of the nation's economic activities, including labor and agriculture, finance and banking, transportation and communication, mining and manufacturing, trades and professions, education and welfare.

Others take the position that these clauses do not authorize these powers in the least degree, and they point to other provisions which they assert specifically deny them. They may cite as their authority Article V of the Bill of Rights which says: "No person shall be . . . deprived of life, liberty, or property, without due process of law; nor shall private property be taken for public use without just compensation."

Which of these opposing views is right; or are they both wrong, with the correct answer lying somewhere in between?

On every question of construction, carry ourselves back to the time when the constitution was adopted, recollect the spirit manifested in the debates, and instead of trying what meaning may be squeezed out of the text, or invented against it, conform to the probable one in which it was passed. (Thomas Jefferson, *Works*, Vol 12, p. 257, Fed. Ed.)

It is extremely difficult, if not impossible, to take a certain provision of the Constitution, isolate it from the balance of the instrument and determine its correct meaning. One sentence or even one
paragraph standing alone may logically be interpreted in a variety of
ways. But when read in connection with the entire document and as
a necessary part of the overall plan or purpose of those who adopted
it, its true meaning may become clear. Let us use this approach in
our attempt to determine the limitations on the power of government
under our Constitutional system.

11.4 GOVERNMENT SHALL NOT ACT CONTRARY TO THE PURPOSES FOR WHICH FORMED

> And now, verily I say unto you concerning the laws of the
> land, it is my will that my people should observe to do all things
> whatsoever I command them.
> And that law of the land which is constitutional, supporting
> that principle of freedom in maintaining rights and privileges,
> belongs to all mankind, and is justifiable before me.
> Therefore, I, the Lord, justify you, and your brethren of my
> church, in befriending that law which is the constitutional law of
> the land;
> And as pertaining to law of man, whatsoever is more or less
> than this, cometh of evil. *(D&C 98:4-7)*

> That they may be conferred upon us, it is true; but when we
> undertake to cover our sins, or to gratify our pride, our vain ambi-
> tion, or to exercise control or dominion or compulsion upon the
> souls of the children of men, in any degree of unrighteousness,
> behold, the heavens withdraw themselves; the Spirit of the Lord is
> grieved; and when it is withdrawn, Amen to the priesthood or the
> authority of that man. *(D&C 121:37)*

The most obvious, the most logical, the most precise limit on
government power is this: It shall not act contrary to the purposes
for which it was created; it shall not destroy that which it has a duty
to preserve; it shall not perform those acts it was directed to forbid
and punish.

When those who established our American Constitutional system of government directed it to preserve freedom, they impliedly
forbade it to destroy freedom. By authorizing it to protect the right
of private property, they denied it the power to abrogate this right.

By assigning it the duty to enforce a Christian code of morality, punish crime and dispense justice, they obligated it never to violate that code, commit crime or act unjustly.

It is assumed that Americans of today are in agreement with the objectives of our Founding Fathers as set forth above. If so, we are also agreed that our governments are without power to act contrary to these purposes. But the critical question is: when are they doing the one and when the other? When are they preserving freedom and protecting the right of private property and when are they acting in opposition to these objectives?

Is it realized that every law they adopt and every act they perform which does not have the effect of accomplishing these purposes has the opposite effect of defeating them? Because of their very nature—the fact that they use force to accomplish their purposes—governments do either good or evil each time they act. Never are the results without moral consequence.

Whenever government uses force and the threat thereof to compel obedience, it unavoidably deprives those affected of either life, liberty or property. If the law is obeyed out of fear of punishment, liberty of action is affected. If it is disobeyed and the punishment inflicted, either life, liberty or property is taken. The purpose and effect of every law is to deprive the citizens of one of these three possessions. But it cannot do this without committing either good or evil because there is no question of greater moral significance than that of determining when it is right to take from a person his life, liberty or property. From this it must be concluded that under the American system, government acts contrary to those harmonious purposes for which it is established whenever it passes any law whatsoever which does not have the effect of achieving these purposes. These purposes define the exact limit of its power.

11.5 *Laws Within And Without The Limits Of Government Power*

Let us examine some of the more familiar types of laws for the purpose of determining whether they are within the limits of those powers granted to accomplish the purposes of our American system of government.

By inflicting punishment on a criminal, government does not contradict its purposes; it does not deprive him of his natural right to life, liberty or property. When he intentionally violates his duty to refrain from crime, he forfeits his right to the possession taken from him as punishment.

Neither does it act contrary to its purpose of protecting private property when it compels the performance of duties between citizens. By forcing a debtor to discharge a debt, it does not take from him anything he has a right to retain. It merely transfers to the creditor that which is rightfully his.

And when a taxpayer is compelled to bear his fair share of the tax burden or the obligations of national defense, his property rights and freedom are not violated. If these duties were not performed, his rights and freedom would not be protected.

But when government has performed these functions, it has completed its assigned tasks and reached the limit of its powers to use force. Anything beyond this destroys man's rights. For instance, when it enforces licensing, regulatory and welfare state laws, it does not protect freedom, the right of private property nor liberty of contract. Neither does it obey the code of private morality, punish crime nor dispense justice. On the other hand, it acts in opposition to each one of these objectives.

11.6 LIMITED VS. UNLIMITED GOVERNMENT

Perhaps there is no better way of understanding the American system of limited government power than by comparing it with one whose powers are unlimited—the Communist form. These two governments are the very antithesis of each other. They have nothing in common and everything in opposition.

The American system was designed by men of deep religious faith and high moral standards. They adopted as their national motto: "In God We Trust." In contrast, the founders of Communism were avowed atheists committed to the destruction of religion and the family along with the moral principles they exemplified and taught.

The Constitution provides for a federal system with the powers of government first divided between the national and the states and a second division within each. The Communist form is a centralized, all powerful dictatorship. The American system gives the people the right to elect their own leaders and alter their laws. Communism denies all rights of self-government. The Constitution contains a Bill of Rights and other detailed limitations on government power. The Communist state recognizes no limits on its power whatsoever.

But the distinction between limited and unlimited power is most clearly seen when a comparison is made between the objectives of the two systems with respect to the right of private property. The Constitution expressly guarantees this right in the same clause of the Fifth Amendment in which it protects the rights to life and liberty. And in this same clause is found this restriction: "nor shall private property be taken for public use without just compensation."

On the other hand, the police power under Communism is used to deny private property rights. The Communist Manifesto, which is generally recognized as the ultimate authority for Communists the world over contains a statement of the basic purposes and program of their form of government, says this: ". . .the theory of the Communist may be summed up in the single sentence: abolition of private property." At another point in this document is found this sentence: "The Communist revolution is the most radical rupture with traditional property relations." The Communist state is completely socialistic. Its ownership and control over property is unlimited. Private ownership and control is forbidden.

Of utmost importance to those who believe in the American system and desire its preservation is the plan outlined in the Manifesto to convert all political systems over to Communism. The avowed purpose of the Communists as stated in the Manifesto is to overthrow all governments and replace them with a Communist form having unlimited power.

11.7 THE METHOD OF CONVERTING CAPITALISM INTO THE COMMUNIST SYSTEM

The method proposed in the Manifesto for replacing Capitalism with Communism is by destroying the right of private property. This they plan to accomplish by inducing the governments of capitalist nations to adopt, over a period of time, a political platform which will ultimately have this effect. Let us quote from the Manifesto itself regarding how the plan is to work:

> We have seen above that the first step in the revolution by the working class is to raise the proletariat to the position of ruling class, to establish democracy.
>
> The proletariat will use its political supremacy to wrest by degrees all capital from the bourgeoisie, to centralize all instruments of production in the hands of the state, i.e., of the proletariat organized as the ruling class, and to increase the total of productive forces as rapidly as possible.
>
> Of course, in the beginning this cannot be effected except by means of despotic inroads on the rights of property and on the conditions of bourgeois production; by means of measures, therefore, which appear economically insufficient and untenable, but which, in the course of the movement outstrip themselves, necessitate further inroads upon the old social order, and are unavoidable as a means of entirely revolutionizing the mode of production.
>
> These measures will, of course, be different in different countries.
>
> Nevertheless, in the most advanced countries the following will be pretty generally applicable:

Then are listed the famous ten points of the Communist Manifesto which are as follows:

1. Abolition of property in land and application of all rents of land to public purposes.
2. A heavy progressive or graduated income tax.
3. Abolition of all right of inheritance.
4. Confiscation of the property of all emigrants and rebels.
5. Centralization of credit in the hands of the state by means of a national bank with state capital and an exclusive monopoly.
6. Centralization of the means of communication and transport in the hands of the state.
7. Extension of factories and instruments of production owned by the state; the bringing into cultivation of waste lands, and the improvement of the soil generally in accordance with a common plan.
8. Equal obligation of all to work. Establishment of industrial armies, especially for agriculture.
9. Combination of agriculture with manufacturing industries; gradual abolition of the distinction between town and country by a more equable distribution of the population over the country.
10. Free education for all children in public schools. Abolition of child factory labour in its present form. Combination of education with industrial production, etc.

11.8 THE IMPLEMENTATION OF THE PLAN OF THE MANIFESTO

The Communist Manifesto has been termed "the starting point of the modern socialist movement." (*Encyclopedia Britannica*, 1960 Ed., Vol. 20, p. 881) And it is generally agreed that its proposals for imposing socialism world-wide have been largely incorporated into the laws of every nation.

Again quoting from the Encyclopedia Britannica:

> The idea of socialism, which until World War I had inspired labour movements almost exclusively in the West, already manifested itself in the interwar period, both as Social Democracy and as Communism in some Asian countries, and after World War ll spread rapidly all over the globe. (*Ency. Brit.* 1970 Ed., Vol 20, p. 756A)

The adoption of the Communist plan here in the United States might be more clearly seen if we note the three main methods governments use in destroying the right of private property and how the licensing, regulatory and welfare-state laws which have been so widely adopted both on a Federal and state level, fit into each category. Those methods and the laws which implement them are:

(1) Prevent people from acquiring property in the first instance.
    a. Licensing laws.
    b. Labor laws.
    c. Zoning laws.
(2) Confiscate private property and property rights thus transferring ownership to government.
    a. Graduated income, estate and gift tax laws.
    b. Welfare state laws.
    c. Laws providing for housing, irrigation and power projects, flood control and parks.
    d. Laws which have abolished the gold and silver standard and substituted irredeemable paper money.
(3) Regulate the people in their use of the property so that control over it is placed in government and taken from private hands.
    a. No list will be attempted here because of the enormous number of laws which should be included. It is merely noted that it would include all of those enactments by legislatures, agencies and commissions by which government regulates agriculture and labor, finance and banking, transportation and communication, mining and manufacturing and virtually every other economic endeavor.

A statement by President David O. McKay concerning the position of The Church of Jesus Christ of Latter-day Saints on Communism.

In order that there may be no misunderstanding by bishops, stake presidents, and others regarding members of the Church participating in nonchurch meetings to study and become informed on the Constitution of the United States, Communism, etc., I wish to make the following statements that I have been sending out from my office for some time and that have come under question by some stake authorities, bishoprics, and others.

Church members are at perfect liberty to act according to their own consciences in the matter of safeguarding our way of life. They are, of course, encouraged to honor the highest standards of the gospel and to work to preserve their own freedoms. They are free to participate in nonchurch meetings that are held to warn people of the threat of Communism or any other theory or principle that will deprive us of our free agency or individual liberties vouchsafed by the Constitution of the United States.

The Church, out of respect for the rights of all its members to have their political views and loyalties, *must maintain the strictest possible neutrality.* We have no intention of trying to interfere with the fullest and freest exercise of the political franchise of our members under and within our Constitution, which the Lord declared he established "by the hands of wise men whom (he) raised up unto this very purpose" *(D&C 101:80)* and which, as to the principles thereof, the Prophet Joseph Smith dedicating the Kirtland Temple, prayed should be "established forever." *(D&C 109:54)* The Church does not yield any of its devotion to or convictions about safeguarding the American principles and the establishments of government under federal and state constitutions and the civil rights of men safeguarded by these.

The Position of this Church on the subject of Communism has never changed. We consider it the greatest satanical threat to peace, prosperity, and the spread of God's work among men that exists on the face of the earth.

In this connection, we are continually being asked to give our opinion concerning various patriotic groups or individuals who are fighting Communism and speaking up for freedom. Our immediate concern, however, is not with parties, groups, or persons, but with principles. We therefore commend and encourage every person and every group who is sincerely seeking to study Constitutional principles and awaken a sleeping and apathetic people to the alarming conditions that are rapidly advancing about us. We wish all of our citizens throughout the land were participating in some type of organized self-education in order that they could better appreciate what is happening and know what they can do about it.

Supporting the FBI, the police, the congressional committees investigating Communism, and various organizations that are attempting to awaken the people through educational means is a policy we warmly endorse for all our people.

The entire concept and philosophy of Communism is diametrically opposed to everything for which the Church stands—*belief in Deity, belief in the dignity and eternal nature of man, and the application of the gospel to efforts for peace in the world.* Communism is militantly atheistic and is committed to the destruction of faith wherever it may be found.

The Russian Commissar of Education wrote: "We must hate Christians and Christianity. Even the best of them must be considered our worst enemies. Christian love is an obstacle to the development of the revolution. Down with love of one's neighbor. What we want is hate. Only then shall we conquer the universe.'

On the other hand, the gospel teaches the existence of God as our Eternal and Heavenly Father and declares: ". . .him only shalt thou serve." *(Matt. 4:10)*

Communism debases the individual and makes him the enslaved tool of the state, to which he must look for sustenance and religion. Communism destroys man's God-given free agency.

No member of this Church can be true to this faith, nor can any American be loyal to his trust, while lending aid, encouragement, or sympathy to any of these false philosophies; for if he does, they will prove snares to his feet. (President David 0. McKay, *Conference Report*, Apr., 1966, pp. 109-110)

I was due here two weeks ago, and had a theme to deliver which I thought was timely and appropriate, but I come with another theme this morning— "Two Contending Forces." Those forces are known and have been designated by different terms throughout the ages. In the beginning they were known as Satan on the one hand, and Christ on the other. . . . In these days, they are called "domination by the state" on the one hand, "personal liberty" on the other; communism on one hand, free agency on the other. . . . Students, two forces are at work. There might be a conflagration such as the world has never known. Mankind will have to choose the one course or the other. (President David O. McKay, *Speeches of the Year*, BYU, May 18, 1960)

(See Also: Ether 8:22-25; 1 Ne. 14:9-16; Hela. 4:22; 5:2; 6:38-39; 7:4-5, 25; 8:1-4; 3 Ne. 6:20-30; 7:1-2, 6; 9:9)

11.9 THE EFFECT OF SUBSTITUTING UNLIMITED FOR LIMITED GOVERNMENT POWER

Thus, today, brethren, we are in danger of actually surrendering our personal and property rights. This development, if it does occur in full form, will be a sad tragedy for our people. We must recognize that PROPERTY RIGHTS ARE ESSENTIAL TO HUMAN LIBERTY.

Former United States Supreme Court Justice George Sutherland, from our own state, carefully stated it as follows:

'It is not the right of property which is protected, but the right TO property. Property, per se, has no rights; but the individual— the man—has three great rights, equally sacred from arbitrary interference; the RIGHT TO HIS LIFE, the RIGHT TO HIS LIBERTY, and the RIGHT TO HIS PROPERTY. The three rights are so bound together as to be essentially ONE right. To give a man his life, but deny him liberty, is to take from him all that makes life worth living. To give him liberty but take from him the property which is the fruit and badge of his liberty, is to still leave him a slave." [From a speech before the New York State Bar Association, January 21, 1921] (President David O. McKay, *Conf. Rep.* Oct. 1962, p. 6)

There are a number of enormously important consequences which attend the transition from limited to unlimited government power—or from the Constitutional system to socialism which is the same thing. Among these are the practical changes wrought in the economy of the nation. An entirely different set of problems are encountered by those who work in the two systems. As the change occurs the student and practitioner of business discovers less and less need for a knowledge of the principles of private business and contract law, and an ever-increasing need to know the current rules and regulations of government. Textbooks and courses in this area are devoting a much greater portion of their attention to relationships between business and government with a corresponding decrease in attention to unregulated relationships between private parties. However, much of this learning may have little practical value because it may become obsolete before it can be put to use.

The most regrettable effect of the change, however, is on the character of the people. It alters their entire value system. That which was formerly evil the law has now made acceptable; and that which was once good is made no longer necessary or desirable. When government destroys the institution of private property, a long train of evils follows. The commandment, "Thou shalt not steal," is legislated out of existence. Government engages in plunder on a massive basis under socialism and by its example justifies the citizens in doing likewise. If it is proper for government to steal, how can it be wrong for the individual to do so? The people are taught that they no longer need to respect the right of private property and when this happens, they tend to lose respect for all other human rights as well.

There is a resulting loss of interest in freedom. Especially the youth who are raised up in the system and have experienced nothing else are unable to appreciate its value. They come to accept the laws which restrict them as necessary and proper. They cannot imagine how freedom would work. They are taught in the schools and elsewhere that it is for the good of the people that they are regulated.

Socialism destroys the people's sense of justice. The idea that each person is entitled to benefit from the fruits of his own labors is in diametric opposition to its underlying principle. Furthermore, the laws under which the socialist state is imposed are unjust because they provide for punishing those who are innocent of evil. They deny the citizens their rightful liberties and physically suppress those who attempt to exercise them.

And finally, the adverse effect upon the family is one of the most lamentable of all. Socialism tends to destroy this organization and with it the very foundation upon which a moral society rests. Parents are relieved of the necessity of providing for, teaching and supervising their own children, and children are absolved from the obligation of caring for their parents. The consequence of this is to destroy family ties. The love and affection which these mutual sacrifices would otherwise beget are lost and with them the finer and nobler restraints of family tradition. No matter from what angle socialism is viewed, it is evil; and so are the welfare-state practices and regulatory measures which lead to it. It is the imposition by force of the doctrine of materialism and has the effect of suppressing and destroying that spiritual or moral nature of man which distinguishes him from the animals. A government with unlimited power is the greatest tragedy which can befall a nation.

...we must learn the principles of the Constitution in the tradition of the Founding Fathers.

Have we read the Federalist papers? Are we reading the Constitution and pondering it? Are we aware of its principles? Are we abiding by these principles and teaching them to others? Could we defend the Constitution? Can we recognize when a law is constitutionally unsound? Do we know what the prophets have said about the Constitution and the threats to it?

President Ezra Taft Benson,
"Our Divine Constitution,"
General Conference, Oct. 1987

CHAPTER XII

PROCEDURES WHICH MUST BE FOLLOWED BY GOVERNMENT IN THE EXERCISE OF ITS POWER

12.1 THE BILL OF RIGHTS

The United States Constitution, as well as those of the States, sets forth a number of procedures which the officers of government must follow in the exercise of their powers. Legislatures, courts and the executive branch have adopted a great many additional rules specifying procedures which pertain to the functioning of government.

We will concern ourselves here only with the provisions in the Federal Constitution and will further limit our discussion to the procedural requirements contained in the Bill of Rights which serve to protect one accused of a crime.

While the Bill of Rights contains provisions not related to procedure, its brevity permits us to quote it here in full:

Article the First

Congress shall make no law respecting an establishment of religion, or prohibiting the free exercise thereof; or abridging the freedom of speech, or of the press; or the right of the people peaceably to assemble, and to petition the government for a redress of grievances.

Article the Second

A well regulated militia being necessary to the security of a free State, the right of the people to keep and bear arms shall not be infringed.

Article the Third

No soldier shall, in time of peace, be quartered in any house without the consent of the owner; nor in time of war, but in the manner prescribed by law.

Article the Fourth

The right of the people to be secure in their persons, houses, papers, and effects, against unreasonable searches and seizures, shall not be violated, and no warrants shall issue, but upon probable cause, supported by oath or affirmation, and particularly describing the place to be searched, and the persons or things to be seized.

Article the Fifth

No person shall be held to answer for a capital or otherwise infamous crime, unless on a presentment or indictment of a grand jury, except in cases arising in the land or naval forces, or in the militia when in actual service in time of war or public danger; nor shall any person be subject for the same offence to be twice put in jeopardy of life or limb; nor shall be compelled in any criminal case to be witness against himself; nor be deprived of life, liberty, or property, without due process of law; nor shall private property be taken for public use without just compensation.

Article the Sixth

In all criminal prosecutions the accused shall enjoy the right of a speedy and public trial, by an impartial jury of the State and district wherein the crime shall have been committed, which district shall have been previously ascertained by law, and to be informed of the nature and cause of the accusation; to be confronted with the witnesses against him; to have compulsory process for obtaining witnesses in his favor, and to have the assistance of counsel for his defence.

Article the Seventh

In suits at common law, where the value in controversy shall exceed twenty dollars, the right of trial by jury shall be preserved; and no fact tried by a jury, shall be otherwise reexamined in any court of the United States than according to the rules of the common law.

Article the Eighth

Excessive bail shall not be required, nor excessive fines imposed, nor cruel and unusual punishments inflicted.

Article the Ninth

The enumeration in the Constitution of certain rights, shall not be construed to deny or disparage others retained by the people.

Article the Tenth

The powers not delegated to the United States by the Constitution or prohibited by it to the States, are reserved to the States respectively, or to the people.

12.2 GOVERNMENTS ARE BOUND BY THE PROCEDURAL REQUIREMENTS OF THE CONSTITUTION

The express purpose of the Bill of Rights is to place restrictions on the power of the Federal government. These restraints were imposed by the people acting through their representatives, and according to the provisions of the Constitution they can be removed only with the consent of the people. Until such time, the officers of the Federal government are duty bound to obey them. It will be recognized that many of the prohibitions and denials of power contained in the Bill of Rights apply equally to State governments either because of similar provisions in their own Constitutions or because the Supreme Court of the United States has decreed them to be so applicable.

12.3 4TH AMENDMENT—UNREASONABLE SEARCHES AND SEIZURES

The first step in a criminal prosecution is to search for and seize evidence of the alleged crime and make an arrest of the suspect.

The Fourth Amendment places restrictions upon these procedures by requiring first that searches and seizures shall not be unreasonable and secondly that warrants for making a search, seizure or an arrest shall not be issued unless someone has stated under oath a probable cause for such, which statement shall describe the place to be searched and the persons or things to be seized.

These requirements protect the citizens against being harassed or bothered by the police unless someone has stated a good cause for doing so and has done so under oath for which he may be prosecuted for perjury if the statement is false.

12.4 5TH AMENDMENT—THE GRAND JURY CLAUSE

The Fifth Amendment contains a number of procedural requirements. One of them guarantees the accused a right to be indicted by
a grand jury in certain cases. It provides that "No person shall be
held to answer for a capital, or otherwise infamous crime, unless on
a presentment or indictment of a Grand Jury, ..." By this clause,
even the authority to formally accuse a person of having committed
a serious crime is taken out of the hands of government and placed
in those of the citizens. It is presumed that a jury will have no special interest in prosecuting a person such as those in government
might have. A person's reputation can be ruined or seriously injured
by being formally accused of having committed a serious crime and
so the power to do this was withheld from the government.

There are exceptions to this rule. As the Fifth Amendment provides, the right to be indicted by a grand jury does not apply "in
cases arising in the land or naval forces, or in the militia, when in
actual service in time of war or public danger."

Generally speaking, "a capital, or otherwise infamous crime" is
one punishable either by death or imprisonment in a state prison or
penitentiary.

12.5 THE DOUBLE JEOPARDY CLAUSE

The Fifth Amendment provides that no person shall "be subject
for the same offence to be twice put in jeopardy of life or limb."

This clause protects a person accused of a crime in two ways:
(1) He cannot be punished twice for the same offense, and (2) He
cannot be tried twice for the same crime whether or not he was
acquitted or convicted in the first trial. Once the accused has been
acquitted by a jury, he is completely free from danger of conviction
of the offense for which he was tried. His case cannot even be
appealed by government to a higher court. The acquittal is the end of
the matter.

If the jury is unable to reach a unanimous verdict in a case and is
discharged by the court, the double jeopardy clause does not pre-
clude a new trial of the same matter.

12.6 THE PRIVILEGE AGAINST SELF-INCRIMINATION

Another procedural restraint contained in the Fifth Amendment provides that no person "shall be compelled in any criminal case to be a witness against himself."

The privilege granted a person to refuse to testify or answer questions regarding a matter for which he might be criminally prosecuted is granted primarily for the purpose of preventing the officers of government from torturing a confession from the accused. This diabolical practice has been, and still is extremely common to governments who are not so restrained.

12.7 THE REQUIREMENT OF DUE PROCESS OF LAW

The last procedural requirement of the Fifth Amendment reads:

> No person shall . . . be deprived of life, liberty, or property, without due process of law.

The term "due process of law" had its origin in the English Common Law, and at the time of the formation of the Constitution had a well-defined meaning. The term can be traced back to the Statutes of Edward III of England for the year 1355. The sentence in which it is contained reads as follows:

> No man of what state or condition he be, shall be put out of his lands or tenements nor taken, nor disinherited, nor put to death, without he be brought to answer by due process of law. (Chapter 3 of 28 Edw. III, 1355)

This statute had its origin in the famous Chapter 29 of the Magna Carta of 1225 in which the king bound himself as follows:

> No free man shall be taken or imprisoned or deprived of his freehold or his liberties or free customs, or outlawed or exiled, or in any manner destroyed, nor shall we come upon him or send against him, except by a legal judgment of his peers or by the law of the land.

Insofar as procedures are concerned then, this "due process of law" clause requires that no person shall be deprived of life, liberty, or property, without a jury trial. To state the matter otherwise, no person shall be punished for a crime without first having been convicted by a jury. There can be no question but that the term, "deprived of life, liberty or property" is referring to punishment under a criminal law. No other meaning can be given to it. For what other reason would government be depriving a person of these possessions? It could take his property for taxes but certainly not his life or liberty. It might also condemn his property for public use but this matter is specifically provided for by the clause which immediately follows which reads: "nor shall private property be taken for public use, without just compensation." The "due process of law" clause then demands that government shall never inflict a punishment without the consent of a jury. We shall treat this matter further in connection with our discussion of the Sixth Amendment.

12.8 6TH AMENDMENT — THE RIGHT TO A JURY TRIAL

The only provision contained in the Sixth Amendment which we shall discuss is the one pertaining to a jury trial. The essential meaning of the other procedural requirements are so clearly stated and easily understood that for our purposes here they need no elaboration. The provision for a jury trial also seems to be so clear that it could not be misunderstood. However, some extremely serious questions have been raised regarding this right which need to be considered.

The first question we will examine is whether or not the protection afforded extends to "all criminal prosecutions" as the amendment clearly states, or only to some of them. The express wording of the provision would seem to place the matter beyond dispute. Further evidence that the Founding Fathers meant to require a jury trial in "all" criminal prosecutions is found in the Fifth Amendment discussed above. We noted that the government is there forbidden to punish any person by depriving him of either life, liberty or property without due process of law and that the term "due process of law" was meant to include a trial by jury.

But this is not the end of the evidence of the meaning intended by this clause. Among the original provisions of the Constitution we find this:

> The trial of all crimes, except in cases of impeachment, shall be by jury. (Art. III, Sec. 2)

Once more we find the word "all" used to describe the criminal prosecutions meant to be covered. The only exception mentioned is that of impeachment and it seems obvious that all other cases were meant to be included. An impeachment trial is in reality not a criminal trial because even though the accused be found guilty, neither his life, liberty nor property can be taken as a punishment. The Constitution provides that: "Judgment in cases of impeachment shall not extend further than to removal from office, and disqualification to hold and enjoy any office of honor, trust, or profit under the United States; but the party convicted shall, nevertheless, be liable and subject to indictment, trial, judgment, and punishment, according to law."

The Supreme Court of the United States has, however, severely abridged the right of citizens to a jury trial. By judicial decision it has eliminated this protection in those very cases where protection against tyranny by government is the most necessary—in cases involving licensing and regulatory laws. In the case of District of Columbia v. Clawans, 300 U.S. 617, (1937), Ethel Clawans was convicted in the District of Columbia police court of engaging, without a license, in the business of a dealer in secondhand property. On arraignment, she demanded a jury trial which was denied. She was convicted by a judge sitting without a jury and fined $300 or, in the alternative, to spend 60 days in jail.

She appealed her conviction to the Court of Appeals which overturned it on the grounds that she had been denied her Constitutional right to a jury trial. The District of Columbia then appealed the case to the Supreme Court which, in a split decision, reversed the Court of Appeals and held that she was not entitled to a jury trial.

The majority contended that since the crime of engaging in a business without a license was, morally speaking, "relatively inoffensive," and since the penalty for violating the licensing statute ($300 fine or 90 days in jail) was not sufficiently "severe," there was no right to a jury trial.

The dissenting justices pointed out that the Constitution provides that even in a civil case where the amount in controversy exceeds

$20, the right to a jury trial is guaranteed. And now here in a criminal case where there is a much greater danger of abuse of government power, the right is refused when the fine is 15 times that amount. This logic is irrefutable, and there was no attempt on the part of the majority to answer it. They simply closed their judicial eyes to the plain meaning of the Constitution.

If additional evidence is needed that the majority denied the people a right which the Founding Fathers meant they should have, it is found by comparing the provisions for a jury trial in the Sixth Amendment with those for a grand jury indictment in the Fifth. The Fifth Amendment states: "No person shall be held to answer for a capital, or otherwise infamous crime unless on a presentment or indictment of a Grand Jury. . . ."

Here the Founding Fathers deliberately limited the right to a grand jury indictment to those cases where the crime charged is "capital" or "infamous." They did not require it where the offense is, relatively speaking, "morally inoffensive," and where the penalty fixed is not "severe." Now had they intended to exempt similar cases from the requirement of a jury trial in the Sixth Amendment, who will deny that they would have done so explicitly? It is contrary to all reason to assume that those wise and careful men who drafted those two provisions meant they were to cover the same crimes. And still, that is essentially what the majority of the Court in the Clowans case has done.

12.9 TRIAL BY JURY—THE BULWARK OF CIVIL AND POLITICAL LIBERTY

The importance of the trial by jury as the guardian of liberty was expressed by the famous Supreme Court Justice, Joseph Story, in these words:

(Trial by Jury) was from the very early times insisted on by our ancestors in the parent country, as the great bulwark of their civil and political liberties, and watched with an unceasing jealousy and solicitude. . . . The great object of a trial by jury in criminal cases is, to guard against a spirit of oppression and tyranny on the part of rulers, and against a spirit of violence and vindictiveness on the part of the people. . . . So long, indeed, as this palladi-

um remains sacred and inviolable, the liberties of a free government cannot wholly fall. (Story, *Commentaries on the Constitution
of the United States*, Sec. 1779)

To appreciate how the right to trial by jury can serve as the bulwark of our liberties, it is necessary to understand the precise role of
a jury in a criminal case. If the provisions of the United States
Constitution are adhered to, the government can convict and punish
no one without the unanimous consent of twelve jurors. This body of
men can stand as an impregnable safeguard against injustice. They
can prevent oppression of any kind. Of course, they can thwart the
conviction of an innocent man who is being prosecuted under a just
law, but they can also prevent the punishment of one of their fellow
citizens who is guilty of having violated a law which is unjust.

It is often stated that it is the function of a jury to determine the
facts while it is the exclusive province of the judge to determine
matters of law. In other words, it is said that the jury cannot consider
the nature of the law they are upholding. But suppose a defendant is
being prosecuted under a law which provides for punishing innocent
behavior. Suppose that the law denies those unalienable rights guaranteed under the Constitution. Is the jury obligated to blindly follow
the law and return a verdict of guilty when they know that the
accused has neither intended evil nor committed harm? Are they to
act as accomplices with the other branches of government in uphold-
ing a law which destroys the defendant's rights as well as their own?

It is in this very type of a case that the jury can truly serve as the
bulwark of our liberties. They have the unquestionable right to find
the accused innocent of a crime and no one can challenge their
authority to do so. It is their function to prevent injustice and more
especially when it comes before them in the form of an unjust law.
Let us quote several recognized Constitutional authorities on this
matter.

One of the clearest expositions is by the celebrated authority on
the Constitution and State Supreme Justice, Thomas Cooley, who
wrote:

> (I)t is . . . an important question whether it is the duty of the
> jury to receive and act upon the law as given to them by the judge,
> or whether, on the other hand, his opinion is advisory only, so that
> they are at liberty either to follow it if it accords with their own
> convictions, or to disregard it if it does not.

In one class of cases, that is to say, in criminal prosecutions for libels, it is now very generally provided by the State constitutions, or by statute, that the jury shall determine the law and the facts. . . . In all other cases the jury have the clear legal right to return a simple verdict of guilty or not guilty, and in so doing they necessarily decide such questions of law as well as of fact as are involved in the general question of guilt. If their view conduce to an acquittal, their verdict to that effect can neither be reviewed nor set aside.

In such a case, therefore, it appears that they pass upon the law as well as the facts, and that their finding is conclusive. (Cooley, *Constitutional Limitations*, pp. 394-5)

James Wilson, who signed the Declaration of Independence as well as the Constitution, and who served as one of the original justices on the United States Supreme Court, made this observation about the right of juries to decide questions of law:

Upon all general issues, the jury find not the fact of every case by itself, leaving the law to the court; but find for the plaintiff or defendant upon the issue tried, wherein they resolve both law and fact complicatedly, and not the fact by itself. . . . Suppose that, after all the precautions taken to avoid it, a difference of sentiment takes place between the judges and the jury, with regard to a point of law: suppose the law and the fact to be so closely interwoven, that a determination of one must, at the same time, embrace the determination of the other: suppose a matter of this description to come in trial before a jury—what must the jury do?—The jury must do their duty, and their whole duty; they must decide the law as well as the fact.

This doctrine is peculiarly applicable to criminal cases; and from them, indeed, derives its peculiar importance. When a person is tried for a crime, the accusation charges against him, not only the particular fact which he has committed, but also the motive, to which it owed its origin, and from which it receives its complexion. The first is neither the only, nor the principal object of examination and discussion. On the second, depends the innocence or criminality of the action. The verdict must decide not only upon the first, but also, and principally, upon the second: for the verdict must be coextensive and commensurate with the charge. (*Works*, pp. 540, 541)

The final authority we quote on this issue is Thomas Jefferson:

. . .(M)agistrates have jurisdiction both criminal and civil. If the question before them be a question of law only, they decide on it themselves; but if it be a fact, or of fact and law combined, it must be referred to a jury. In the latter case, of a combination of law and fact, it is usual for the jurors to decide the fact, and to refer the law arising on it to the decision of the judges. But this division of the subject lies with their discretion only. And if the question relate to any point of public liberty, or if it be one of those in which the judges may be suspected of bias, the jury undertake to decide both law and fact. (*Works*, Vol IV, p. 37)

But even though it were assumed that juries are restricted to determining issues of fact only, the most important fact they must determine in every criminal case is that of a criminal intent. Without this there can be no crime. This is so even though the accused has caused harm. Even though he has caused a death, the jury must still decide whether it was accidental, committed in the act of self-defense or perhaps even in an attempt to help the victim. Unless they determine that the accused had a criminal intent, it is their duty to see that he is not punished.

And this should be their function in every case they are called upon to decide. Unless the prosecution proves to them beyond a reasonable doubt that the defendant had an evil intent in committing the act with which he is charged, it is not only their right but their duty to refuse to convict. Therefore, if a law provides for inflicting punishment without proof of an evil intent, it is their obligation as just men and as guardians of the liberties which such laws would destroy, to refuse to enforce such laws.

On questions of good and evil or right and wrong, juries are the sole arbiters. No judge and no legislator should be allowed to usurp this function nor prevent them from performing it. They are the body whose exclusive right it is in cases which come before them, to determine whether a moral law has been violated. This is the question of fact which they pass upon when they decide the existence or non-existence of a criminal intent. The enforcement of every freedom-destroying, licensing or regulatory law could be prevented by juries if they were made aware of their proper function and were allowed to perform it.

Other Quotes Regarding Jury Trial

I consider trial by jury to be the only anchor ever yet imagined by man, by which a government can be held to the principles of the constitution. (Thomas Jefferson, *Works* 3:71)

But there is another check, . . . superior to all the parchment checks that can be invented . . . the people themselves have it in their power effectually to resist usurpation, without being driven to an appeal to arms. An act of usurpation is not obligatory; it is not law; and any man may be justified in his resistance. Let him be considered as a criminal by the general government, yet only his own fellow-citizens can convict him; they are his jury, and if they pronounce him innocent, not all the powers of Congress can hurt him; and innocent they certainly will pronounce him, if the supposed law he resisted was an act of usurpation. -Mr. Parsons, delegate to the Massachusetts convention as he argued for the adoption of the Federal Constitution. (*Elliot's Debates*, v. 2, p. 94)

Trial by jury, as applied to the repression of crime, appears to me an eminently republican element in the government . . . (for) it always preserves its republican character in that it places the real direction of society in the hands of the governed, . . . and not in that of the government. . . .

The true sanction of political laws is to be found in penal legislation; . . . He who punishes the criminal is therefore the real master of society. Now, the institution of the jury raises the people itself. . . to the bench of judges. The institution of the jury consequently invests the people. . . with the direction of society. . . .

It teaches men to practice equity; every man learns to judge his neighbor as he would himself be judged. . . . The jury teaches every man not to recoil before the responsibility of his own actions and impresses him with that manly confidence without which no political virtue can exist. . . .

The jury contributes powerfully to form the judgment and to increase the natural intelligence of a people; and this, in my opinion, is its greatest advantage. It may be regarded as a gratuitous public school, ever open, in which every juror learns his rights, enters into daily communication with the most learned and enlightened members of the upper classes, and becomes practically acquainted with the laws. . . I think that the practical intelligence and political good sense of the Americans are mainly attributable to the long use that they have made of the jury. . . .

Thus the jury, which is the most energetic means of making the people rule, is also the most efficacious means of teaching it how to rule well. (Alexis de Tocqueville, *Democracy in America*)

(T)he trial by jury ever has been, and I trust ever will be, looked upon as the glory of the English law. And if it has so great an advantage over others in regulating civil property, how much must that advantage be heightened, when it is applied to criminal cases . . . it is the most transcendent privilege which any subject can enjoy, or wish for, that he cannot be affected either in his property, his liberty, or his person, but by the unanimous consent of twelve of his neighbors and equals. . . . It is therefore, upon the whole, a duty which every man owes to his country, his friends, his posterity, and himself, to maintain to the utmost of his power this valuable constitution (jury trial) in all its rights; to restore it to its ancient dignity, if at all impaired. . . or otherwise deviated from. . .; to amend it wherever it is defective; and, above all, to guard with the most jealous circumspection against the introduction of new and arbitrary methods of trial, which, under a variety of plausible pretenses, may in time imperceptibly undermine this best preservative of English liberty. (Blackstone, *Commentaries On The Laws Of England*, v. 3, pp 379, 381)

The Founding Fathers well understood human nature and its tendency to exercise unrighteous dominion when given authority (D&C 121:39-40). A Constitution was therefore designed to limit government to certain enumerated functions, beyond which was tyranny.

President Ezra Taft Benson,
(The Constitution: A Heavenly Banner, p.21)

CHAPTER XIII

ADMINISTRATIVE LAWS AND THE LAW OF STEWARDSHIPS

13.1 THE IMPORTANCE OF ADMINISTRATIVE LAWS

The term "administrative laws" is used herein to mean all of those rules, regulations, decrees and enactments of administrative agencies, legislatures and others by which governments regulate and control the economic and social affairs of the community. They include licensing laws by which the state dictates who may and who may not enter into businesses, trades and professions; zoning laws through which it specifies the uses of land and the structure of buildings; welfare state laws under which it collects and redistributes hundreds of billions of dollars in wealth each year; regulatory laws which give it supervision and control over employers and employees, mining and manufacturing, finance and banking, transportation and communication, forestry and agriculture along with a host of other activities.

For many years following the formation of this nation, administrative laws were declared by the courts to be unconstitutional. Not only were they regarded as an infringement of the right of private property and an interference with freedom of contract, but law-making by administrative agencies was considered a violation of the constitutional principle of separation of powers which decrees that only legislatures have been authorized by the people to make laws. The federal Constitution, for example provides in Article I, Section I that:

> All legislative powers herein granted shall be vested in a Congress of the United States, which shall consist of a Senate and House of Representatives.

That attitude has completely changed in recent years and today the Supreme Court of the United States has in effect taken the position that both Federal and state governments have unlimited power to regulate the people in any manner they choose. With respect to regulation by state governments the Supreme Court has declared:

> The day is gone when this Court uses the Due Process Clause . . .to strike down state laws, regulatory of business and industrial conditions, because they may be unwise, improvident, or out of harmony with a particular school of thought. (Williamson v. Lee Optical of Oklahoma, 348 U.S. 483, 488 [1955])

And concerning regulation by the Federal Government the Supreme Court has stated:

> It is not for this court to reweigh the relevant factors and, perchance, substitute its notion of expediency and fairness for that of Congress. . . . This court is not a tribunal for relief from the crudities and inequities of complicated experimental economic legislation. (Secretary of Agriculture v. Central Roig Refining Co., 338 U.S. 604, 618 [1949])

The growth of administrative agencies in recent years and the increase in their powers has been nothing short of phenomenal. This growth continues apace as both legislatures and agencies continue to pour forth a veritable flood of new laws, rules and regulations each year. To appreciate the extent of this growth one need only compare the budgets of governments today with those of say 50 years ago. While the effects of inflation serve to distort the picture, the change is still astounding. For example the total annual federal budget in the early 1930's was somewhere between four and five billion dollars. Today it is around 500 billion most of which goes to finance administrative law programs. It is plainly apparent that the impact of such laws on society today are greater than that of all other areas of the law combined.

13.2 ADMINISTRATIVE LAWS NEITHER PUNISH CRIME NOR PROTECT RIGHTS

There is extensive disagreement over the utility of administrative laws and the extent to which they should be adopted. On the one hand are the believers in socialism who favor complete government ownership and control of the instrumentalities for producing and distributing goods and services. At the other extreme are those who advocate no government controls whatsoever and would confine state ownership of property to that amount necessary to enable it to punish crime, settle disputes and provide for the national defense.

The great majority of the people, seem to take a position somewhere between these two views. However, there is hardly any agreement regarding exactly what that position should be. Very few seem able to justify in their own minds why they favor laws of this nature at all nor can they explain why there should not be more or less than the ones they do favor.

It is suspected that at least a part of this confusion and disagreement arises from a belief on the part of some that administrative laws are necessary to punish crime or to enforce individual rights or both. A clear understanding of these laws and of the scope of the criminal, tort and contract laws will reveal that administrative laws have neither of these consequences. Let us observe why.

If, while doing an act which is punishable under administrative law, a person commits a crime or does something evil, he is punishable under the criminal laws. They are sufficiently broad that they cover every type of conduct which is considered evil and punishable. Administrative laws therefore can add nothing to them which would help achieve this purpose. Similarly if a person while doing an act forbidden by an administrative law causes harm either intentionally or negligently, the injured party may recover under either the tort or contract laws. These together with the laws of domestic relations provide restitution for every type of injury considered compensable. From this it is apparent that the adoption of administrative laws to protect rights are as unnecessary as when adopted to punish crime.

13.3 *ARE ADMINISTRATIVE LAWS NECESSARY TO PROTECT THE RIGHTS OF MINORITIES?*

Even though the laws of torts, contracts and domestic relations adequately protect the rights of individuals, there is prevalent today a belief that administrative laws are necessary to protect the rights of certain minority groups, who, it is contended, are being discriminated against by the majority. To correct this alleged injustice, anti-discrimination laws and equal rights amendments to constitutions are being widely advocated. The main complaint of those who sponsor these movements seems to be that employers are not allocating jobs and setting wage rates on the basis of race or sex, but are using some other criteria such as the ability of the employee to perform the task. The legislation proposed would deny employers their freedom to choose employees and set their wages according to competency, experience, training or integrity if such choices happened to result in the hiring of a smaller or larger number of the minority groups than government dictates is proper. In other words such laws would give government employees the power to establish hiring policies and wage scales and take it away from the business owner. These laws would also provide for making the employer a criminal and punishing him with a jail sentence or a fine if he selected his employees or paid wages other than as those in government direct.

Are such laws just? Do they protect rights or destroy them? It is obvious that they restrict the employer's right to select his own employees and pay them according to merit. But what is the effect upon the rights of the workers whether they belong to the majority group or the minority? Perhaps an illustration will help us visualize the effect more clearly.

Let us assume that an employer has been prosecuted under an antidiscrimination law and found guilty of having hired a disproportionate number of white males in his factory. In addition to being fined or sent to jail, let us also assume that the court or administrative agency which tried the case ordered him to discharge some of his employees so that he can make room for more females or members of a minority race. Will someone explain the justice of this order to the discharged employees who, when they ask for an explanation are told that it is not because they have failed to do their work properly but because they are white and male? Can someone convince a group of white males seeking work at this factory that they are not being discriminated against on the basis of both race and sex?

Anti-discrimination laws do not prevent discrimination, they compel discrimination. They do not protect the rights of either the employer or the employee but on the other hand destroy the rights of both by transferring control over jobs to government. There is no such thing as group justice. There is only individual justice. Rights and duties, punishments and rewards can be dispensed only according to individual merit and not at all according to membership or non-membership in any particular group. The idea of group justice is a mirage or an illusion because justice cannot be administered to groups. It is nothing but a clumsy fraud designed to increase the power of government at the expense of human rights.

Is it not apparent that it is impossible for government to "create" rights in one person or group without destroying the rights of another? When it gives special privileges to one it must deny them to someone else. This result is unavoidable because when government creates a "right" in one person, it must at the same time create a "duty" in someone else. A right is without any substance unless there is someone against whom it can be enforced. But the one against whom it is enforced is saddled with a duty he did not formerly owe. The law compels him to do something or refrain from doing something and punishes him if he refuses. But you cannot compel a person against his will, nor can you punish him, without taking from him either his right to life, his right to liberty or his right to property. Thus the law has destroyed his rights in attempting to create "rights" in someone else. Under the anti-discrimination law described above, both the rights of the employer and also the rights of the majority were destroyed by attempting to create "rights" in the minority.

13.4 ADMINISTRATIVE LAWS VIOLATE THE RULES OF PRIVATE MORALITY

We have undertaken to demonstrate that administrative laws do not have the effect of either punishing crime nor protecting rights. What then is their effect? Like all other laws, they use force and the threat of force on humans. But force cannot be used on humans without moral consequences and therefore to appraise the total effect of these laws we must examine these moral consequences along with any others. For this purpose let us divide administrative laws into these three categories:

(1) Licensing laws
(2) Regulatory laws, and
(3) Welfare state laws

We will then test the moral consequences of each by observing the effect of doing outside of government that which such laws direct be done within its framework.

(1) Licensing Laws.

Assume that some non-governmental group engaged in a particular trade or profession undertook to enforce their own licensing law by threatening to punish anyone who competed against them without first complying with a list of costly and time-consuming requirements similar to those demanded by government-enforced licensing laws. Assume further that they actually do physically punish those who compete without their prior permission.

This crude attempt to establish a monopoly would be branded as racketeering, gangsterism and extortion (And it should be.). To forcibly restrain competition and punish a person for no other reason than that he had tried to make an honest living shocks the conscience. Every moral person will agree that this group has committed an evil act for which they should be punished under the criminal laws. But such a use of force should be equally offensive when government employs it because the consequences are much the same. In both instances a monopoly is created, innocent people are threatened and punished and the public is denied their freedom to patronize whom they please.

(2) Regulatory Laws.

To illustrate the effect of regulatory laws let us assume that some private group interested in bettering the working conditions of employees were to use violence and the threat thereof to compel employers to raise wages. Let us also assume that, not being satisfied with the working conditions in factories and being critical of how the owners are operating their businesses otherwise, they use violence to impose their own ideas of management. To take over and regulate the affairs of private owners in this manner is not only a denial of the right of private property but is a form of slavery condemned by the laws of every state. But is there any essential difference when government does the same thing?

(3) Welfare-State Laws.

To test the morality of welfare-state laws we will assume that some private charitable organization such as the Red Cross, the Salvation Army or some church were to undertake to help the poor by using violence to collect all of the contributions they considered necessary for this purpose. Even though their motives may be noble, this would be characterized and punished as robbery or plunder. Like all other administrative laws, welfare-state laws violate the same rules of moral behavior which governments are organized to force the people to obey.

13.5 WHY DO PEOPLE FAVOR ADMINISTRATIVE LAWS?

If, as has been concluded, the effect of enforcing administrative laws is to commit crime rather than punish it, to destroy rights rather than to protect them and to violate the rules of private morality rather than enforce them, why are they favored by so many people?

Unquestionably the failure to understand the nature and effect of these laws would explain why some support them who otherwise would not. A second reason closely related to the first is the assumption made by many that: ANYTHING WHICH IS LEGAL IS MORAL, and IF IT IS THE LAW IT IS RIGHT. While it is most desirable that people respect and obey the laws insofar as they are worthy of respect, if we close our eyes to the possibility that laws can be, and ofttimes are, evil and that men in government are as likely to be as wicked and subject to error as others, we suffer from one of the most dangerous delusions possible.

But aside from the fact that many accept administrative laws through blindness or folly, there are others who favor them for reasons which are plainly dishonest. It is obvious why members of a licensed profession, trade or business would, for selfish reasons favor government-enforced monopolies in their field. When competition is thus restricted and the public is compelled to patronize them or go without, they can obtain more business and charge higher prices than would be possible in a free market.

It is equally apparent why indolent and covetous people on welfare would vote for laws which compel others to support them and why greedy employees would support laws forcing their employer to pay higher wages and provide more benefits than he would do if the government allowed him his freedom to contract.

With respect to regulatory laws, no one benefits financially from these except possibly the bureaucrats who administer them and who would lose their jobs if they were repealed. In fact such laws not only deny the people freedom to conduct their own business and private affairs, but increase the tax burden enormously. We must therefore find reasons for the support of these laws other than in greed and covetousness. A partial explanation might be the almost universal disposition to abuse authority. When the mass of the people have the reins of government placed in their hands and nothing to restrain them but their consciences, they are apt to yield to that very prevalent weakness of the human race to exercise unrighteous dominion.

But there is still another explanation for the general acceptance of administrative laws which, while it might include and be an outgrowth of all of the factors mentioned above, is so important that it deserves special attention. This is the deeply imbedded and widespread fear of the free enterprise system on the one hand and an equally widespread and deeply held faith in, and worship of, the state on the other. The belief seems to be quite general that if private enterprise were left free, the wealth of the nation would soon be concentrated in a few hands to the injury of the masses. There is a fear amounting almost to a phobia, that without government intervention, giant monopolies would arise and use their economic power to enslave the people. It is also assumed by many that given economic freedom, the rich would get richer and the poor would get poorer with the latter eventually starving. To prevent such catastrophes the people turn to the state and invest it with power to control the capitalists and take from the haves and give to the have nots. Are these fears and these assumptions justified?

13.6 WOULD THE OWNERSHIP BY A PRIVATE INDIVIDUAL OF A LARGE SHARE OF THE LAND BE INJURIOUS TO THE PUBLIC?

Inasmuch as the greatest fear of an unregulated free enterprise system seems to be that it would permit a small group of greedy and heartless capitalists to acquire ownership and control over certain essential goods and products, let us postulate a situation wherein one person does acquire a large share of some essential form of wealth. Then let us observe whether he could use his monopolistic powers to injure society.

It is probably true that the only type of property without which men cannot survive is land. If one has ownership and control over land, he may raise plants and animals for food and clothing. He can mine ores for his machinery, extract gas, coal and oil for his energy needs, harvest trees for his buildings and provide himself with all other things necessary to sustain and enjoy life. He has a spot on earth whereon he may construct a home and rear a family, build a church and worship God, or erect a school and gain an education. In short, the ownership of land by the people makes them independent and enables them to achieve their purposes regardless of how much of the other forms of wealth are owned by the few.

On the other hand if the people are denied ownership of land and cannot obtain what it produces, they are indeed at the mercy of those who do own it. This being so, let us assume that a single individual is the owner of a large portion of the land area in the nation. To give our illustration realism and to get the reader deeply involved in the problem, let us assume that all of the land in the United States now owned by government except that needed by it for national defense and the exercise of its police powers, were immediately transferred to you. Reputedly this will amount to approximately one-third of the total land mass. Let us also assume that even though you are not a greedy, heartless capitalist, nonetheless you will attempt to strengthen your monopolistic position by acquiring more land and will also try to make huge profits at public expense. In other words let us assume that you set out deliberately to do that which the unregulated capitalist is generally charged with doing—abuse economic power to harm the people.

13.7 THE PROBLEMS OF A LARGE LAND-OWNER

Probably the first problem which will come to your attention as a large land owner is that of taxes. Whereas the property did not help bear the land tax burden while owned by government, to the great delight and benefit of other taxpayers, you must now share their load. Your share may amount to billions of dollars annually. You must immediately face the problem of raising that money by the end of the tax year and each year thereafter.

Another financial problem of perhaps even greater importance is that of managing your vast domain. While you might be able to supervise a few hundred acres, you must hire literally thousands of competent employees to oversee the other millions of acres and protect them against squatters, campers, hunters and other acquisitive souls. You must be prepared to fight fires and diseases in your forests; maintain dams, canals, fences and bridges; establish offices, communication and transportation facilities and do a thousand other things which the ownership of this much land will surely require. The tax burden may seem small indeed when compared with the payroll and other expenses you must meet.

The sheer enormity of your problems may tempt you to sell much of what you own but remember that you are a monopolist at heart and your desire is to increase, not decrease your holdings. And even though you did sell some of your land to private owners, they would face the same problems you are contending with. You might ask yourself how government, the previous owner was able to handle an acreage of this size. How did it meet all of these ownership expenses? And then you recall that in the first place it did not pay taxes and in the second place it could use its taxing powers to compel the public to foot its bills.

13.8 THE PROBLEMS OF THE OWNERS OF LARGE BUSINESSES

It occurs to you that there is one and only one way you can meet all of your ownership expenses and retain your lands and that is by doing what government did—get the public to pay the bill. Only your problem is not so simple. While it could compel the people to give it money, you must induce them to do so voluntarily by offering them goods and services which they are both willing and able to purchase. In other words you must make your land productive. You must put it to beneficial use.

You consider the possibilities. Certainly some of it can be farmed. There should be much mineral wealth under it along with huge deposits of coal, gas and oil. The millions of acres of timber land will enable you to enter the lumber business in a big way. The very extensive grazing lands will allow you to go into sheep and cattle ranching and to lease land to private ranchers. There are enormous opportunities to establish recreation facilities and resorts and make profits in that area. You can even become a giant land developer, a home builder and the owner of great shopping centers. The possibilities seem almost endless.

But if you thought you had money problems as a land owner, contemplate the investment capital which will be required to enter even one of the above business ventures not to speak of all of the others. Nonetheless you realize that no matter how much money is required to enter business you must raise it. If you do not there will be no income. And if there is no income it will be impossible to pay your taxes and defray the other enormous expenses which must be borne.

13.9 THE IRON LAW OF STEWARDSHIPS

As you contemplate which of the many business opportunities you should select and ponder the amount of capital and management ability which will be required for each, you decide that you must proceed with caution and commence only one business at a time. Just one of those huge enterprises will tax your skill, ingenuity, and management ability to the utmost.

It is at this point in your deliberations that you come face to face with the iron law of stewardships. This law decrees that the private owner of property must use it or lose it. He must produce or perish. He must utilize it for the benefit of the public or surrender it to someone who will. If he lets it lie idle, it will be a burden rather than a benefit. It will not even bear its ownership expenses, much less produce a profit.

There is no escape from this implacable law. It imposes its demands upon every private owner regardless of the size of his holdings. The large landowner as well as the small must either put his property to productive use, dispose of it, or make enough on other operations to cover the loss. No smart businessman will retain idle assets for any length of time. He cannot afford to. They will destroy him if he attempts it. And so you have no alternative other than to immediately put all of your land to productive use or suffer the losses which this unused property always causes.

You ask yourself how government was able to survive the

demands of this inexorable law. Upon reflection you see that the law of stewardships does not apply to government. The state does not need to put a single acre to productive use. It does not need to produce one dollar of income or satisfy one customer. It can use its taxing power to finance its losses.

13.10 CAN THE WEALTHY CAPITALIST USE HIS ECONOMIC POWER TO INJURE THE PUBLIC?

Let us assume that in spite of the tremendous problems which had to be faced and overcome, you were able to establish profitable business operations on all of your land which was susceptible of use.

The reader will have recognized long before now how utterly preposterous it is to assume that he or any other person could manage and control a business operation of this magnitude. The severe limitations each of us have with respect to time, energy and ability makes it inconceivable that this much wealth could be efficiently controlled even by several hundred individuals much less one. But because huge concentrations of wealth in a few hands is what people seem to fear, we have assumed it is possible.

It is so often forgotten by those who fear the free enterprise system that the severe physical limitations each of us has requires that when we accomplish tasks of any magnitude we must employ the services of others. To do this we must pay them what they think they are worth. As soon as they get to that point where they believe they can do better by acquiring their own business or by taking a job with another employer, they will leave. And this is constantly happening.

Every employer finds himself continually in danger of being crushed between the conflicting demands of the employees on the one hand and the buying public on the other. Employees are constantly demanding more pay for the same or less work which forces a raise in selling prices to cover the increased labor costs. On the other hand consumers demand more and better products for less money which compels a lowering of the selling price. Of course the employee and the consumer are very often the same person but whether he is making demands in the one capacity or the other, you must satisfy him or lose him. The overwhelming majority of enterprisers who enter business go under within a relatively short period because they are unable to do this.

But you with your millions of employees and consumers are a very remarkable person. You have been able to attract employees away from other employers with your high wages and at the same time you have been able to win over his consumers with your low selling prices and high quality products. You now have a stranglehold on the production of many of the necessities of life. Can you use your monopoly position to harm the public? Can you raise prices to great heights, gouge the public and make exorbitant profits? You decide to try it. What happens?

According to economic law, with every raise in prices there will be a corresponding decrease in sales. Some of the lower income people you had been serving will be compelled to do without. Others will consume less.

The money formerly being spent on your products and services will not go as far and therefore there will not be as much consumed. But if the public cannot or will not buy, you cannot sell. And if you cannot sell you cannot produce. And if you cannot produce, some of your production facilities must lie idle. And when this occurs they become a burden to you rather than a benefit. You must dispose of them or bear the losses which idle facilities always cause. If you sell them, then the buyer will start using them to serve the public and you will lose your monopoly. Thus your attempt to gouge the public is self-defeating. It cannot be accomplished. The iron law of stewardships operates to prevent you from profiting from your own greed.

And let us observe that the law of stewardships which compels the owner of land to put it to productive use or lose it, operates with even greater rigor with respect to the ownership of depreciable property or property which may become obsolete. The owner of such facilities not only must pay taxes and bear the other ownership expenses incurred by land owners, but he must face the fact that if he allows it to lie idle, the natural agents of decay or the invention of better facilities will likely render it valueless after a relatively short period of time.

13.11 LARGE PROFITS—A CURSE OR A BLESSING?

Let us assume that in spite of the operation of the law of stewardships you are still able to maintain your prices at a level high enough to produce what might be termed exorbitant profits. Would this harm the public?

Before attempting to answer this question, let us note that there are three main uses to which you can put your profits: (1) Consume them by purchasing consumer goods, (2) Bury them, or (3) Reinvest them. Since, as a wealthy person you are already consuming all that you desire, you will not use profits for this purpose. As a shrewd businessman you realize that only a fool will bury his profits. Like other kinds of property, profits must be put to productive use if they are going to benefit you. This means that your profits will be reinvested. This means that you increase your production facilities so that you may produce more goods and services.

Who is benefitted by this action? The consumers of course. The more you produce, the more you must sell. The more you must sell, the lower must be your prices. The lower your prices the greater the number of people in the lower and middle income brackets who will enjoy your products and services. If you once made large profits by charging your customers high prices, you must now benefit those customers by charging them lower prices which the reinvestment of profits and increased production will bring about.

13.12 ADMINISTRATIVE LAWS INTERFERE WITH THE OPERATION OF THE LAW OF STEWARDSHIPS

The same reasons which compel the conclusion that private ownership is to be preferred over ownership by the state also compel the conclusion that private management is to be preferred over state management. To the exact extent that government controls a business the owner does not and to this same extent he is prevented from serving the public as he would do in the absence of such control. As we have observed, the great object of the private business owner is to satisfy the public on their own terms. It is to produce goods and services which the people want and can afford. It is to make profits which can be reinvested to produce even more for public consumption.

Administrative laws interfere with the attainment of this purpose and the operation of the law of stewardships is defeated to this same extent. Not only does this interference restrict production, but it increases the prices the public must pay by: (1) Increasing productions costs and (2) Raising taxes. Both of these costs must be passed on to the buying public in the form of higher prices.

13.13 PEOPLE SHOULD FEAR GOVERNMENT OWNERSHIP AND TRUST PRIVATE OWNERSHIP

The only monopoly people need fear is that which is created by force, and the worst of all monopolies is that which is created or maintained by the force of government. That is the one organization which can use its ownership and control of property to make slaves and paupers of the people. That is the one owner which can sit on the nations wealth and allow it to lie idle.

In the socialist nation where the state owns the land, the people are literally in bondage to their own government. It was only to be expected that the first of the Ten points of the Communist Manifesto which Marx and Engels suggested be adopted by governments to bring about socialism was:

> Abolition of property in land and application of all rents of land to public purposes.

But the abolition of property in land can be achieved not only by outright confiscation by government but also by the adoption of a set of administrative laws which transfer control over land to government. Such laws can, if numerous enough, prevent the operation of the law of stewardships as effectively as state ownership.

On the other hand where the free enterprise system is allowed to operate without regulation, the rich do not get richer while the poor get poorer, but they all become rich together. The rich can neither gain nor retain large amounts of wealth except by serving the public and creating numerous jobs. The same inexorable law of stewardships which prevents a person from owning extensive wealth without making it productive, thus sharing it with many consumers, prevents him from making it productive without sharing it with many employees. And in each case he must share with them on their own terms.

It is strange indeed that the private capitalist which the people should trust, they stand in fear of, while the government owner and regulator which they should fear, they place their trust in.

In Summary

Some people think it is a dreadful sin for a people like the Latter-day Saints to claim that they believe with all their souls that the world would be better if only the laws of God could be enforced in this world. Some people think that if God's authority, if God's law, if God's righteousness were to be enforced among the children of men that would debase and degrade them. We do not look at this in this way. We believe that God's will is to exalt men; that the liberty that comes through obedience to the Gospel of Jesus Christ is the greatest measure of liberty that can come to man. There is no liberty that men enjoy or pretend to enjoy in the world that is not founded in the will and in the law of God and that does not have truth for its underlying principle and foundation. It is error that makes bondsmen. It is untruth that degrades mankind. It is error and the lack of knowledge of God's laws and God's will that leaves men in the world on a par with the brute creation; for they have no higher instincts, no higher principle, no higher incentive, no higher aspiration than the brute world if they have not some inspiration that comes from a higher source than man himself.

I believe in God's law, I believe that it is His right to rule in the world. I believe that no man has or should have any valid objection in his mind to the government of God, and the rule of Jesus Christ, in the earth. (President Joseph F. Smith, *Conf. Rep.* Apr. 1904, pp. 3-4)

The Kingdom of God, is the government of God, on the earth, or in the heavens. . . . If the world be the Lord's, He certainly has a right to govern it; for we have already stated that man has no authority, except that which is delegated to him. He possesses a moral power to govern his actions, subject at all times to the law of God; but never is authorized to act independent of God; much less is he authorized to rule on the earth without the call and direction of the Lord; therefore, any rule or dominion over the earth, which is not given by the Lord is surreptitiously obtained, and never will be sanctioned by him. (President John Taylor, *Government of God*, pp. 1, 58)

The kingdom of God is an order of government established by divine authority. It is the only legal government that can exist in any part of the universe. All other governments are illegal and unauthorized. God having made all beings and worlds, has the supreme right to govern them by his own laws, and by officers of his own appointment. Any people attempting to govern them-selves by laws of their own making, and by officers of their own appointment, are in direct rebellion against the kingdom of God. (President Joseph Fielding Smith, *Seek Ye Earnestly*, p. 22, Deseret Book, 1970)

Next to being one in worshipping God, there is nothing in this world upon which this Church should be more united than uphold-ing and defending the Constitution of the United States. (David O. McKay, *Statements on Communism and The Constitution*, Deseret Book Co., 1966, p. 6)

Brother Brigham took the stand, and he took the Bible, and laid it down; he took the Book of Mormon, and laid it down; and he took the Book of Doctrine and Covenants, and laid it down before him, and he said: "There is the written word of God to us, concerning the work of God from the beginning of the world, almost, to our day." "And now," said he, "when compared with the living oracles those books are nothing to me; those books do not convey the word of God direct to us now, as do the words of a Prophet or a man bearing the Holy Priesthood in our day and generation. I would rather have the living oracles than all the writing in the books." That was the course he pursued. When he was through, Brother Joseph said to the congregation: "Brother Brigham has told you the word of the Lord, and he has told you the truth.

(President Wilford Woodruff, CR-10/97:18-9)

UNITY

One of Daddy's concerns was that those who felt concern about this principle of agency sometimes allow that concern to cause them to break the law, thinking that would show their willingness to follow the prophet. Others, upon learning about the principle of agency, would become angry with the Lord, His prophet, His local leaders, because so little is being done or said about it in His Church. Their concern for having the principle of agency hammered into others RIGHT NOW is exceeded only by their ignorance of the Lord's plan of allowing men agency to reject Him and His prophet. Possibly He feels many would reject His prophet, even if it was hammered, and hence they will be under less condemnation for rejecting less exposure to the opportunity to believe. Suppose He has other reasons our minds haven't conceived of. If 1/3 part of us rejected Christ and agency in the pre-existence, and in coming to the earth all but our Savior brought with us weaknesses and faults which might again lead us to fall away from Christ, who are we to steady the Ark? God and His prophet see that we each get exactly what we deserve, past, present and future *(Alma 29:1-8)*. Absolutely nothing happens to us, save that which we deserve, and whether we see it as best for us or not, it is. All is designed to take us back, if we will but once again follow Christ. It may take faith, but nothing else has changed.

All that we do is for our Father in Heaven, our Savior, the Holy Ghost and the leaders Christ chose to organize and lead us. We are fortunate to have this knowledge. We were led by such leaders in the pre-existence, and we are once again here on earth. Christ leads us, and we have no more right to "improve" on His decisions here, than we did there. Satan's sin of pride led him to be angry, to refuse counsel, to refuse to follow his leader. Pride and its resulting anger will reap another harvest here, of those who refuse to be loyal to Christ and His prophet.

Over the years, President Benson has given many copies of Daddy's books to many people, always encouraging them to read them. President Benson was a constant source of encouragement to him.

Daddy received a lot of calls and letters from people who love President Benson, who are concerned about our freedom, and wanted to know what they should do. Below is a copy of a letter he sent to one such person, five months before he (Daddy) died on July 16, 1992.

I am in receipt of your recent letter regarding my book, *The Great and Abominable Church of the Devil* and I do hope I can help you solve the problems you face. Since as you say in your letter, you already believed the things written in the book before you read it, the philosophy expressed therein did not cause a turmoil in your own mind. However as I understand it, by voicing those beliefs, you have encountered some opposition from others.

It probably will not surprise you to learn that the difficulties you are experiencing are quite common among politically conservative Church members. Perhaps some of the discourses delivered by our prophets will help explain why.

In the April, 1966 general conference of the Church, President David O. McKay who was then the prophet, issued a statement entitled: "Statement concerning the position of The Church of Jesus Christ of Latter-day Saints on Communism." You probably are quite familiar with that pronouncement. At the time it was issued, I was teaching at the Brigham Young University and discovered to my consternation that the statement caused considerable contention among those I associated with.

In the October, 1967 general conference, President McKay, seeming to sense the discord, delivered another address entitled, "A Plea for Unity." In that talk he again condemned communism and charged that those subscribing to its philosophy were causing contention both in this nation and others. He asked that members who were unable to solve their problems on a local level, to appeal to the brethren in Salt Lake who would give the needed help.

President McKay waited another eighteen months and then in the April, 1969 general conference, he repeated some of the things he had said against communism three years earlier, but suggested that those fighting communism should not do so in such a way as to cause contention. It is my suggestion to you that you obtain these three addresses by President McKay, study them carefully and prayerfully, and then follow his advice.

You apparently have become aware that it is virtually impossible to discuss either communism, socialism or welfare statism in Church meetings without causing contention. For this reason we do not now hear much from the pulpit on these subjects as was formerly the case. This does not mean however that we should not study and take a stand on these matters as President McKay advised in 1966 when he said:

We therefore commend and encourage every person and every group who is sincerely seeking to study constitutional principles and awaken a sleeping and apathetic people to the alarming conditions that are. . . .

We should still follow that advice, provided we do so without causing discord. As you are doubtless aware, our living prophet has perhaps been more vigorously outspoken on these matters than anyone and he has never indicated that he has changed his mind. On the other hand he has continued to admonish us to read the Book of Mormon and beware of secret combinations. No prophet has ever advised that we ignore the warnings of Moroni expressed to us Gentiles in Ether 8, nor can this be done without rejecting the Book of Mormon.

The prophecies of Nephi contained in 2 Ne. 27 through 2 Ne. 31:1 seem to explain what is now happening in the Church. Since these chapters are explanations of Isaiah's writings which the Lord has admonished us to search diligently, *(3 Ne. 23:1, 2),* they should be very meaningful to us today.

But even though we can no longer publicly discuss what President McKay has called the greatest satanical threat to peace, prosperity, and the spread of God's work among men which exists on the face of the earth, we can educate ourselves, our families, and our close friends . . . and I hope that the Lord will continue to bless you as you try to follow the prophets and stand up for that which they stand for. (H. Verlan Andersen, Letter to a member, 2/20/1992)

WHAT IS SOCIALISM?

We here in the United States, in converting our government into a social welfare state, have ourselves adopted much of socialism. Specifically, we have to an alarming degree adopted the use of the power of the state in the control and distribution of the fruits of industry. We are on notice according to the words of the President, that we are going much further, for he is quoted as saying:

We're going to take all the money we think is unnecessarily being spent and take it from the "haves" and give it to the "have nots." (1964 Congressional Record, p. 6142, Remarks of the President to a Group of Leaders of Organizations of Senior Citizens in the Fish Room, March 24, 1964)

That is the spirit of socialism: We're going to take. The spirit of the United Order is: We're going to give. (Romney, Marion G., *Conference Report,* April, 1966, p. 98)

As Bastiat pointed out over a hundred years ago, once government steps over this clear line between the protective or negative role into the aggressive role of redistributing the wealth and providing so-called "benefits" for some of its citizens, it then becomes a means for what he accurately described as legalized plunder. . . .

How is the legal plunder to be identified? Quite simply. See if the law takes from some persons what belongs to them, and gives it to other persons to whom it does not belong. See if the law benefits one citizen at the expense of another. . . . (*The Law*, p. 21, 26)

. . .In the end, no one is much further ahead, and everyone suffers the burdens of a gigantic bureaucracy and a loss of personal freedom. . . . (Ezra Taft Benson, *An Enemy Hath Done This*, p. 136-7)

IS SOCIALISM SATAN'S PLAN OF GOVERNMENT?

Force, on the other hand, emanates from Lucifer himself. Even in man's pre-existent state, Satan sought power to compel the human family to do his will by suggesting that the free agency of man be inoperative. If his plan had been accepted, human beings would have become mere puppets in the hands of a dictator, and the purpose of man's coming to earth would have been frustrated. Satan's proposed system of government, therefore, was rejected, and the principle of free agency established in its place. (McKay, David O., *Conference Report*, April 1950, pp. 33-35)

I was due here two weeks ago, and had a theme to deliver which I thought was timely and appropriate, but I come with another theme this morning— "Two Contending Forces." Those forces are known and have been designated by different terms throughout the ages. In the beginning they were known as Satan on the one hand, and Christ on the other. . . . In these days, they are called "domination by the state" on one hand, "personal liberty" on the other; communism on one hand, free agency on the other. . . .

Students, two forces are at work. There might be a conflagration such as the world has never known. Mankind will have to choose the one course or the other. (Mckay, David O., "Two Contending Forces," Speech at BYU, May 18, 1960)

WHAT TO DO, TO HAVE UNITY WITH THE PROPHETS

. . .Thus, according to the gospel plan under which the Church is established and operates, the care of the widow, the orphan, and the poor, is a Church function, is a part of the brotherhood of man which underlies our whole social and religious life. As God's children all, and as brothers and sisters in Christ, we must as a matter of spiritual responsibility and pursuant to positive divine command care for the helpless, the unfortunate, and the needy. Furthermore, it is essentially a neighbor to neighbor obligation. It is not a function of civil government. This is fundamental. . . .

The primary aim of this program is to provide for the material wants of faithful members of the Church who find themselves now in difficulty, to rebuild them spiritually, and to restore to them the proper concept, pride, and appreciation of American citizenship. . . . No effort has been spared to teach the people to be self reliant, independent, to take a humble, righteous pride in being, individually and as communities, fully self supporting. . . .

These things have been told in order that you may have a background and understanding of what we are now to say.

Viewing all of these things it will be easy for you to understand that the Church has not found it possible to follow along the lines of the present general tendency in the matter of property rights, taxes, the curtailment of rights and liberties of the people, nor in general the economic policies of what is termed the "New Deal". The great bulk of what these people are trying to do is, in the final analysis, absolutely contrary to the fundamental principles of which we have spoken. It is the considered, long considered opinion of President Grant and those who are associated with him, that our nation cannot be preserved if the present governmental policies shall continue. We do not believe that any other great nation or great civilization can be built up or maintained by the use of such policies. . . . As we see it, there is no way in which we can, to use your own words, "preserve and perpetuate our freedom—freedom to govern ourselves, freedom of speech, and freedom to worship God according to our own light," except we shall turn away from our present course and resume the normal course along which this great country traveled to its present high eminence of prosperity, of culture, of universal education, and of the peace and contentment which we enjoyed prior to the inauguration of the "New Deal.'

We have done in the past, we are doing now, and we shall continue in the future to do everything within our power to secure this turning of which we speak. We confess to you that it has not been possible for us to unify our own people even upon the necessity of such a turning about, and therefore we cannot unfortunately, and we say it regretfully, make any practical suggestion to you as to how the nation can be turned about. But the President of the United States could do it in good part if he were willing to exert his effort along that line, but this he appears not to be willing to do.

. . .this we feel we can definitely say, that unless the people of America forsake the sins and the errors, political and otherwise, of which they are now guilty and return to the practice of the great fundamental principles of Christianity, and of Constitutional government, there will be no exaltation for them spiritually, and politically we shall lose our liberty and free institutions.

Returning to your original letter and our reply thereto regarding the selling of Defense Bonds. The Church as a Church does not believe in war and yet since its organization whenever war has come we have done our part . . . we do thoroughly believe in building up our home defenses to the maximum extent necessary, but we do not believe that aggression should be carried on in the name and under the false cloak of defense. We therefore look with sorrowing eyes at the present use to which a great part of the funds being raised by taxes and by borrowing is being put. . . . We believe that our real threat comes from within and not from without, and it comes from the underlying spirit common to Naziism, Fascism, and Communism, namely, the spirit which would array class against class, which would set up a socialistic state of some sort, which would rob the people of the liberties which we possess under the Constitution, and would set up such a reign of terror as exists now in many parts of Europe. . . .

We trust you will pardon this long letter, but we feel we must say that you invited it.

Trusting that the Lord will point out some way, will somehow bring about a rejuvenation of the American spirit along with a true love of freedom and of our free institutions, and for Constitutional government, we are, Faithfully yours, /s/ Heber J. Grant, J. Reuben Clark, Jr., David O. McKay. (First Presidency letter to U.S. Treasury, September 30, 1941)

Now, we may rest assured of this: if there is no devil, there is no God. But there is a God and there is a devil, and the bringing of peace requires the elimination of Satan's influence. Where he is, peace can never be. Further, peaceful coexistence with him is impossible. He cannot be brought to cooperate in the maintenance of peace and harmony. He promotes nothing but the works of the flesh. . . .

As a prelude to peace, then the influence of Satan must be completely subjugated. Even in heaven there could be no peace with him after his rebellion. There, in the world of spirits, the Father and the Son could find no ground upon which they could cooperate with him. He had to be cast not - not compromised with, but cast out. (Marion G. Romney, First Presidency Message, *The Ensign*, Oct. 1983, p. 5)

How is it possible to cut out the various welfare-state features of our government which have already fastened themselves like cancer cells onto the body politic? Isn't drastic surgery already necessary, and can it be performed without endangering the patient? In answer, it is obvious that drastic measures are called for. No half-way or compromise actions will suffice. Like all surgery, it will not be without discomforts and perhaps even some scar tissue for a long time to come. But it must be done if the patient is to be saved, and it can be done without undue risk.

Obviously, not all welfare-state programs currently in force can be dropped simultaneously without causing tremendous economic and social upheaval. To try to do so would be like finding oneself at the controls of a hijacked airplane and attempting to return it by simply cutting off the engines in flight. It must be flown back, lowered in altitude, gradually reduced in speed and brought in for a smooth landing. Translated into practical terms, this means that the first step toward restoring the limited concept of government should be to freeze all welfare-state programs at their present level, making sure that no new ones are added. The next step would be to allow all present programs to run out their term with absolutely no renewal. The third step would involve the gradual phasing-out of those programs which are indefinite in their term. In my opinion, the bulk of the transition could be accomplished within a ten-year period and virtually completed within twenty years. . . . (Ezra Taft Benson, *An Enemy Hath Done This*, p. 141-2)

For it must needs be, that there is an opposition in all things. If not so, my first-born in the wilderness, righteousness could not be brought to pass, neither wickedness, neither holiness nor misery, neither good nor bad. . . .

Wherefore, the Lord God gave unto man that he should act for himself. Wherefore, man could not act for himself save it should be that he was enticed by the one or the other.

(2 nephi 2:11, 16)

HANDLING OPPOSITION

This book, *The Moral Basis of a Free Society* is probably the one my father worked on more than any other. He used it as a syllabus for his business law classes at BYU. I found more drafts, more changes, more years of effort with this one that all his others put together. Over the years he was continually refining it, adding to it and honing it to answer the opposition and make it as presentable as possible to college students, many being of a more liberal philosophy than himself. He felt he had just the one semester to try and align his students with the prophets as to law and government. Because in most instances he was the first exposure most of his students would have to correct principles, and very possibly the last, he felt a heavy responsibility to teach it as clearly as possible. He used this book the first two weeks of his class to establish the "why" of government.

He told me he often had some angry opposition from his students. He didn't enjoy this part of it, because he believed that once someone became angry with you your ability to teach them anything left, because the spirit leaves the angry one. He told me much of this opposition continued until the last few years when he tried a new approach. He would ask the students to put themselves in the position of the lawmaker. They were to write up a code of justice and determine when it was just to compel a man with force (government), not persuasion. Only when they had to wrestle with their own conscience, the "light of Christ," the innate Golden Rule, were they brought to deal with when it is right or wrong to use government. Only those who were already steeped in socialism failed to contemplate what the prophets believed and taught about government. Sometimes students were already too attached to socialism because of public education indoctrination, their own participation in government welfare, their parents employment etc.

Daddy received dozens of letters over the years from many students who thanked him for what he had done. Many said his was the only class they recalled from their years at BYU because of his effort to cause them to think about right and wrong.

Outside the classroom he experienced other opposition. At one point the head of the college came to Daddy and asked him to quit teaching, *The Moral Basis of a Free Society.* He explained that professors in other departments and colleges were complaining that students would take what Daddy had taught them and use it to argue with them. It was causing contention.

Daddy was more than a little familiar with a letter President McKay had sent to President Wilkinson, which had been sent to all the professors at BYU with their annual contract renewal. Much of that letter is quoted in the Introduction to this book. He pulled that out, gave it to him, and told him that he wanted to do exactly what the prophet wanted. Daddy did not have to change.

Daddy used to debate professors in other BYU colleges on campus when the teachers wanted to have contrasting opinions. Many of these were live debates, and others were filmed. Some who invited him to participate placed the restriction on him that he could not use scriptures or the words of the prophets during their debates. Since he died I have spent many hours going through his journals, correspondence, letters, etc. I came across one memo from the BYU Communications Dept. which was filming one of these debates. It says in part,

> To allow a little margin of safety, this lecture-discussion, "The Role of Government in the United States," which will be presented to the History 170 class on January 11, should be taped on Wednesday, January 4. The normal taping period is 3:10 to 5:00 p.m., in the TV studio in the basement, . . .
>
> We have agreed, I believe, that each of you will present a 12-15 minute lecture, to be followed by 15 minutes for questions. The questions can be agreed upon in advance and included in the outline if desired. You can decide by coin-flip or some rational process which should speak first. We have agreed to avoid citation of scripture and doctrinal disputation; . . .

To teach the principles of agency and the proper role of government to non-mormons or BYU students who do not have living prophets or the scriptures for a guide is difficult.

A year after Daddy died I was out looking at a piece of property with a client. He had brought along another friend, a BYU professor from one of the more liberal departments at BYU. I asked him if he had known my father and he said he had, but not well. We got into a discussion. He said the thing which made his colleagues most unhappy with Daddy was that they couldn't understand how a man of his intelligence could have thrown himself in with those kind of people (conservatives) and with those kind of views. He knew Daddy was in the top 10% of his class at Stanford, and number one at Harvard Law School, as did the others. They were unanimous with their opinion that people of such intelligence just don't do that.

Just before he died some friends had attempted to honor him with a large contribution to BYU with the suggestion that a chair be set up to honor him but it was not done.

He served two terms in the Utah Legislature. He was elected on the Republican Party ticket. While in the legislature he was awarded a small trophy which had engraved on it, "MR. NO." for having voted against more legislation than any one up there. He believed what Washington had said about political parties, so while he would encourage people to make contributions to individual candidates his encouragement for party contributions was lacking. He would also speak to many groups, including American Party groups who invited him to speak on the proper role of government. These activities got him into hot water.

On one occasion the heads of the Republican Party called him on the carpet to charge him with disloyalty to the Republican Party. Before he went he found out "what was up," so he took with him a copy of the Republican Party National Platform, August 6th, 1968, Miami Beach Florida. In going through his papers I found this platform and the sections he had marked. While I wasn't there, and I'm trying to recall a conversation 25 years back, his markings and notes on the platform speak for themselves. Of course, some of these men were conservative, so put yourself in their shoes as Daddy raised these issues to them from their own Republican platform.

> By contrast, Republican leadership in Congress has: . . . — Created a National Institute of Law Enforcement and Criminal Justice to conduct crime research and facilitate the expansion of police training programs. (page 6)

This promotes federal funding and control of local police. It is unconstitutional.

> Enactment of legislation to control indiscriminate availability of firearms, safeguarding the right of responsible citizens to col-

lect, own and use firearms for legitimate purposes, retaining primary responsibility at the state level, with such federal laws as necessary to better enable the states to meet their responsibilities. (page 8)

Here we see gun control legislation and the 2nd Amendment trampled.

To help assure excellence and equality of educational opportunity, we will urge the states to present plans for federal assistance which would include state distribution of such aid to non-public school children and include non-public school representatives in the planning process. Where state conditions prevent use of funds for non-public school children, a public agency should be designated to administer federal funds. . . . To help colleges and universities provide this opportunity, we favor grant and loan programs for expansion of their facilities. (page 9)

Here we see Federal aid to education being proposed.

The inability of the poor to cope meaningfully with their environment is compounded by problems which blunt opportunity—inadequate income, inferior education, inadequate health care, slum housing, limited job opportunities, discrimination and crime.
Full opportunity requires a coordinated attack on the total problem through community human development programs. Federal revenue sharing would help provide the resources to develop such coordinated programs. (page 10)

Here we see proposed expansion of federal welfare programs.

Elderly Americans desire and deserve independence, dignity, and the opportunity for continued useful participation. We will strengthen the Social Security system and provide automatic cost of living adjustments under Social Security and the Railroad Retirement Act. An increase in earnings permitted to Social Security recipients without loss of benefits, . . .

Here we see proposed increasing the cost of social security and expanding it. (page 14)

We support an equitable minimum wage for American workers—one providing fair wages without unduly increasing unemployment among those on the lowest rung of the economic ladder—and will improve the Fair Labor Standards Act, with its important protections for employees.

The forty-hour week adopted 30 years ago needs re- examination to determine whether or not a shorter work week, without loss of wages, would produce more jobs, increase productivity and stabilize prices. (page 17)

This addresses minimum wage laws and more federal involvement.

Farm policies and programs which will enable producers to receive fair prices in relation to the prices they must pay for other products. (page 20)

Here we see price supports expansion. There were several others dealing with education, poverty, transportation, Viet Nam, etc., etc., which were also marked. Daddy, when mentioning this meeting later said when he left them they were "understandably confused." Daddy did to them what Paul did to the Jews who wanted to stone him after he had been in the temple.

. . .I am a Pharisee, the son of a Pharisee: of the hope and resurrection of the dead I am called in question.
And when he had so said, there arose a dissension between the Pharisees and the Sadducees: and the multitude was divided. . . .
And there arose a great cry: and the scribes that were of the Pharisees" part arose, and strove, saying, We find no evil in this man: but if a spirit or an angel hath spoken to him, let us not fight against God. *(Acts 23:6-9)*

Conservatives work hard at the local level, coming up with strongly worded conservative platforms to express their political views. Most never even know of the disappearance of their views altogether by the time it reaches the national platform writers.

By the 1972 election Daddy's legislative boundaries had been gerrymandered to such an extent he had little chance of re-election. Mama felt no remorse when he got beat. He used to come home many nights in tears, both for his failure and the eternal consequence he feared for the vast majority in the legislature. He had some idea what he was up against. In a letter to his mother shortly after he was elected he wrote,

I am trying to get ready to go to the legislature next month and so this keeps me pretty well occupied. I am somewhat apprehensive about how much good I will be able to do as a legislator since my ideas of what power government should possess are so far removed from the ideas of practically all people I know. I find it a real challenge to occupy the rather isolated position I do. I am going to try and visit with each member of the legislature prior to the time it convenes next month and give them each a copy of my book. The probability is that I will have but little influence nevertheless I have become convinced the LDS people will have to come back to the fundamental principles of constitutional government voluntarily or the Lord will punish us so harshly that we will be led back to them to escape our sufferings. Practically every one of the members of the state legislature belongs to the Church and so this gives me a starting point for my conversion work. (Letter to his mother, Mynoa Andersen 12//1968)

I recall him telling me that he worked hard to get legislators to vote against some bills, and would succeed. He felt he was making real progress, but then a week later the same bill would come up again and they would switch their votes. It was very disconcerting to him to see no standards, no principles used. Few even attempted to use such principles.

Immediately after losing the election it appeared that even the majority of the people in his own ward had voted against him, so it was probably best he not be elected. Below is most of a "letter to the editor" by a prominent republican, published in the Daily Herald January 18, 1968.

It has been very enlightening to read the "Your Legislators Speak" series in the Herald—a real service both to the legislators and the public.

For instance, while most of the legislators have gotten down to the real problem of financing the services demanded and needed by the people, we find the lonely voice of H. Verlan Andersen demanding an end to free public education, the national income tax, and all welfare programs of the government, and well he ought to be lonely with such unrealistic proposals.

It is worthy to note that he was willing to run for office as a Republican—a party that supports all these programs in both state and national platforms, and in spite of the fact that last spring he was busily engaged in supporting the presidential candidacy of George C. Wallace. [This was not true. That spring Daddy was working on Ezra Taft Benson's candidacy and George Wallace was talking to Ezra Taft Benson.] I hope the citizens of the 41st District are keeping a sharp eye on this pseudo-Republican, who, judging by his public utterances, seeks to change or destroy programs of both parties, including our cherished system of free education for all. If he really feels such programs are unconstitutional, I would suggest that Mr. Andersen take a close look at Article I, Section 8 of the U.S. Constitution and note that "Congress shall have the power to lay and collect taxes to . . . provide for the common defense and general welfare of the United States."

If we as a community and nation really want to avoid collapse and possible revolution, we ought to be working to strengthen all levels of our government, and our excellent school systems, through increased fiscal and personal support, led by such outstanding civic groups as the Chamber of Commerce who truly want positive programs that make "golden years" happen. Then will this country be strong enough to overcome and resist the threats to it from the Communists, the student anarchists, the racists, and the so-called "study groups" that join the others in teaching attitudes of social disruption which are the real fodder of social revolution.

Several BYU professors and some political science classes made it a project to defeat Daddy. They were successful. Democrats seldom even ran in this district, so the battles were always between Republicans.

While in the legislature Daddy received many notes and letters. One letter from a liberal Democrat reads in part:

> Just a short note to let you know how much an impression you made upon me during the two sessions earlier this year. We all have our honest convictions and, at times, we differ philosophically in our approaches to the same problems. Oft times, as I looked at the electronic board, [Their votes are displayed on an electronic board at the state legislature.] I felt the feeling of how lonesome you must be.
>
> Your voting record showed the convictions of a man truly dedicated to the least governed, the best governed . . . wherein we all act with self-restraint, with self respect, and with the highest esteem for man's right to dignity. I salute you. (Personal letter received 12/22/71)

One bill he introduced titled, "Compulsory Charity" begins: "An act defining and prohibiting compulsory charity and providing for the phase out of appropriations to fund all public welfare programs and payments." This would have eliminated all government welfare. Another bill he introduced, titled "Freedom to Buy and Sell Act" begins: "An act relating to business crimes, guaranteeing to the public the freedom to purchase from whom they please; prohibiting punishment of the manufacture, sale, production or purchase of goods or services unless a crime is involved." This would have eliminated all business licensing laws. One legislator, after reviewing these bills said he thought they would eliminate about 90% of the laws on the books. They did not pass.

Some LDS bookstores refused to carry his books, even after he became a general authority. I contacted some of these stores five different times with letters and phone calls to let them know they were not out of print. A few years after he died they began to carry them again.

One of his opportunities which he enjoyed the most was participating in Education Week. Education Week Programs, for some popular teachers went on throughout the summer. One month my sisters travelled with him was detailed on a "Campus Memorandum" to him outlining their travel in June, 1968. Las Vegas, June 1, 3, 4, Mesa, June 6, 7, 8, Scottsdale, June 10, 11, 12, Phoenix, June 13, 14, 15, El Paso, June 17, 18, 19 and Snowflake, June 22, 24, 25.

He participated in this because it gave him an opportunity to travel throughout the Church and teach truth. Once again, however, opposition came. After several years one of the heads of it came to him and told him they loved to have him, but some Education Week lecturers had complained that what he taught was in conflict with what they taught. Contention is not good. They wanted Daddy to continue with them, but to change what he taught. Because it was what he taught that caused him to even consider spending as much time away from his family as he did during the summers he gave it up.

In his papers was a talk given by Harold B. Lee July 18, 1968 to seminary and institute teachers. At the end of it he said,

> You and I to be worthy of our places in God's Kingdom must be defenders of the faith and as someone has written, "If you have no enemies you say, alas, my friend, the boast is poor. He who has mingled in the fray of duty that the brave endure must have made foes. If you have none, small is the work you have done. If you have hit no cup from purged lips, you have never turned a wrong to right, you have been a coward in the fight."

Below are some of his writings on opposition, and his attitude toward it and how to handle it. I've put in just a small list of opposition he experienced during his life, but it's enough to help the reader see how and why he also had to deal with opposition. The first reference is part of a letter to his mother about five months after he lost his election for a third term in the Utah Legislature.

You are right in surmising that we are going through somewhat of a period of trial. It certainly is a different type of a trial than I have ever experienced before and I suppose that it stems mainly from my book writing activity. I have thought many times that if what I have said in these books is true, and I am as convinced of their truth as I am of the other gospel truths, that I would face considerable opposition. I do not believe that a person can contend against the church of the devil as D&C 18:20 puts it, and not suffer tribulation because of it. However, there is one thing of which I am convinced, and that is that the Lord will not allow us to be tested beyond our ability to allow us to exercise freedom of choice between good and evil.

It is completely beyond man's comprehension how God could so plan our lives that such plans take into consideration the conditions which arise from the choices made by those around us whose lives affect and hinge upon our own. Our inability to comprehend how God could solve such an infinitely complicated problem does not alter the fact that such is the case. He is able to predict perfectly the life of each of us.

A fellow member of my High Council stated not long ago that I was an outcast in my own ward. The thing which is more difficult than anything is to see this ill will directed against my children.

I hope that you will not concern yourself unduly however. The Lord has blessed me with a very strong testimony and I know that He rules in the lives of both men and of nations. I know that justice will be done in spite of anything that happens, therefore my only concern is to see that I am obedient to His commandments. . . .

I am so grateful for your testimony of the truthfulness of what I have said in the "devil book." I feel that my efforts here are in partial fulfillment of the promise made to me in my patriarchal blessing which says:

> Your voice shall be raised in the defense of truth and many shall rejoice and glorify God on account of your diligent labors in bringing knowledge and light to them.

I was also promised that if I would keep my mind and talents on the higher ideals of life,

> . . .knowledge and wisdom shall come to you that you may
> fully understand the plan of life and salvation.

But if I am able to accomplish anything worthwhile in this life, I
know that the credit therefore shall largely be due my parents, and
since father has been gone for such a long time, and you have been
left to bear the responsibilities of parenthood alone for so many
years, a great deal of credit should be due you for the Patriarch
stated:

> Dear Brother, great blessings await you for the prayers of
> your parents will continually plead in your behalf before the
> Almighty, and you shall have strength and wisdom and knowledge
> to accomplish a wonderful work upon the earth.

And so Mother let me here once again express my deep love and
appreciation for your faithfulness, your concern, your love and your
prayers. Regarding my being tried my blessing also says:

> Trials will meet you in life but inasmuch as you are sincere
> and humble, the Lord will sustain you and His angels will guard
> you and warn you against temptation and snares which shall meet
> you on your journey in life.

I do not really feel that I have had to undergo any great trials yet
and so perhaps if I live properly I have them to face in the future. I
hope that the Lord will continue to bless you and preserve you in
health and strength that I might continue to feel the spiritual support
and strength which you have always given me, for I may need such
more than ever during the coming years. (Letter to Mother, Mynoa
Andersen, 3/4/1973)

When we allow the evil words and actions of others to influence
us to do evil we are listing to the voice of Satan. It is carnal nature to
return hate for hate, evil for evil.

When we elected to come to earth rather than to follow Satan,
we agreed to become acquainted with both good and evil here, not
just to observe evil acts being done to others but to also experience
our own share of unkind words, false accusations, cheating and even
bodily harm.

One of the most urgent needs of a man is to recognize what his own reaction should be to the evil done to him. The first and foremost virtue is to restrain the natural reaction of ill-will. This is much easier to do if we recognize that God is just and He will allow nothing to happen to a child of His which is not deserved or for his best good.

When one is the victim of an evil deed, he has the opportunity then and there to develop the Christ-like quality of charity which is the pure love of Christ *(Moro. 7:47)* and without which we cannot become as Christ is. In one sense we should welcome such opportunities, not that we should become masochists, but we should recognize that the trials of life are the crucible through which our souls must pass to become refined and developed.

A cursory glance at the lives of the most righteous men who have dwelt upon the earth reveals that they have received the worst treatment. Is this justice? Does a righteous life merit suffering and even martyrdom in return? Certainly by man's shallow standards the answer is no. Our laws are designed to punish the wicked, not the righteous. But in the infinite wisdom of a kind and loving Father who is both just and merciful, these martyrs who have suffered the most rank human injustice which could be inflicted have thereby been provided with the opportunity to become as God is. (Personal Journal, / /1962)

It is the Lord and not man, who controls the number and severity of the trials, tests and challenges which come into our lives. He carefully and constantly watches over each one and allows us to experience those circumstances, and face those situations and difficulties we need, and to which our past conduct entitle us.

Some might contend that if the Lord intervenes this intimately in our affairs, He would thereby deprive us of our free agency. But let it be noted that although He ofttimes prevents us from carrying out our desires, never does He interfere with their formation. The scriptures relate numerous instances where the Lord has intervened to prevent people from fulfilling their intentions, and still there are many others where He has permitted evil actions even though it may appear to us to be unjust. While He allowed the wicked leaders in the city of Ammonihah to burn innocent women and children to death, He directly prevented them from slaying Alma and Amulek. While He allowed King Noah and his priests to martyr Abinadi, when a robber tried to kill Ammon, he was stricken dead. While He allowed Lamanite armies to slay tens of thousands of righteous Nephites, He intervened to prevent them from slaying even one of the two thousand sons of Helaman.

On the other hand, we are all conscious of the fact that the Lord does not interfere with the formation of our desires. In accordance with the following scripture, He constantly entices us to do good and He permits Satan to constantly entice us to do evil:

> Wherefore, the Lord God gave unto man that he should act for himself. Wherefore, man could not act for himself save it should be that he was enticed by the one or the other. [2 Ne. 2:16]

(Personal Notes, / /1989)

Everything which happens to you is either good for you or you deserve it; otherwise there is no justice. In order to be just the Lord must control and regulate every event in our lives except our freedom to choose between the alternatives He places before us. (Talk on the Mormon Exodus, Virdan, New Mexico, 12/30/1990)

To conclude I wanted to say something about those people who are similarly concerned, as my father was, about what is happening in our country. Often when we LDS ". . .awake to a sense of your awful situation. . ." *(Ether 9:24)* we wish to awake all those around us. We would like to ". . .speak with the trump of God, with a voice to shake the earth, . . ." *(Alma 29:1)*.

So far so good, but we often go a step further and ask why the Church doesn't take the lead in this battle. Sometimes Church leaders, seeing the zeal of this new born free agency mormon will counsel with him. The free agency mormon may feel this counsel is generated by the leaders lack of loyalty to the prophet or lack of understanding. The free agency mormon has entered a dangerous situation if he does not handle it right.

The Church, to protect itself from apostasy, must maintain control of those who are teaching what is or is not doctrine. Anyone teaching what is Church doctrine outside the established line of authority has the potential to get off course. To keep the doctrine that is taught correct, auxiliary leaders and teachers are called by those in authority. For our own protection, and the Church's protection, they may counsel us for our benefit. We are obligated to accept and obey that counsel, as obedience is the first law. We should never allow pride to lead us. If pride were a disease it would be the worst, because the victim is blinded to an awareness of the symptoms of it to the exact degree the disease has gotten hold of him.

A great deal could be written about this, but after all is said, obedience and submission to authority will be the only right answer. Our Father in Heaven loves all His children. He gives us our agency to accept or reject the benefit of His love and counsel. In the pre-existence man had his agency. Did God put a heavy hand on us there? He did not. While the war continues here, minus our memories of the last one, we are again given agency. The Lord runs His Church. The Lord decides what the prophet says. Without the Lord, His prophet and His Church, what do we have of worth?

AND now it came to pass that in the three hundred and sixty and third year the Nephites did go up with their armies to battle against the Lamanites, out of the land Desolation.

And it was because the armies of the Nephites went up unto the Lamanites that they began to be smitten; for were it not for that, the Lamanites could have had no power over them.

But, behold, the judgments of God will overtake the wicked; and it is by the wicked that the wicked are punished; for it is the wicked that stir up the hearts of the children of men unto bloodshed.

(Mormon 4:1, 4, 5)

JUSTIFIED AND UNJUSTIFIED WARFARE

[In 1990 and 1991 Daddy became extremely concerned that the U.S. might enter into a war of aggression, and eventually suffer the same consequences the Nephites did, when they waged aggressive war against the Lamanites. In an effort to spare at least the mormons from voting for such a war, he wrote the LDS senators and congressmen. Daddy was aware of only one who agreed with him, and voted against the war. After the war was won, even that one said he made a mistake voting against the war. Daddy believed that eventually our nation will have to suffer terribly for that act. There were ten LDS congressmen and three LDS senators who received letters almost identical to the one below.]

It has come to my attention that the Congress of the United States is debating the possibility of waging war against the nation of Iraq in the event that their nation fails to withdraw its armed forces from Kuwait on or before a specified deadline. I wonder if in considering this matter you are aware of the Laws of God which state in the clearest of words that aggressive warfare is forbidden.

I am enclosing for your considerations, some statements from the LDS scriptures which I urge you to ponder. As you will note, they state that war is justifiable in the eyes of the Lord only in the defense of life. No one can logically claim the action the United States is now contemplating against Iraq falls in that category.

If I am correctly informed, you feel aggressive action against Iraq is justified at this time to forestall the possibility of a nuclear war—if and when Saddam Hussein comes into possession of nuclear weapons. The scriptures deal with the idea of preventive war and indicate disaster for the aggressor *(3 Nephi 3:20-21* and *Mormon 4:4-5).*

Even though you choose to believe that this scripture is not applicable to the present situation, surely you realize that anyone of a dozen other nations can, and probably will, pose a similar threat within the near future, and eliminating one of those possible aggressors will do little to obviate that danger.

Inasmuch as only those who accept the scriptures of the LDS Church understand clearly the will of the Lord with respect to war, we have a very heavy responsibility to utilize that knowledge for the benefit of ourselves and others. If we fail to do so, our punishment for the terrible crime of waging aggression will be far heavier for us than for others because we sin against the light.

As a final item, I note that the United States Constitution gives to Congress the exclusive power to declare war. This places upon you and fellow members of Congress the awesome responsibility of making decisions relative to this matter.

May the Lord bless you in the discharge of your heavy responsibilities. Sincerely,

—Elder H. Verlan Andersen

He attached to the above letter the following:

Scriptures Forbidding Aggressive Warfare

Now the Nephites were taught to defend themselves against their enemies, even to the shedding of blood if it were necessary; yea, and they were also taught never to give an offense, yea, and never to raise the sword except it were against an enemy, except it were to preserve their lives.

And this was their faith, that by so doing God would prosper them in the land, or in other words, if they were faithful in keeping the commandments of God that he would prosper them in the land; yea, warn them to flee, or to prepare for war, according to their danger;

And also, that God would make it known unto them whither they should go to defend themselves against their enemies, and by so doing, the Lord would deliver them; and this was the faith of Moroni, and his heart did glory in it; not in the shedding of blood but in doing good, in preserving his people, yea, in keeping the commandments of God, yea, and resisting iniquity. *(Alma 48:14-16)*

Nevertheless, thine enemy is in thine hands; and if thou rewardest him according to his works thou art justified; if he has sought thy life, and thy life is endangered by him, thine enemy is in thine hands and thou art justified.

Behold, this is the law I gave unto my servant Nephi, and thy fathers, Joseph, and Jacob, and Isaac, and Abraham, and all mine ancient prophets and apostles.

And again, this is the law that I gave unto mine ancients, that they should not go unto battle against any nation, kindred, tongue, or people, save I, the Lord, commanded them.

And if any nation, tongue, or people should proclaim war against them, they should first lift a standard of peace unto that people, nation, or tongue;

And if that people did not accept the offering of peace, neither the second nor the third time, they should bring these testimonies before the Lord;

Then I, the Lord, would give unto them a commandment, and justify them in going out to battle against that nation, tongue, or people.

And I, the Lord, would fight their battles, and their children's battles, and their children's children's, until they had avenged themselves on all their enemies, to the third and fourth generation. *(D&C 98:31-37)*

Cursed is he that putteth his trust in man, or maketh flesh his arm, or shall hearken unto the precepts of men, save their precepts shall be given by the power of the Holy Ghost. *(2 Nephi 28:31)*

Now the people said unto Gidgiddoni: Pray unto the Lord, and let us go up upon the mountains and into the wilderness, that we may fall upon the robbers and destroy them in their own lands.

But Gidgiddoni saith unto them: The Lord forbid, for if we should go up against them the Lord would deliver us into their hands; therefore we will prepare ourselves in the center of our lands, and we will gather all our armies together, and we will not go against them, but we will wait till they shall come against us; therefore as the Lord liveth, if we do this he will deliver them into our hands. *(3 Nephi 3:20-21)*

Let no man think he is ruler; but let God rule him that judgeth, according to the counsel of his own will, or, in other words, him that counseleth or sitteth upon the judgment seat. *(D&C 58:20)*

. . .the crowding in of the socialistic reform programs . . . are threatening the very foundation of the Church, . . . I warn you that government subsidies are not the Lord's way; and if we begin to accept, we are on our way to becoming subsidized politically as well as financially.

(Harold B. Lee, *The Teachings of Harold B. Lee,* [1996], p. 314-15)

WHO OPPOSES SOCIALISM

At one point in my life I attempted to find justification for the position taken by members who opposed President Benson, and whose opposition to him did not slacken, one whit, even after he became the prophet.   —*Hans V. Andersen, Jr.*

JOSEPH SMITH

> *Wednesday, 13. I attended a lecture at the Grove, by Mr. John Finch, a Socialist, from England, and said a few words in reply. . .*
>
> *Thursday, 14. I attended a second lecture on Socialism, by Mr. Finch; and after he got through, I made a few remarks, alluding to Sidney Rigdon and Alexander Campbell getting up a community at Kirtland, and of the big fish there eating up all the little fish. I said I did not believe the doctrine.* (Joseph Smith, *History of the Church,* Vol. 6, p. 33)

BRIGHAM YOUNG

> *We heard Brother Taylor's exposition of what is called Socialism this morning. What can they do?*
>
> *Live on each other and beg. It is a poor, unwise and very imbecile people who cannot take care of themselves.* (Brigham Young, *Journal of Discourses,* Vol. 14, p. 21)

JOHN TAYLOR

> *. . .the world have generally made great mistakes upon these points. They have started various projects to try to unite and cement the people together without God; but they could not do it. Fourierism (authors note: Francois Fourier was a French socialist and writer), Communism—another branch of the same thing—and many other principles of the same kind have been introduced to try and cement the human family together. And then we have had peace societies, based upon the same principles; but all these things have failed, and they will fail, because, however philanthropic, humanitarian, benevolent, or cosmopolitan our ideas, it is*

impossible to produce a true and correct union without the Spirit of the living God, . . . (John Taylor, *Journal of Discourses*, Vol. 18, p. 137)

I was speaking, a while ago, about the people there being divided into three classes. One of them you may call infidel, under the head of socialism, fourierism, and several other isms. Communism is a specimen of the same thing, . . . (John Taylor, *Journal of Discourses*, Vol. 1, p. 23, August 22, 1852)

WILFORD WOODRUFF

You may wish to know why I make these remarks. I will tell you. Because God himself grants this right to every human being upon the earth irrespective of race or color; it is part of the divine economy not to force any man to heaven, not to coerce the mind but to leave it free to act for itself.

He lays before His creature man the everlasting Gospel, the principles of life and salvation, and then leaves him to choose for himself or to reject for himself, with the definite understanding that he becomes responsible to Him for the results of his acts. (Wilford Woodruff, *Journal of Discourses*, Vol. 23, p. 77)

LORENZO SNOW

In things that pertain to celestial glory there can be no forced operations. We must do according as the Spirit of the Lord operates upon our understandings and feelings. We cannot be crowded into matters, however great might be the blessing attending such procedure. We cannot be forced into living a celestial law; we must do this ourselves, of our own free will. And whatever we do in regard to the principle of the United Order, we must do it because we desire to do it. . . .

The United Order is not French Communism. (Lorenzo Snow, *Journal of Discourses*, Vol. 19, p. 346, 349-350)

JOSEPH F. SMITH

. . .We must choose righteous men, good men to fill these positions. Hence if you will only get good men to fill these offices no one should care who they are, so that you have agreed upon them, and were one. We want you to be one both in temporal, political and religious things, in fact, in everything you put your hands to in righteousness. We want you to be one, one as God and Christ are one, seeing eye to eye. Do not try to crush anybody, or build yourselves up at the expense of your neighbor. Do not do it; it is a custom of the world, and it is a wrong principle. (Joseph F. Smith, *Journal of Discourses*, Vol. 25, p. 251)

HEBER J. GRANT

. . .Among the Latter-day Saints they speak of their philosophy and their plans under it, as an ushering in of the United Order. Communism and all other similar "isms" bear no relationship whatever to the United Order. They are merely the clumsy counterfeits which Satan always devises of the gospel plan. Communism debases the individual and makes him the enslaved tool of the state to whom he must look for sustenance and religion; the United Order exalts the individual, leaves him his property, "according to his family, according to his circumstances and his wants and needs," (D&C 51:3) and provides a system by which he helps care for his less fortunate brethren; the United Order leaves every man free to choose his own religion as his conscience directs. Communism destroys man's God-given free agency; the United Order glorifies it. Latter-day Saints cannot be true to their faith and lend aid, encouragement, or sympathy to any of these false philosophies. They will prove snares to their feet. (Heber J. Grant, J. Reuben Clark Jr., David O. McKay, The First Presidency, CR, April, 1942, p. 90)

GEORGE ALBERT SMITH

Consider the condition in the world, the number who are determined to take from the rich man not what belongs to themselves, but that which belongs to the others. God has permitted men to get wealth, and if they obtained it properly, it is theirs, and he will bless them in its use if they will use it properly. . . .

We must not fall into the bad habits of other people. We must not get into the frame of mind that we will take what the other man has. Refer back to the ten commandments, and you will find one short paragraph, "Thou shalt not covet." That is what is the matter with a good many people today.

They are coveting what somebody else has, when as a matter of fact, many of them have been cared for and provided with means to live by those very ones from whom they would take property. (President George Albert Smith, Prophets, Principles and National Survival, p. 343 [compiled by Jay Newquist], CR-10/49:171-2)

God gave this nation the Constitution. No nation in the world has a constitution that was given to it by our Heavenly Father except the United States of America. I wonder if we appreciate that. The Lord gave us a rule of life for this great nation, and as far as we have lived up to it and taken advantage of it, the nation has grown, and the people have been blessed. But there are many people who prefer, or at least they seem to prefer something else.

As one man said to me, "Why not try what Russia has tried and what Germany has tried?" And my answer to him was, "Why try something that has already failed? Why not hold on to what the Lord has given?" (The Teachings of George Albert Smith, Bookcraft, Salt Lake City, [1996], p. 171)

DAVID O. MCKAY

We are placed on this earth to work, to live; and the earth will give us a living. It is our duty to strive to make a success of what we possess—to till the earth, subdue matter, conquer the glebe, take care of the cattle, the flocks and the herds. It is the Government's duty to see that you are protected in these efforts, and no other man has the right to deprive you of any of your privileges. But it is not the Government's duty to support you. That is one reason why I shall raise my voice as long as God gives me sound or ability, against this Communistic idea that the Government will take care of us all, and everything belongs to the Government. It is wrong! No wonder, in trying to perpetuate that idea, they become anti-Christ, because that doctrine strikes directly against the doctrine of the Savior. . .

No government owes you a living. You get it yourself by your own acts! —never by trespassing upon the rights of a neighbor; never by cheating him. You put a blemish upon your character the moment you do. (David O. McKay, *Statements on Communism and the Constitution of the United States,* p. 23)

During the first half of the twentieth century we have traveled far into the soul-destroying land of socialism . . . (David O. McKay, *Gospel Ideals,* p. 273)

JOSEPH FIELDING SMITH

We have all been taught the doctrine of personal free agency and that no individual is ever compelled by force or other means to comply with divine edicts and philosophy. We have been informed that a long time ago in the pre-existence there was a rebellion in heaven, and because one notable character, who had been entrusted with great authority, rebelled and led many away with him, he had to be cast out of the kingdom. However we should remember that every principle and law existing in the celestial kingdom has been proved to be perfect through the eternities through which they have come. If any individual proves himself worthy for the exaltation in that kingdom, it will be by strict obedience to every principle and covenant here existing. Therefore we may be assured that every law and principle thereunto pertaining is perfect and cannot be amended or discarded because of it perfection. (Joseph Fielding Smith, *Answers to Gospel Questions,* Vol. 4, p. 69)

The modern trend of the nations is towards dictatorship. It is taking form in two great camps, but, nevertheless, the direction is the same, although it is being reached by different routes. On the one side the direction to make an end of all nations, is through communism; . . . (Joseph Fielding Smith, *The Progress of Man,* p. 397)

HAROLD B. LEE

There are some things of which I am sure, and that is that contrary to the belief and mistaken ideas of some people, the United Order will not be a socialistic or communistic setup; . . . (Harold B. Lee, *Stand Ye in Holy Places*, p. 280)

Now, keep in mind with all the crowding in of the socialistic reform programs that are threatening the very foundation of the Church, we must never forget what the Lord said, "that the church may stand independent above all other creatures beneath the celestial world" (D&C 78:14). Whenever we allow ourselves to become entangled and have to be subsidized from government sources-and we think that it's the expedient way to do business in this day-or when we yield to such pressures, I warn you that government subsidies are not the Lord's way; and if we begin to accept, we are on our way to becoming subsidized politically as well as financially. (Harold B. Lee, *The Teachings of Harold B. Lee*, [1996], p. 314-15)

SPENCER W. KIMBALL

. . . Assume that you become the world leader of Socialism and in it have marked success, but through your devotion to it you fail to live the gospel. Where are you then? Is anything worthwhile which will estrange you from your friends, your Church membership, your family, your eternal promises, your faith? You might say that such estrangement is not necessarily a result of your political views, but truthfully hasn't your overpowering interest in your present views already started driving a wedge? (0/0/45) (Spencer W. Kimball, *Teachings*, pp. 408-409)

EZRA TAFT BENSON

The fifth and final principle that is basic to our understanding of the Constitution is that governments should have only limited powers. The important thing to keep in mind is that the people who have created their government can give to that government only such powers as they, themselves, have in the first place. Obviously, they cannot give that which they do not possess.

By deriving its just powers from the governed, government becomes primarily a mechanism for defense against bodily harm, theft, and involuntary servitude. It cannot claim the power to redistribute money or property nor to force reluctant citizens to perform acts of charity against their will. Government is created by the people. The creature cannot exceed the creator. (Ezra Taft Benson, *Ensign*, Sept. 1987, p. 8)

No true Latter-day Saint and no true American can be a

socialist or a communist or support programs leading in that direction. (Ezra Taft Benson, *Title of Liberty*, p. 190)

Our nation will continue to degenerate unless we read and heed the words of the God of this land, Jesus Christ, and quit building up and upholding secret combinations, . . . (Ezra Taft Benson, *Ensign*, July, 1988, p. 80)

We must keep the people informed that collectivism, another word for socialism, is a part of the communist strategy. Communism is essentially socialism. (Ezra Taft Benson, *This Nation Shall Endure*, p. 90)

HOWARD W. HUNTER

. . .we know from both ancient and modern revelation that Satan wished to deny us our independence and agency in that now forgotten moment long ago, even as he wishes to deny them this very hour. Indeed, Satan violently opposed the freedom of choice offered by the ather, so violently that John in the Revelation described "war in heaven" over the matter. (Rev. 12:7) Satan would have coerced us, and he would have robbed us of that most precious of gifts if he could: our freedom to choose a divine future and the exaltation we all hope to obtain. . . .

To fully understand this gift of agency and its inestimable worth, it is imperative that we understand that God's chief way of acting is by persuasion and patience and long-suffering, not by coercion and stark confrontation . . . (Howard W. Hunter, *That We Might Have Joy*, pp. 77-78)

GORDON B. HINCKLEY

I am confident that it was out of what he saw, the bitter fruit of dictatorship that he developed his strong feelings, almost hatred for communism and socialism. That distaste grew through the years as he witnessed the heavy handed oppression and suffering of the peoples of eastern europe under what he repeatedly described as godless communism. These experiences further strengthened his love for the land of his birth. . . .

He never got over his boyhood love for freedom. Rather, it grew within him. Nurtured by what he saw of oppression in other lands, and by what he observed first hand of a growing dominance of government in this land over the lives of the people. (Gordon B. Hinckley, Talk given at the funeral of Ezra Taft Benson, June 4, 1994)

—A—

Abinadi, 199
Abraham, 205
Administrative Laws, *iii,* 101, 163-
 165, 167, 169-171, 173, 175-177,
 179
Adultery, 12-13, 28
Agency, Free, 10, 144-145, 184,
 199-200, 209-210
Alma, *iv,* 12, 25, 28, 30, 32, 44-45,
 78, 95, 125, 181, 199-200, 204
Ammonihah, 199
Amulek, 78, 199
Apostasy, 200
Armed forces, 7, 26, 203

—B—

Banking, 102, 105, 137, 143, 163
Banks, 133
Bastiat, Frederic, 115
Benson, Ezra Taft, 52, 120, 127,
 162, 184, 187, 194, 211-212
Bill of Rights, 70, 136-137, 141,
 149, 151
Blackstone, William, 6, 68
Book of Mormon, 180, 183

—C—

Charity, *xi,* 107, 195, 199, 211
Children, *xiii,* 15, 22, 29, 72, 75, 78,
 81, 93, 108, 113, 138, 142, 147,
 178, 185, 192, 197, 199, 201-202,
 205
Christ, 41, 80, 144-145, 178, 181-
 182, 184-185, 189, 199, 208, 212
Church members, 144, 182
Church of the Devil, 182, 197
Cicero, 5
Clark, J Reuben, 186, 209
Clawans, Ethel, 155
Coinage Act, 126
Commandments, *xvi,* 4-5, 49, 64,
 73, 79, 197, 204, 209
Communism, *v,* 140-141, 143-145,
 179, 182, 184, 186, 207-210, 212
Communist Manifesto, *v-vi,* 141-
 143, 177
Conscience, 11, 24-25, 29, 31, 44,
 64, 75, 78, 81, 168, 189, 209
Constitution, *iii, vi, xvi-xvii,* 11, 17,

20, 38, 46, 48-49, 52-53, 55-61,
 63-65, 70, 77, 100, 120, 125-128,
 131-132, 136-138, 140-141, 144,
 149-151, 153, 155-158, 160-163,
 179, 186, 195, 204, 209-211
Cooley, Thomas, 157
Crime, 27-29, 35, 38-39, 42, 44, 59,
 67-69, 71-82, 84-85, 88, 96, 98,
 100, 102, 139-140, 149-152, 154-
 160, 164-165, 167, 169, 191-192,
 196, 204

—D—

de Tocqueville, Alexis, 160
Deception, 14, 100
Discrimination, 166, 192
Division, *v,* 53, 58-59, 97, 122, 140,
 159
Dominion, unrighteous, 30, 162,
 170

—E—

Earth, 2, 15, 33, 41, 53, 80, 108-
 115, 136, 144, 171, 178, 181,
 183-184, 198-200, 208, 210
Education, *vi, xviii,* 15, 102, 137,
 142, 145, 171, 185, 189, 192-196
Eternal life, 115
Evil, *viii-xii, xiv-xv, xvii,* 8, 13, 17,
 21, 27-28, 31, 39-40, 42, 48-50,
 64-65, 69-73, 75, 78-82, 98-101,
 130, 138-139, 146-147, 157, 159,
 165, 168-169, 193, 197-200
Extortion, 76, 100, 168

—F—

Family, 13, 22-23, 32-33, 83, 85,
 99, 140, 147, 171, 184, 196, 207,
 209, 211
Fascism, 186
Father, 12, 38-39, 46, 54, 58, 145,
 181, 186, 189-190, 198-201, 209
Federal, *vi,* 35, 53-63, 70, 93, 126-
 128, 130, 133, 136-137, 140, 143-
 144, 149, 151, 160, 163-164, 191-
 193
Founding Fathers, *xvi-xvii,* 6, 45,
 49, 58, 64, 97, 130, 137, 139,
 148, 154, 156, 162
Free, *iv, vi, viii, x-iv, xvi, xviii,* 2, 4,

6-8, 10-14, 16-18, 20, 22, 24, 26,
28, 30-32, 34, 36, 38, 40, 42-44,
46, 48-50, 52, 54, 56, 58, 60-62,
64, 66, 68-70, 72, 74, 76, 78, 80,
82, 84, 86, 88, 90, 92, 94, 96, 98,
100, 102-104, 106, 108, 110, 112,
114-116, 118, 120, 122, 124, 126,
128, 130, 132, 134, 136, 138,
140, 142, 144-146, 148-150, 152-
154, 156-158, 160, 162, 164, 166,
168-170, 172, 174, 176-178, 180,
182, 184, 186, 188-190, 192, 194,
196, 198-200, 202, 204, 206, 208-
210, 212, 214, 216, 218, 220, 222

Freedom, *iii, ix, xi, xv-xvi,* 3, 8-21,
23, 25-35, 37, 40, 44, 48, 50, 64-
65, 69, 71-73, 76, 81-82, 84, 86-
87, 90, 94, 96-99, 101, 105-107,
113, 116, 118-119, 134, 138-140,
144, 147, 149, 163, 166, 168-170,
182, 184-186, 195, 197, 200, 212

—G—

Gadianton, 79
Gadianton Band, 79
Gilmer, Francis, 35
God, iv, xvii-xviii, 2-6, 10, 17, 24-
25, 28-31, 38-39, 44, 48-49, 52,
54, 64, 72-73, 75, 78-79, 81, 115-
116, 140, 144-145, 171, 178-181,
183, 185-186, 188, 193, 196-197,
199-205, 207-210, 212
Gold, *vi,* 56, 120, 124-127, 130-
133, 143
Golden Rule, *iii, xi,* 37, 39-45, 47-
49, 51, 65, 71, 189
Governeur Morris, 128
Government, *iii, vi-xvii,* 3-7, 9-11,
14, 16, 18-21, 24-35, 37-38, 40,
42-65, 67-72, 76-77, 81-82, 94-
95, 98, 100-102, 106-107, 119,
121, 123-131, 133-141, 143-147,
149, 151-157, 160, 162, 164-174,
176-179, 183-187, 189-191, 194-
195, 206, 210-212
Graduated income tax, 142
Grant, Heber J, 186, 209

—H—

Hamilton, Alexander, *xiv,* 46
Hate, 18, 145, 198
Hatred, 128, 212

Heaven, *xviii,* 3, 29, 52, 80, 181,
186, 201, 208, 210, 212
Helaman, 8, 25, 79, 200
Honest, 80, 120, 127, 168, 195
Honor, 144, 155, 191

—I—

Individual, *xiv, xvii,* 7, 10-11, 14-
15, 19, 24, 31-32, 34, 40, 42, 44-
45, 47-48, 50, 62, 64-65, 81, 83,
98, 117, 119, 144-147, 165-166,
170-171, 191, 209-210
Intelligence, 1-4, 14, 18, 116, 118,
160, 191
Intent, 17, 22, 31, 42, 68-71, 73-78,
82, 84, 88, 98, 102-103, 159
Isaac, 205

—J—

Jacob, 205
Jefferson, Thomas, 35, 63, 137,
158, 160
Jessel, George, 97
Judges, *xviii,* 4, 24, 37-38, 60-61,
74, 78-80, 85, 89, 125, 158-160
Judgment, 3, 10, 24, 30, 41, 45, 48,
61, 104, 121, 135, 153, 155, 160,
205
Justice, *iii, ix-x, xvi,* 5, 9, 18, 24, 31,
37-41, 43, 45, 47-49, 51, 64-65,
73, 75-78, 81, 84, 94, 97, 100,
119, 139-140, 146-147, 156-157,
166-167, 189, 191, 197, 199-200

—K—

Keynes, John Maynard, 132
Kimball, Spencer W., 211
Kingdom of God, 178-179
Knowledge, *xi,* 1, 3, 9, 12-21, 23,
28, 76, 80, 88, 96, 104, 116, 118,
146, 178, 181, 197-198, 204

—L—

Law(s),
   Administrative, *iii,* 101, 163-167,
   169-171, 173, 175-177, 179
   Licensing, *vi, xii-xiii,* 100-106,
   134, 140, 143, 155, 159, 163,
   167-168, 196
   Natural, *iii, vii,* 1-4, 6-9, 14, 19,
   21-27, 29-35, 37, 48, 65, 67-68,
   71, 73, 80-84, 86, 89, 94, 96, 98,

110-113, 116, 119, 140, 160, 175, 199
Lee, Harold B., 196, 206, 211
Legal tender, 57, 127, 129-130
Lenin, 132
Liberty, *v, ix-xi, xiv,* 6-10, 15-17, 19-21, 23, 28-29, 31, 34, 40, 43-44, 46-47, 50, 60, 63, 67, 70-71, 76, 80, 82, 87, 96-97, 104, 115, 130, 136-137, 139-141, 144-146, 150, 153-157, 159, 161, 167, 178, 184, 186, 212
Life, *ix, xi,* 4, 6, 8, 10-17, 19-21, 23-24, 28-29, 31, 34, 37, 40-41, 43, 47, 50, 60, 71, 74, 76, 82, 96, 103-104, 110-111, 113-115, 134, 137, 139-141, 144, 146, 150, 152-155, 167, 171, 175, 185, 196-199, 203-204, 207-209
Locke, John, 5, 20
Lord, *xviii,* 4-5, 8, 10, 17, 25, 29, 33-34, 45, 48, 53-54, 72, 78, 80, 108, 113, 136, 138, 144, 178, 180-181, 183, 186, 188, 194, 197-201, 203-206, 208-209, 211

—M—
Madison, James, *xiv,* 46, 58, 61, 128
Man, *xiv,* 1-4, 6, 9-13, 15-21, 24-35, 38, 40-41, 44-45, 47-48, 51, 53, 63, 65-66, 68, 70, 74, 79, 81, 84, 90, 95-98, 100, 104, 108-115, 117-119, 132, 135, 138, 140, 145-147, 153, 157, 160-161, 178, 180, 184-185, 188-189, 191, 193, 195, 197, 199-201, 205, 208-210
Manifesto, *v-vi,* 141-143, 177
McKay, David O, *xvi,* 10, 16, 137, 144-146, 179, 182, 184, 186, 209-210
Money, 2, 16, 22, 57, 76, 94, 96, 105, 107, 118, 120, 122-134, 143, 171-175, 183, 211
Montesquieu, 59
Moral, *iv, vi, viii-xii, xiv, xviii,* 2, 4, 6-10, 12-14, 16, 18, 20, 22, 24, 26, 28, 30, 32, 34, 36, 38-40, 42, 44, 46, 48-52, 54, 56, 58, 60, 62, 64-66, 68, 70, 72, 74-82, 84, 86, 88, 90, 92, 94, 96, 98, 100, 102, 104, 106, 108, 110, 112, 114,

116, 118-120, 122, 124, 126, 128, 130, 132, 134, 136, 138-140, 142, 144, 146-148, 150, 152, 154, 156, 158-160, 162, 164, 166-170, 172, 174, 176, 178, 180, 182, 184, 186, 188-190, 192, 194, 196, 198, 200, 202, 204, 206, 208, 210, 212, 214, 216, 218, 220, 222
Morality, *viii-x, xiii, xvii,* 17-18, 50, 64, 70, 139-140, 167-169
Mormon, *xvii,* 180, 183, 200, 202-203
Moroni, 183, 204
Moses, 5, 38-39, 41, 64, 72-74
Murder, 7, 12-13, 17, 27-28, 38, 41, 47, 72, 74, 76

—N—
Negligence, 32, 83-84, 86, 90-93, 106
Nephi, 2, 54, 72, 79-80, 115, 183, 188, 203-205
Noah, 199
Nuisance, 91

—O—
Obedience, *xviii,* 2-4, 9, 22, 31, 41-42, 73, 139, 178, 201, 210
Organizations, 10, 43, 145, 183

—P—
Paper Money, 57, 127-131, 133, 143
Peace, 11, 24, 27, 31, 39, 55, 58, 72-73, 79, 84, 132, 144-145, 149, 183, 185-186, 205, 207
Plunder, 147, 169, 184
Political, *v, viii, xi, xiii-xvi,* 1, 4-5, 8-9, 16, 19-20, 36, 45-46, 48-50, 53, 62-64, 71, 130, 141-142, 144, 156, 160, 186, 191, 193, 195, 208, 211
Poor, *vi,* 34, 108, 113, 117, 168, 170, 177, 185, 192, 196, 207
Precepts of men, 205
Preserved, 16, 119, 150, 185
Press and Speech, 15
Pride, 18, 29, 138, 181, 185, 201
Priesthood, 29, 138, 180
Property, *iii, ix-xi, xiii,* 7-8, 11-12, 14-17, 19-21, 23-24, 28-29, 31, 34, 40, 42-44, 47, 50, 57, 59, 67,

71, 74, 76-77, 82, 87-88, 93-94,
96-97, 100, 103-104, 107, 118-
119, 121-125, 127, 129-143, 146-
147, 150, 153-155, 161, 163, 165,
167-168, 171, 173, 175-177, 185,
190, 209, 211
Prophet, *xvii,* 5, 144, 180-183, 190,
200-201, 207
Prosperity, 58, 144, 183, 185

—R—
Racketeering, *xii,* 168
Regimentation, 13
Regulation, *vi-vii, xv,* 7, 67, 126,
164, 177
Regulatory, *xii,* 100-101, 106-107,
134, 140, 143, 147, 155, 159,
163-164, 167-169
Religious, *viii, xvi-xvii,* 7, 10, 16,
29, 44, 49-51, 81, 140, 185, 208
Rights, *vii,* 6, 8-10, 15, 17, 19-26,
28-29, 32, 34-35, 37-38, 44-48,
59-63, 65, 67, 70, 77, 81, 83-84,
89-90, 92, 96-97, 100, 121-125,
127, 129-138, 140-144, 146-147,
149-151, 157, 160-161, 164-167,
169, 185, 210
Romney, Marion G, 184, 187
Russia, *v,* 63, 209
Russian Commissar of, 145

—S—
Satan, 145, 181, 184, 186, 198, 200,
209, 212
Separation of Church and state, 48
Sin, 2, 178, 181, 204
Slavery, 168
Smith, *xvii,* 120, 127, 144, 178-179,
207-210
• George Albert, 209
• Joseph, Jr, 207
• Joseph F, 178, 208
• Joseph Fielding, 179, 210
Snow, Lorenzo, 208
Socialism, *iii, v,* 143, 146-147, 164,
177, 182-184, 189, 207-208, 210-
212
Socialized, 137
State, *xiii, xvii,* 7, 11, 30, 37, 42, 44-
50, 53, 55-60, 62-63, 67, 69-70,
74-76, 80, 83-84, 97, 101, 103-
104, 107, 111, 116, 124, 126-128,

130, 133-134, 136, 140-147, 149-
154, 157-158, 163-165, 167-168,
170, 174, 176-177, 183-184, 186,
192, 194-195, 203, 209
Stewardship, 33
Story, Joseph, 156

—T—
Taxpayer, 43, 140
Taylor, John, 179, 207-208
Teachers, 190, 196, 200
Ten Commandments, *xvi,* 5, 64, 73,
209
Tort, *iii, x, xii,* 32, 50, 59, 82-94, 96,
121, 123-124, 165
Truth, *viii, xii,* 9, 20, 39-40, 46, 80,
88, 104, 119, 178, 180, 196-197

—U—
United Order, 184, 208-209, 211
United States, *iii, xvi-xvii,* 6, 46, 49,
52-53, 55, 57-61, 63, 65, 68, 70,
77, 80, 125-131, 133, 136-137,
143-144, 146, 149-151, 155, 157-
158, 163, 171, 179, 183, 186,
190, 195, 203-204, 209-210
Unity, *iii,* 16, 55, 181-182, 185
Utah, 74, 103, 127, 191, 197

—W—
Wealth, *iii,* 14, 109-119, 121, 132,
137, 163, 170-172, 174, 177, 184,
209
Welfare, *xiii, xvii,* 55, 75, 99, 134,
137, 140, 143, 163, 167, 169,
182-183, 189, 192, 194-195
Wilson, James, 158
Woodruff, Wilford, 180, 208

—Y—
Young, Brigham, *xvi-xvii,* 137, 182,
207

(Product Availability and Prices Subject to Change)

Conservative America-CD

It's here! It's New! It's Yours! The greatest conservative library of all time. Never before has this been available! With ease you can do research instantly by word or phrase. Search in a particular publication or entire library. It's all available on CD-Rom. Upgrades will be available as books and periodicals are added. Over 100,000 pages of text. Why spend thousands of dollars on hard to find books and even more for periodicals. It's all yours for only $149.95. (Makes a great gift!)

Includes American History...

Ever wished you had a library of the works of the Founding Fathers? You Can!!

- Elliot's Debates (5 vol)
- Thomas Jefferson (6 vol)
- Alexis de Tocqueville (2 vol)
- Alexis de Tocqueville (2 vol)
- The Conservative Mind
- The Roots of American Order
- Many Papers of the Presidents
- The Tragedy of American Compassion
- James Madison (4 vol)
- Original Intent and the Framers of the Constitution
- Right from the Beginning
- Church, State and the Constitution
- George Washington, Edmund Burke, *and many more...*

Includes Current Periodicals (2 yrs. plus)...

When you research, you will have immediate access to:

- Phyllis Schlafly Report (4 yrs+)
- Human Events (past 2 yrs)
- Family Voice
- Wirthlin Report
- Crisis
- Commentary
- Woman's Quarterly
- Campus
- Modern Age
- Intercollegiate Review
- Imprimis (past 10 yrs)
- David Barton's Wallbuilders, *and many more...*

Includes Current Books...

- Unlimited Access (Gary Aldrich)
- Abortion and the Constitution
- Crime and Freedom
- God and Men at Yale
- Enviromental Overkill
- Who Killed the Constitution
- Enviromental Gore
- Abortion and the Constitution
- The Freedom Revolution
- Remembering Reagan
- Darwin on Trial, *plus over 100 more...*

Also Available

THE NEW AMERICAN MAGAZINE/DOS/Disks

1988 thru 1995!! Complete Text, Reference and Index! Only $24.95/Yr. (+$5 s&h)

Visit Our Web Site! http://www.itsnet.com/~eleccons

(Product Availability and Prices Subject to Change)

Computer Software-Infobases (CD's)...

____Conservative American Win-Mac *(See Front Page)*..149.95
____LDS Collector's Library (95) Win 149.95
____LDS Collector's Library (95) Mac.............................149.95
____LDS Basic Library CD Win 19.95
____"Sunday... That One Day" Win-Mac 19.95
____LDS Family History Suite Win 99.95
____CD Sourcebook of American History Win-Mac...........39.95
____CD Sourcebook of American History DOS 39.95

Computer Software (Disks)...

____The New American Magazine-DOS..(1988-95 per/yr) 24.95
____Ancestral Quest LDS Ver 2.0 ....29.97
____LDS Scriptures (Quad) DOS 3.5 ....14.95
____LDS Scriptures (Quad) Mac 14.95
____Deluxe Set-Win 3.5 ....119.95
____Deluxe Set-DOS 3.5 ....99.95
____Deluxe Set-Mac...119.95
____LDS Clips I-Win/DOS 29.95
____LDS Clips I-Mac...29.95
____LDS Clips II-Win/DOS 29.95
____LDS Clips II-Mac...29.95
____Where Jesus Walked Screen Saver-Win 14.95
____Church History Tour Screen Saver-Win 14.95
____Book of Mormon Lands Screen Saver-Win 14.95
____Journey West Coloring Book-Win 9.95
____Journey West Coloring Book-Mac...............................9.95

Books...

____Again May God Forgive Us/*Robert Welch*.....................4.95
____America: To Pray or Not To Pray/*David Barton*............6.95
____America's Steadfast Dream/*E Merrill Root* 7.95
____An Enemy Hath Done This/*Ezra Taft Benson* 12.95
____Anglo-American Establishment, The/*Carroll Quigley* ..14.95
____Animal Farm/*George Orwell*......................................4.95
____Blue Book of John Birch Society,The/*Robert Welch* 5.95
____Book of Mormon and The Constitution,The/*Andersen* 12.95
____Boche and Bolshevik/*Nesta Webster, Kurt Kerlen* 5.95
____Bulletproof George Washington,The/*David Barton* 5.95
____Can Mormons be Patriots/*Ron Sinclair* 9.95
____Changing Commands/*John F McManus* 8.95
____Conspiracy Against God and Man/*Rev. Clarence Kelly* 7.95
____Constitution, A Heavenly Banner, The/*Ezra T Benson*..3.50
____Communist Manifesto, The/*Karl Marx* 3.00

____Creature from Jekyll Island, The/*G Edward Griffin* ......
____Economics in One Lesson/*Henry Hazlitt* 7.95
____Elders of Isreal and Constitution/*Jerome Horowitz*.......9.95
____Establishment's Man, The/*James J Drummey* 3.95
____Federalist Papers, The/*Hamilton, Madison, Jay*...........5.95
____Financial Terrorism/*John F McManus* 8.95
____Foundations of the Republic/*Herman S Frey* 4.95
____Freedom on the Altar/*William Norman Grigg*...............8.95
____Global Tyranny Step by Step/*William F Jasper*..........12.95
____Great and Abominable Church of the Devil/*Andersen* 11.95
____Insiders, The: Architects of the NWO/*John McManus*..2.95
____Kiss the Boys Goodbye/*Monica Jensen-Stevenson*....12.95
____Mainspring of Human Progress, The/*Henry Weaver*....5.95
____Many are Called but Few are Chosen/*HV Andersen*....6.95
____Mises Made Easier/*Percy L Greaves, Jr.* 11.95
____Moral Basis of a Free Society/*HV Andersen* 12.95
____New Lies for Old/*Anatoliy Golitsyn* 14.95
____None Dare Call it Treason (25 yrs later)/*John Stormer*.5.95
____Original Intent/*David Barton*..................................12.95
____Parents' Rights/*John W Whitehead*..........................7.95
____Perestroika Deception, The/*Anatoliy Golitsyn* 19.95
____Pink Swastika, The/*Lively and Abrams* 9.95
____Politician, The/*Robert Welch* 4.95
____Proofs of a Conspiracy/*John Robison* 7.95
____Proper Role of Government, The/*Benson-Andersen*.....3.95
____Prophets, Principles and National Survival/*Newquist*..15.95
____Romance of Education, The/*Robert Welch* 6.95
____Secret File on John Birch, The/*James, Marti Hefley* ...12.95
____Secret Side of History, The/*Dee Zahner* 9.95
____Shadows of Power, The/*James Perloff* 10.95
____Socialist Network, The/*Nesta Webster*......................9.95
____Surrender of an Empire/*Nesta Webster* 11.95
____Teddy Bear/*Zad Rust* 4.95
____That Everyman Be Armed/*Stephen P Halbrook*.........16.95
____The Law/*Frederic Bastiat* 3.95
____The Unseen Hand/*Ralph Epperson* 15.95
____To Harrass Our People/*George Hansen* 6.95
____We Hold These Truths/*Lawrence McDonald*..............9.95

Videos...

____A More Perfect Union/*Brigham Young University*........20.00
____America's Godly Heritage/*David Baron* 20.00
____Keys to Good Government/*David Baron* 20.00
____Spirit of the American Revolution, The/*David Baron* ...20.00

- *Add 10% Shipping and Handling.*
- *Order 10 or more Items and Receive 25% Off Prices Listed!*
- *Sorry, No Discounts on Videos.*

Name: _____

Address: _____

City/ST/Zip: _____

Payment: $_____ ☐Check ☐Money Order

Send to:

Electronic Conservative
1160 S. State #190A
Orem, UT 84097

Or Call: (801) 225-0396

Cut and Return Entire Order Form!

Visit Our Web Site! http://www.itsnet.com/~eleccons